The Knave
of
Boston

The Knave
of
Boston

& Other Ambiguous Massachusetts Characters

Francis Russell

with an introduction by
William F. Buckley, Jr.

QUINLAN PRESS
BOSTON

Published by Quinlan Press
131 Beverly Street
Boston, MA 02114

Library of Congress Cataloging-in-Publication Data

Russell, Francis, 1910-
  The knave of Boston.

  1. Politicians—Massachusetts—Biography. 2. Irish Americans—
Massachusetts—Biography. 3 Massachusetts—Biography. 4 Crime and
criminals—Massachusetts—History. I. Title.
F63.R87 1987   974.4'04'0922   86-43248
ISBN 0-933341-79-2

Printed in the United States of America
June 1987

ἦ μεγάλα χάρις δώρῳ σὺν ὀλίγῳ

for
Sara Letitia Stephanie Russell

CONTENTS

INTRODUCTION

Y OU WONDER, IF SO UNLUCKY AS NOT TO HAVE COME FROM THERE, JUST
what it is about Boston that has on its native sons such impact.
It is tempting to say that in order to discover why it is so, it is
only necessary to read this collection by Francis Russell; but that is not
enough. As much entertainment, history and excitement could, by the
proper belletrist and cultural intelligence, be decocted from a study
of San Francisco, or New York, or—well, or Yoknapapatawpha County. Boston has plenty to individuate it, and Francis Russell, looking
out for what is distinctive, has a jeweler's eye. He grew up in Dorchester,
with Blue Hill Avenue as its artery. ''Blue Hill Avenue was for me *the*
Avenue before I knew there were other avenues, a Via Appia running
die-straight from Blue Hill to Boston on the horizon that to my child's
eye was London and Paris and Rome and all the world's fabled and
fabulous cities.''

That was not many years after Francis Russell was born, in 1910. His
memory astonishes, but there is no inclination to doubt him when
he tells you, offhandedly, that he remembers a 1914 August afternoon,
his father coming up the walk in a stiff straw hat and carrying a
newspaper with flaring headlines—that the four-year-old could not yet
read—announcing the outbreak of the First World War. ''It will only
last six weeks,'' his father said.

Throughout his productive lifetime Francis Russell has collected the
quiddities of Greater Boston, which preoccupation, by the way, takes
him in this volume to the Vermont of Calvin Coolidge. As governor

of Massachusetts, Coolidge was after all a Bostonian; a Bostonian who uttered that most proper pronouncement, that there is no right to strike against the public at any time, anywhere: a declaration of civic virtue, emanating as it did from the capital of civic corruption, so nationally incandescent as to elevate him to the White House, via the Vice Presidency. Charles Ponzi was reared in Italy, John Boyle O'Reilly in Ireland and Britain: but they became a part of Boston, and here Francis Russell finds them and weaves them into his tapestry with an eye a sociologist would envy, and a pen no sociologist disposes of—Francis Russell cannot write an awkward sentence, let alone an ugly one.

*   *   *

I met him many years ago, in the early days of *National Review*. Russell was the quiet, scholarly Bostonian who had done postgraduate work in Ireland, and was busy fashioning meticulously wrought pieces about prominent men and women of letters, in books and periodicals, most conspicuously *American Heritage*. Along the way he set out to exonerate Sacco and Vanzetti definitively, but in mid-course he became convinced that the story was not at all as the received legend of their martyrdom would have it. Francis Russell, in the mind's eye, is the sedentary scholar whose work, like William Prescott's, is done in library stacks. It is in fact quite otherwise. Whether it is the room in remote Vermont in which Calvin Coolidge was sworn in as President of the United States (Russell had actually to *see* it), or the actual letters written to his mistress by Warren Harding (it was Francis Russell who brought them for the first time to light), Russell wants to experience history to the extent it is possible to do so. He tracked down and went through the extensive legal maneuvers necessary to arrange for new tests on the weapon found on Sacco's person when he was arrested that night on the streetcar as he was travelling with Vanzetti from Bridgewater to Brockton: and lo, test bullets bore the unmistakable markings of the bullet taken from the dead guard Sacco and Vanzetti were eventually electrocuted for murdering.

Tragedy in Dedham was followed by a second book with yet fresher material on the controversial subject, although there is probably no controversial question on which history ever entirely closes its book to the exclusion of all alternative hypotheses however implausible. One can find books and articles affirming not only the innocence of Sacco, Vanzetti and Alger Hiss, but the guilt of Dreyfus and Socrates. After a point it becomes a diversion, if that is what diverts one: material for Father Brown, not for the historical jurist.

These biographical essays are remarkable for many things, among them the quality of historical patience shown by the author. Francis Russell understands that perceptions and indeed criteria change, in art as well as politics. For a while, John Boyle O'Reilly was thought to be a truly gifted poet. "His reputation became for a time international. In 1882 he was chosen to read his poem "America" at the reunion of the Army of the Potomac with General Grant presiding. Grant later asserted that it was the grandest poem he had ever heard—which may well have been true." Russell does not forgive the incineration of Evelyn Wagler in a side street in Dorchester by six black youths; his protest is internalized. He visited the scene of the crime (as one would expect him to do), only blocks away from where he grew up. He writes about it that "Blue Hill Avenue itself was [now] empty, a scarecrow boulevard, like an artery drained of blood. I could see a planet over the dark hull of the Lewenberg School, Venus or Jupiter, I wasn't sure which. I knew that then, when everyone else had forgotten her, I should not forget Evelyn Wagler. I knew that I should not come that way again."

The final, the ultimate rebuke; the protest of the sentient, but civilized man of conscience. The protest of the fatalist who disdains organized action not because he deems protest ineffective, but because it is not his way. My father, in protest against the course of political history in America, resolved in 1941 never again to vote. A hazardous resolution, in its implications: If no one were ever again to go to Blue Hill Avenue, nothing ever would be done about Blue Hill Avenue. If no one were to vote, who knows what would be the consequences? But there is a purity in the eremitical withdrawal; and without a hint of rodomontade, Russell knows when, gently, to close the covers of a book, and to lay it down forever.

His attitude toward the vicissitudes of Boston's political history is patient, yet judgmental. He names this volume, after all, after one "knave" of Boston, Daniel Coakley. Men are as they are, and social conditions are as social conditions are. Russell knows this. He quotes another knave, the ruthless Ben Butler, "God made me only one way. I can't change it, and upon the whole I don't want to." Who will fail to make some allowances for the political knavery that followed the Irish immigration? "They had been forced to leave a broken land to become the lowest level of the new-world proletariat. The Irish immigrants in the eastern seaboard cities lived and died like animals. Their somber fate played itself out obscurely, below the levels of literary understanding.''

Any wonder, then, that "the men of the great Irish tradition, men like O'Brien and Collins and of whom O'Reilly was the honored leader, were followed by the little venal men, the Honey Fitzes, the Coakleys and their blackmailing rings, the 'Bath-House' John McCoys, the Dowds and the O'Dwyers, Curley (who liked to quote O'Reilly)''? Russell is fascinated by—and fascinates the reader in recounting—the scale of the corruption. In his autobiography, Curley openly doubted that there was a single transaction conducted while he was mayor that did not yield an extra-level favor to someone. But the folkways and mores that gave Boston the Fitzgeralds, the Curleys, the Butlers, came to a gradual end about the time of the Second World War. Mayor Curley discovered on his return to Boston from a five-month sojourn in the federal prison at Danbury that "the city was not the same. His personal openhandedness as boss of old Ward 17, and in his many years as mayor had now become a more impersonal function of government. Voters were no longer gratefully held in line by a job shoveling snow, by the odd ton of coal, by the perennial Thanksgiving turkey and Christmas basket. Social Security and unemployment insurance and the psychiatric social worker had taken over.''

That, broadly speaking, is the scope of this volume, though the lens is wide, giving us a taste of entirely nonpolitical actors. The rise of Irish-American power; and, now, the decline of it, as Russell notes that two recent gubernatorial elections in Massachusetts have been won by Italians, and that the state's present governor is Greek. And where the Jews once moved in, taking over Dorchester as the Irish extravasated out into the middle class suburbs, the blacks have come, reasserting the cynical observation of the late Saul Alinsky that an integrated neighborhood is defined as the time between the arrival of the first black, and the departure of the last white. Francis Russell does no projecting here. We are on our own, but wiser for having read this engrossing book: more sensitive to nuances of politics and social assertion.

WILLIAM F. BUCKLEY, JR.

After his June 13, 1941, impeachment as governor's councilor, Dan Coakley, cigar in hand, tips his hat to the world.

THE KNAVE OF BOSTON

THEY ARE ALL GONE, THOSE VIVID AND VENAL CHARACTERS WHO FOR HALF a century up to World War II moved with insouciant relentlessness across the spotted field of Boston politics. One could scarcely forget Honey Fitz Fitzgerald jigging on the top of a cab on election eve as he sang "Sweet Adeline," or Jim Curley in an iron mike at a rally mellifluously reciting the Lord's Prayer, then pausing to whisper to an aide: "Get the son of a bitch that's heisting my coat!" But the lesser figures are recalled only by old men turning over the memories of the gaslit polling places of their youth: Martin Lomasney, the lantern-jawed Mahatma of Ward 8, who commandeered such loyalty in his ward that the dead rose annually from their graves to vote for him; blue-eyed Pat Kennedy behind his East Boston bar pronouncing that "to the spalpeens belong the spoils"; the portly invert, Senator David Ignatius Walsh; Pea Jacket Maguire, the South End tailor turned politician, who sewed up mayors and buttoned down city patronage; Smiling Jim Donovan, Pea Jacket's successor; Diamond Jim Timilty, fingers, cuff links and stickpin asparkle with brilliants, ending his speeches with "Honest to God, min, I'm your fri'nd!"; Knocko McCormack, all three hundred pounds of him, in the pale-blue jester's uniform of the "Forty and Eight," riding a dray horse in the St. Patrick's Day parade. They were indeed a splash of color in the drab Puritan city. There was something to be said for them even in their roguery—although the retreating old-line Yankees were not the ones to say it—at times as much to be said for them as against them. Their reputations are mottled. Only one emerges in consistently dark shades, though he was of the cleverest, Daniel Coakley. If others could have reached their goals on the straight way they might even have preferred it. Coakley found the devious route more interesting, varied, exciting, better suited to his restless, malicious temperament. Clever enough to have made an honest fortune, he preferred trickery, the double-deal, turning the tables.

His early years ran in the normal success-story pattern of his contemporaries like Jim Curley and Honey Fitz. At fourteen he quit school to work as a teamster. Later he spent a few months at Boston College but ran out of money and had to take a job as conductor on the Cambridge Street Railway Company. Evenings he filled in as a bartender in Haymarket Square. When he was caught stealing fares the company discharged him "for negligence." He moved on to New York where he picked up shorthand and went to work as a reporter for the *Sun*. The following year he returned to Boston as sports reporter for the *Herald* and soon grew noted for his pungent vocabulary. He also made a local name for himself as a boxing referee. When the *Herald* sent him to Mississippi to cover the John L. Sullivan–Jake Kilrain fight he managed to scoop all the other reporters by renting a burro and riding it headlong through the swamps to the nearest telegraph station with the news of the "Boston Strong Boy's" victory.

He was only twenty-one, a slight, easy-featured young man with cold blue eyes and wavy blue-black hair, a polysyllabic vocabulary and a voice that could be as sonorous as a church organ or as sharp as chalk on slate. Yet he could see no power for the grasping in the newspaper world. His brother Timothy had become a lawyer, and he now set out to read law on his own in Timothy's office. It did not take the active-minded young man long to pass his bar examination, and almost at once he developed a reputation as an "injury case" lawyer. His experience as a conductor had taught him all the ins, and more particularly the outs, of streetcars. Anyone who tripped, fell or stumbled on public transportation soon learned to come to Coakley. Over his desk he kept a framed copy of his "negligence" discharge. Not many months after he had set up practice he was winning more and larger damages against the Boston Elevated Railway Company than any other lawyer in the city.

With his brother—whom he would later have put away as an alcoholic—he set up the firm of Coakley, Coakley, Dennison &

Sherman, the last two names being merely Anglo-Saxon window dressing. When he was twenty-nine he moved to Brighton, the stagnant saloon ward near the abattoir, and proceeded to make it into his political bailiwick. Boston, although in the power of the Irish Democrats, never produced an all-controlling boss like Tammany's Crocker. Instead there were district and ward bosses. Occasionally uniting in unlikely combinations, they fought each other at every election. In 1905 Smiling Jim Donovan and Honey Fitz squared off as candidates for mayor. When, with Coakley's support, Honey Fitz was elected he rewarded Coakley with the unpaid but patronage-weighty post of park commissioner. After Honey Fitz's enemy Jim Curley became mayor in 1914, Coakley resigned, which, Curley declared, "relieved me of the task of removing him." Yet Coakley remained a potent political force, and at a dinner given on his fiftieth birthday a year later at the Exchange Club it was Mayor Curley who made the speech presenting him with a thousand-dollar hall clock, to the applause of assembled congressmen, former mayors including Honey Fitz, district attorneys, sheriffs, judges and lesser officials. In a further gesture of conciliation Curley made Coakley a trustee of the Boston Public Library. Within months Coakley practically controlled that institution. He became the mayor's personal lawyer and fixer, the man behind the scenes in the first Curley administration. In Cambridge he grew equally influential, even seeing to it that city funds were deposited in the unsteady Tremont Trust Company of his friendly collaborator Simon Swig.

As he approached middle age Coakley had turned from tort cases to criminal law and the larger civil suits. Notoriety dogged his footsteps. He defended Big Bill Kelliher, who had been caught looting the National City Bank of Cambridge, but even he could do little for Big Bill, who was sentenced to eighteen years. As a retainer he had given Coakley some twenty-three thousand dollars in tainted money, and he claimed from prison that he had paid his lawyer to bribe the United States district attorney and the jury. A sensational charge, but who could disbelieve Coakley's eloquent defense of his own integrity? Certainly not his friend District Attorney Joseph Pelletier of Suffolk County for whom he had once acted as campaign manager.

Coakley and Pelletier and District Attorney William Corcoran of Middlesex County formed a smoothly operating triumvirate. Those who feared they might be prosecuted for some previous delinquency found that the district attorneys concerned could be "reasonable" if approached by Coakley. It was soon nosed about among the more knowledgeable in Suffolk and Middlesex Counties that Pelletier and Corcoran would understandingly nol-pros cases brought to their attention by that tribune of the people, Dan Coakley. The understanding was expensive. Some of the less sympathetic would even call it bribery. Coakley considered it more a matter of oiling the wheels of justice.

His most publicized case in the fugitive years before the entry of the United States into World War I was the breach of promise suit brought in 1915 by Elizabeth "Toodles" Ryan against Henry Mansfield, proprietor of the Ferncroft Inn, a roadhouse and gambling joint on the Newburyport Turnpike.

Toodles, a blonde, full-bosomed woman in the overblown style of the period, had lived from 1910 to 1914 at the Ferncroft, where Mansfield taught her how to read marked cards, to operate a rigged roulette wheel and to perform other gamblers' tricks. She showed herself an apt pupil. Before long he put her in charge of his gambling room where she proved an amiable and accommodating hostess as well as his "right arm in the conduct of business."

Mansfield paid her seventy-five dollars a week plus her keep. He also gave her presents, took her to Bermuda and Europe, signing her into hotels as his wife. In 1914 she suggested that a more substantial arrangement would not be amiss. When he demurred she packed her bags, shouting at him that "as a grandfather you're fine, but as a man you're rotten. I've got you now on gambling. I've got you on white slavery!"

Using Coakley on the advice of her bosom friend Honey Fitz, Toodles then brought a breach of promise suit against Mansfield. The Mansfield–Ryan case exercised all Coakley's formidable histrionic talents. Toodles and Henry he referred to as Beauty and the Beast. Mansfield was a "card cheat, guller of his friends, liar and piece of gross flesh." Stalking up to the quivering defendant and shaking his finger under his fleshy nose, Coakley declaimed: "Oh, the dog! Oh, the dog!" After hours of deliberation the jury failed to agree. Rather than face another such trial, Mansfield through Coakley made a settlement with Toodles. She had the last word. "I wouldn't marry that fat old slob anyway," she told reporters.

For Corcoran, Coakley and Pelletier their Celtic inheritance was part of their stock in trade. The Pelletiers of French-Canadian name had long been absorbed into the Boston-Irish current, retaining only their alien patronymic. Like Coakley, Pelletier had built up a strong local political organization. In particular he was felt to have a warm heart. A faithful son of the Church, he was one of the leaders of the Knights of Columbus in Massachusetts, the first grand knight of the Franklin Council. However enmeshed he and Coakley were in the affairs of their working-class constituents, they also saw to it that golden threads ran from their offices to State Street and the Boston business world. Republican bosses like the Back Bay's Charlie Innes were intimate with Pelletier, and the district attorney carried much weight in the Republican-dominated state legislature. Prominent Republicans like Louis Liggett of the drugstore chain took pains to be friendly with him.

When Coakley waved his wand over the two district attorneys' offices, indictments vanished, prosecutions were stopped in their tracks. Later, after Corcoran was succeeded by a born-in-the-wool Yankee, Nathaniel Tufts, the new district attorney proved no less amenable than his predecessor. A call from Coakley's office, a quick conference, and charges of larceny, fraud, theft, practicing medicine without a license, abortions, adultery, assault, receiving stolen goods, running a disorderly house, vanished from the files like snow in April.

From this rewarding field it was only a step further for the triumvirate to create charges, concoct compromising situations. Here Coakley refined the technique of the old "badger game" in which a man is maneuvered into the arms of a woman, then blackmailed. He developed his own "poison gas squad" of manipulative young women, ostensible husbands and ostensible detectives to appear at the climactic moment, and photographers to record that moment. As early as 1915 he had shaken down Hollis Hunnewell of the wealthy Wellesley family. Hunnewell had kept a woman for some years in Cambridge as his mistress and had paid her regularly. As his affections waned so did his payments, and when they stopped she turned to Coakley, who sent a note to Hunnewell at the Somerset Club. A few days later Hunnewell met Coakley and Pelletier at the Parker House. There Hunnewell agreed to a ten-thousand-dollar settlement for the woman and five thousand dollars for a suddenly materialized husband. But this was by no means the end. Coakley had got hold of Hunnewell's love letters, and before the cooled lover could reclaim them he was forced to hand over to Coakley an additional hundred and fifty thousand.

Other unwarily ardent Bostonians with Social Register names like

Bigelow, Fiske and Searles got themselves entangled in Coakley's web. His most profitable coup, and one of the more pathetic, was his shakedown of an elderly Beacon Street bachelor, Edmund Barbour. In 1906, when Barbour was sixty-five, he had somehow made the acquaintance of sixteen-year-old Mae Daly. Over a period of years she would visit him at his office, or sometimes on Sundays in his Beacon Street town house, sit on his lap and let him ''pet'' her. As she herself admitted later, he never went any further. From time to time he gave her expensive presents.

Then on an afternoon in 1918 when he was sitting in his swivel chair in his State Street office with Mae on his lap, he suddenly saw two faces appear over the transom and heard a gruff voice call out: ''Ah, now we've got you!'' Two men burst into his office to identify themselves as officers of the law representing District Attorney Corcoran. As soon as they left, Mae suggested that she and Barbour had better see a lawyer and took him to Coakley's office. Coakley told the humiliated Barbour that it would take a great deal of money to solve his dilemma and suggested a down payment of seventy-five thousand dollars plus a twenty-five-thousand-dollar fee. In the next few years the bearded old man, in failing health and going old and blind, paid Coakley almost three hundred thousand dollars.

Whatever the triumvirate's victims had paid, most of them preferred to keep their mouths shut. Coakley's most notorious case, the one with the most extensive ramifications, concerned Mishawum Manor, an inn of dubious reputation in Woburn run by one Brownie Kennedy. Early in 1917 a group of moving picture magnates—among them Adolph Zukor, Jesse Lasky and Hiram Abrams—gave a dinner for the film star Fatty Arbuckle at Boston's Copley Plaza. After the dinner the others left Arbuckle, and a party of about fifteen headed for the Manor, where Brownie and her girls were awaiting them. Brownie was understanding, and the girls, between trips upstairs, were accommodating enough to take off their clothes. What followed, in the prim language of the Massachusetts Supreme Judicial Court, was ''an orgy of drink and lust...a debauch in a bawdy house...a stench in the nostrils of common decency.'' When the movie men left the following morning, they gave Brownie a check for twelve hundred dollars and thought that was the end of the party. In a few days they learned otherwise: they were informed that they might be indicted on a series of morals charges. Coakley had the bad news relayed to them by Mayor Curley, who personally put through the fateful telephone call. Lawyers for the movie men met with Coakley and finally agreed to pay a hundred thousand dollars to have the party forgotten.

For friendship's sake Coakley was even willing to practice blackmail in reverse, as when Boston Republican leader Guy Currier came to him with an account of his stand-up by a manicurist in a Cleveland hotel. Coakley advised him to take sick and get sent to a hospital. While Currier was there, the manicurist arrived at his room and demanded twenty thousand dollars. Coakley, who had stationed himself within hearing, stepped forward and threatened to take her before District Attorney Pelletier as a blackmailer if she did not at once sign the release he had in his pocket. She signed.

Coakley and Pelletier, with Corcoran and Tufts in tow, had come to think of themselves as impregnable. Most Bostonians aware of their activities were inclined to agree with them. One who stubbornly did not was Godfrey Lowell Cabot, treasurer of the New England Watch and Ward Society. Cabot, one of Boston's wealthiest men, was a Brahmin of Brahmins, being both a Lowell and a Cabot, a first cousin and college classmate of Harvard's President A. Lawrence Lowell, a cousin of Supreme Court Justice Oliver Wendell Holmes and a double third cousin of Senator Henry Cabot Lodge.

That singular Yankee institution, The Watch and Ward Society, had been founded in 1878 to watch over the morals of the once-Puritan city and to ward off influences—mostly sexual—detrimental to it, particularly in the fields of literature and the theater. Once Cabot had set out in self-righteous indignation to destroy Coakley and Pelletier, he was able to use the Watch and Ward's well-endowed facilities in the pursuit. He was quite prepared to use his own resources as well, and the more he unearthed about the two men the more determined he became to bring them down regardless of the cost. As the word spread that Cabot was out to get Coakley and Pelletier, numerous informative letters, some anonymous, began to arrive at his Watch and Ward command post. All of them he investigated. Much to his surprise he found difficulty in engaging lawyers. None of the proper Bostonian law firms, all of whom should have been happy to represent a Lowell-Cabot, showed any desire to tangle with two politicians of such power and influence. "You can go out to kill a lion and get lots of people to help you," he reminisced long afterward, "but when you go out to kill a skunk you've got to do it yourself." He was willing to do it. Through one of his detectives, posing as an electrician, he managed to plant a dictaphone in the district attorney's office and for some months was able to listen in on Pelletier's intimate conversations. At his command post he set up a rogues' gallery of the men and women of Coakley's blackmail team, and at one point even succeeded in working an agent into Coakley's office to steal incriminating documents.

Wary of their implacable antagonist, Coakley and Pelletier took countermeasures. One of Cabot's detectives turned out to be a secret Coakley agent. Pelletier even attempted to trap Cabot with a prostitute. Cabot spent three years and over a hundred thousand dollars of his own money before he was ready to act. In the welter of moves and countermoves, threats and counterthreats, he had come to fear for his life. (In fact he was to live to be 101.) Finally he persuaded two sympathetic Republican senators to introduce a bill in the Massachusetts senate calling for an investigation of District Attorney Pelletier's office by a governor's commission. Somehow, for all its Republicanism, the senate remained immobile. That same year, 1917, Cabot petitioned the state supreme court for the impeachment of Pelletier.

"This," Pelletier replied with a confidence that was just the least bit forced, "is an attempt to discredit. Mr. Cabot has justified the use of the most outrageous methods that would bring a blush of shame to any decent man."

When the supreme court in turn declined to act, Cabot took his documents to the Boston Bar Association, which had stood by impotently for years but now felt compelled to deal with the massive evidence of corruption he had brought to light. In 1918 the association, with Cabot at its elbow, began a three-year inquiry into the activities of Pelletier, Coakley, Corcoran and Tufts. The quartet struck back, securing an indictment for larceny against Cabot and two of his lawyers after Cabot had been found in possession of documents stolen from Coakley's office, among them Hunnewell's love letters.

Like a cuttlefish squirting clouds of ink to cover his trail, Coakley inserted an advertisement on the front pages of the Boston papers under the heading: HUNNEWELL MYTH EXPLODED.

> Lying sick in bed I have been reading the current gossip of the gutter that I spend most of my time in the criminal courts. This gossip has been invented and diligently cultivated by ex-convicts, dope fiends and "pimps" (I have their names) who have been

and are on the payroll of the archfanatic.

Starting thus in the underworld these yarns have by dint of persistent repetition penetrated the circles of decent society and whenever people gather who do not know the high character and integrity of Joseph C. Pelletier. My praise can add not a cubit to his stature.

As a car conductor, as a teamster, as a bartender, as a reporter, I seem to have escaped these cultured antagonisms which of late have beset me. Perhaps it was a mistake to have moved onward from these humble but honorable occupations. In the canons of my antagonists it is in such callings that I and such as I belong.

Even as a lawyer, arriving somewhat late in life, my career occasioned no alarm to anyone, until I got my head far enough above water to look horizontally at some of those on whom Fortune had pinned the blue ribbon. . . .

In December 1920, a month after the advertisement had appeared and Cabot's trial had begun, the court ruled that Coakley's open letter had made it impossible for the defendants to receive a fair trial from jurors who had read it, and ordered the case taken from the jury. Adroitly Cabot's lawyer managed to obtain a not-guilty verdict for him on a technicality.

Several months later the Bar Association filed petitions in the Massachusetts Supreme Court for the removal from office of Tufts and Pelletier, and the disbarment of Corcoran and Coakley on grounds of "deceit, malpractice and other gross misconduct." Attorney General J. Weston Allen led the court battle. Tufts's case was the first to be heard. He was refereeing a football game between Princeton and Swarthmore in September 1921 when the news came that he had been ousted from office.

The trial of Coakley and Pelletier was still to come. For them Boston's mayoralty election in November seemed a way to avoid Tufts's fate. If the popular Pelletier could get himself elected mayor with energetic help from Coakley, he could then thumb his nose at the Bar Association. Against this hope, Curley now came forward to announce that he would again be a candidate. With Curley and Pelletier splitting the vote, the odds were that the reformist John R. Murphy, brother-in-law of John Boyle O'Reilly, would be elected. Somehow Curley was able to apply enough pressure to persuade Pelletier to withdraw. But, though re-elected, Curley did not forgive Coakley's desertion.

Even under the shadow of the Bar Association's inquiry, Coakley remained undaunted. The Watch and Ward Society he characterized as "the gang of hounds that have been chasing me for years." He, Pelletier and Corcoran appeared before the supreme court in 1922. Corcoran confessed—he would later serve a jail term—after which Coakley and Pelletier and Corcoran declined to offer any defense. Found guilty of conspiracy and gross misconduct, they were disbarred, Pelletier being removed from office. This still left them open to criminal prosecution, something they finally faced in 1924. Rather than subject himself to this, Pelletier committed suicide, although it was given out that he had died of a broken heart.

When Corcoran and Coakley finally went on trial, a sympathetic jury promptly acquitted them on all charges. Crowds of Coakley's supporters surrounded the courthouse to cheer him as he emerged after shaking hands with each juror. He then announced confidentially that he would be the next mayor of Boston.

Although Coakley could not officially practice law, business in his office still hummed. A dozen lawyers worked for him. Thanks to the trial publicity the Internal Revenue Service was becoming interested in the mention of large fees apparently not accounted for in his tax returns. In 1928 the service notified him that he owed over four million dollars in back taxes from 1915 to 1922. He finally reached some settlement with the government. What it was has never been revealed.

In 1928 Coakley did indeed run for mayor. Curley could not be a candidate since the law forbade a mayor to succeed himself. Coakley's main issue was the downfall and death of Pelletier whom he accused other politicians of crucifying. In a field of ten he finished fourth, about what he had expected. Enough for him to have ruined the chances of Curley's candidate, Fire Commissioner Theodore Glynn. Four years later the flamboyant Curley was himself eligible. He was opposed this time by Frederick W. Mansfield, a man of somewhat dull integrity, more noted as a labor lawyer and past president of the Boston Bar Association than as a politician. Coakley too ran again, not with any thought of winning but with the hope of garnering enough votes to defeat Curley. Night after night over the radio he begged Curley to release him from his oath as a lawyer "so that I can tell the people the truth about you." "Dapper Dan," Curley taunted him in reply, "you know the man who was responsible for the ruin of Pelletier. It was you, Dapper Dan!" Coakley received only a few thousand votes, failing even to carry his own Brighton ward, and Curley defeated Mansfield by a comfortable margin.

By the following year the oncoming depression had begun to take its political toll in Massachusetts. The Democrats had not elected a governor since 1914, but now the smooth-running Republican escalator that had carried so many Republican politicians to the governor's chair was beginning to clank. All signs pointed to 1930 as a Democratic year. The two leading candidates for governor were Boston's Honey Fitz and Joseph B. Ely, an old-line Yankee. The odd permutations of Massachusetts politics found Curley supporting Honey Fitz and denouncing Ely as an enemy of the Irish "for whom no one with a drop of Irish blood in his veins would vote." In supporting Ely, Coakley devoted his vituperative talents to attacking Curley in a series of radio addresses over Boston's station WEEI. Never in Massachusetts, possibly never before in the country, had anyone been attacked on the air with the invective Coakley now unleashed on Curley. Technicians stood by, hand on the switch during the broadcasts, ready to cut Coakley off as soon as his lips began to form an obscenity. Although ostensibly speaking for Ely, in turning to Curley he really let himself go, jeering at the "double-barrelled voice," the "Oxford accent" that, when Curley was aroused, "reverts to type." Then, he continued,

> the brass knuckles and blackjack are taken from the safe; he [Curley] bursts out in the language of the old Ward 17 days. His voice is raucous and he takes to the high road with the old cap and sweater.

Coakley's attacks on Curley—"CUR-ley," he always called him, stressing the first syllable—reached a climax in a midnight broadcast the night before the primaries. Trembling with hate, Coakley told his audience:

> Since I last talked to you, two hours ago, my young son, Gael Coakley, a boy of 130 pounds, has been brutally assaulted by that masquerading thug, who, God save the mark, is mayor of Boston. In this station, two hours ago, Jim Curley, the bravo, surrounded by a band of twenty blackguards, dashed into the broadcasting room where Chairman Frank Donahue of the State Committee had just finished giving a truthful talk about this marauding mayor.
>
> In language unprintable, the guttersnipe language of his old jailbird days, this blackleg mayor, backed by his brigands, rushed

at Donahue. "I'll get you, you son of a bitch, if it's the last thing I ever do!" My young son, alone with Donahue in the room, stepped before him. "Don't, Mr. Mayor," he said. "Get out of the way, you little son of a bitch!" shrieked the mayor as, grabbing him by the arm, he held him close and, lifting his leg, kneed him in the groin. Then the gunmen companions of the mayor struck the boy twice from behind. "Give it to him again," said their gunman leader.

Without his crew of bruisers behind him, he'd never have dared attack even that little chap. He's a bully and a braggart. He's a yellow cur. It's a slander on a yellow dog to call Curley such. In the early days he always attacked in this method, in this manner, the normal thug style, backed by his brigand band. He has all the traits of a mental, moral and physical coward. Duck debate when he meets a real debater, while he poses as an orator; cringe and whine when he meets a real test of moral courage; run, when alone, if he meets his real physical equal. Until this campaign he has gotten away with it, but politically he's dead tonight. Tonight he uncovered himself in public. After tonight you don't need anyone to *tell* you he's a thug.

Tomorrow will see him in the dust.

Several weeks before the primaries Honey Fitz had announced that he was no longer an active candidate, and Ely won the nomination easily. At a victory rally just before the election, the audience tittered slightly as Mayor Curley, presiding, introduced Ely as "the clean, able, brilliant leader of Democracy from western Massachusetts." And among those cheering Curley from the balcony, indeed sitting in the front row, was none other than Dapper Dan Coakley. "Why not?" he replied affably to an inquiring reporter. "We're all good Democrats out to win."

Ely defeated Republican Governor Frank Allen by only 16,000 votes in over a million cast, but his election would mark the end of Massachusetts as a Republican state. Two years later he was re-elected by a 122,000-vote margin. During Ely's two terms Coakley was a frequent visitor to the executive chambers. Whatever hold the disbarred lawyer had over the governor—and it was clear that he did have a hold—Coakley during the Ely administration could get what he wanted in the way of favors and appointments.

In 1932 Coakley scored a vindication by winning a nomination to the Governor's Council from the Fourth District. Although not even a resident of the district and unaided by Democratic party leaders, he received 40,000 votes to 13,000 for his nearest opponent. In that solidly Democratic section, nomination was the equivalent of election, and Coakley was elected without opposition.

The Governor's Council, composed of eight members plus the lieutenant governor, is a curiously anachronistic survival from the prerevolutionary days of royal governors. Until its wings were clipped finally after World War II, it had the veto power over all government's appointments, pardons, etc. Though a councilor's pay was small, he held great strategic power, since governors were forced to deal with - him and consider his patronage and other demands.* It was a position made to order for Coakley.

As a councilor Coakley felt that the time had now arrived for his legal rehabilitation. In September 1933 he petitioned the state supreme court for readmission to the practice of law, presenting over four hundred endorsers of his position. They included dozens of Catholic priests, two bishops, the Jesuit presidents of Boston College and Holy Cross, former district attorneys, a United States district court judge and even Al Smith. After Coakley had appealed to Cardinal O'Connell, that urbane prelate replied with brief ambiguity:

> I have noted the contents of the letters to you from many distinguished people of the highest reputation for probity, and their prayers—to which I add my own—will, I feel sure, be answered and the cloud of adversity lifted forever.

When the hearing on the petition opened before Supreme Court Justice Fred T. Field, Coakley produced several hundred more character witnesses including such prominent political figures as Senator Walsh, former Assistant United States Attorney General William A. Lewis—a black and former all-American Harvard football star— Congressman John McCormack, Governor Ely and James Roosevelt. Ely felt sure that if Coakley was reinstated "there would never be cause to criticize you again." James Roosevelt wrote that he had found Coakley's attitude "to have been on the highest plane at all times. . . an example which any citizen might choose to follow." Charlie Innes, from the Republican

---

*Such blatant wheeling and dealing went on in the Council Chamber that at one point five of the councilors were under indictment.

side of the fence, thought that Coakley had taken his disbarment manfully and that if readmitted he would "observe scrupulously proper standards of professional ethics." Finally Coakley appended endorsements from 3,740 Massachusetts lawyers and 65 district court judges.

Coakley grew so eloquent in his own defense that it was difficult to say whether he was asserting his innocence or expressing contrition. Judge Field finally asked him to make up his mind. Coakley decided that he was contrite. "I am very, very, very penitent for the things I have done that I shouldn't have done," he answered dramatically, then, pointing to his wife and five children in the courtroom, he added: "I offer my wife and my children as a concrete piece of evidence vouching for my future conduct. . . . No future act of mine shall ever renew their suffering." He ended his plea with a stage whisper: "I ask you to be merciful."

His petition was opposed by the crusty, white-haired president of the Bar Association, Robert Dodge, who maintained that Coakley had shown no real sense of penitence or guilt and that many of his recent public statements had been manifest lies. Judge Field agreed. On March 29, 1934, he denied the petition.

That November Coakley was re-elected to the council at the same time that Curley was elected governor. But the archenemies now discovered themselves strangely compatible. Within weeks of Curley's inauguration he and Coakley were meeting like old friends. In a sense it was a friendship of convenience, for councilor and governor needed one another. Curley's term was the most flamboyantly corrupt since that of the droop-eyed Ben Butler a century before. During those hectic years Coakley helped organize the governor's purge of officeholders and was the prosecutor in a number of removal proceedings. What Curley wanted in and through the council Coakley saw that he got, and the governor returned the favors. In November 1935, Coakley, in speaking at a Parker House luncheon with Curley present, hailed the "bully and blackleg" of only four years before as "the greatest governor the Commonwealth has had in fifty years."

The next month Coakley celebrated his seventieth birthday. He announced that he was looking forward to the next ten years as the best in his life and hinted he might run for governor the following year as "Boston's champion harmonizer." However, by the autumn of 1936 he was ready to settle for another term as councilor. Although his vote margins varied, he seemed undefeatable in the Fourth District, being again elected in 1938 and 1940.

Even in his first term Coakley was recognized as the key man in the council, and with each election his influence expanded, extending beyond party lines, mysterious and potent. No one could ever quite explain why former Governor Allen, that sterling Republican, should approach the chief justice of the Massachusetts Supreme Court to ask diffidently if there was any chance of Coakley's being reinstated at the bar. But much about Coakley could not be explained.

During the Ely and Curley administrations the quality of Massachusetts mercy grew so strained that more convicts seemed to be leaving prison than entering, not only the misadventured amateurs but well-known professionals. Without the consent of the council no pardon could be granted, and most of the pardon petitions seemed to emanate from Councilor Coakley.

After one term as governor Curley was nominated for the United States Senate, only to be defeated in the election by the grandson and namesake of old Senator Henry Cabot Lodge. He was succeeded by Lieutenant Governor Joseph "Chowderhead" Hurley, who had campaigned vaguely as a reformer. For a time under Hurley the pardon stream diminished, only to increase to torrent force in his last weeks. The difficulty with pardons, though, was that they were so apparent. Indictments might be quashed, prosecutions dropped, with no one the wiser. But a released convict became an all-too-obvious presence, particularly if he happened to get into further difficulties with the law. Publicity was unavoidable, and this would in the end prove Coakley's undoing.

In December 1938, shortly before leaving office, Hurley signed a Coakley-endorsed pardon petition for Raymond Patriarca, a Providence hoodlum already on his way to becoming New England's Mafia chief. Patriarca had been pardoned after serving only eighty-four days of three concurrent three-to-five year sentences for armed robbery in Massachusetts. With his release the long-simmering pardon scandal at last boiled over.

Reaction against the Coakley-Hurley years was so sharp that in November 1938 Democratic Massachusetts elected Republican Leverett Saltonstall governor and a Republican legislature as well. After taking office Saltonstall appointed a special commission to investigate pardons and paroles over the previous ten years. Following some nineteen months of investigation the commission concluded that pardons and paroles had been freely granted to notorious criminals and that "substantial sums of money have been paid out for the procurement of certain pardons." Without accusing Coakley directly of taking bribes, the commission nevertheless charged that he had delayed and hindered its probe and had been involved in most of the pardons it had condemned. The members concluded that he should be charged by the legislature with "misconduct and maladministration because of his improper activities."

Following the commission's report the speaker of the House of Representatives, Christian Herter, appointed a committee of three Republicans and two Democrats to study its recommendations. After some weeks—with one Democrat and one Republican dissenting—the committee reported that Coakley should be impeached.

According to the Massachusetts Constitution, "the House of Representatives shall be the grand inquest of this Commonwealth; and all impeachments made by them shall be heard and tried in the Senate." Under this article Coakley was charged on fourteen counts of official misconduct and malfeasance that included acceptance of bribes, the sale of pardons to felons and acting "for his own profit and gain in violation of his oath of office."

The House inquest was scheduled for June 13, 1941. Several days before this Coakley sent a four-page letter to each representative adroitly presenting his version of the prison controversy and assuring the legislators that "when the truth is known, I am sure that ultimately I will be as pure as snow." On June 12 he spent the day in the State House corridors and the House lobby buttonholing members of both parties. He asked to be heard on the floor in his own defense, but this Herter refused to allow as unprecedented. Then he announced he would be present in the visitors' gallery.

At the opening session the gallery was jammed. Coakley, sitting beside his son and daughter, seemed grimly confident as he listened to Speaker Herter appeal to the legislators not to make their vote a party matter. In spite of the speaker's plea the voting followed party lines. After three hours of debate, 130 Republicans and 14 Democrats voted for the impeachment resolution, while 70 Democrats and 5 Republicans were opposed.

As soon as the result was announced, reporters flocked around Coakley to ask if he planned to resign. "Of course I don't," he snapped at them. "I intend to fight these impeachment charges to the end, because I am not guilty. I've been indicted before," he added pugnaciously, "but I've never been convicted." He announced that he would try his own case. "The Mud Bath," knowing politicians labeled the forthcoming senate trial. It was an apt designation for the first trial held in the senate in 120 years.

On August 23 it opened in the sedate eighteenth-century senate chamber under the Wedgwood blue-and-white lining of the State House's gilt dome, with twenty-four Republicans and fifteen Democrats ranged in a circle to decide Coakley's fate. The proper Yankee and proper Republican Attorney General Robert Bushnell, a stocky man with thick reddish hair, a thin moustache, long nose and slow but aggressive voice, was in charge of the prosecution.

In his opening statement Bushnell declared that he would prove Coakley guilty of fraud, falsehoods and "tissues of lies" in obtaining pardons. The most telling evidence would be Patriarca's pardon petition, drafted personally by Coakley, in which he had called the Providence gangster "a virtuous young man eager to be released from prison so that he might go home to his mother."

On the fourteen articles of impeachment, seven were concerned with the Patriarca pardon. In his petition Coakley had clipped eight years from the thirty-year-old Patriarca, making him a youth of twenty-two who had erred chiefly through inexperience and bad company, and naming three priests eager to endorse Patriarca's petition: a Father Garneri of Quincy; Patriarca's Providence pastor, Father Fagen; and Father Sextus Brambilla of East Boston.

The trial, roiled and vituperative as only Coakley could make it, lasted all September. Bushnell presented Patriarca's record going back to 1926, showing him to be a gunman, thief, bootlegger, hijacker, gambler, pimp, racketeer and murder suspect. The attorney general then revealed that Father Garneri—actually the Reverend Philip Guarino of Waverly—never knew Patriarca. In a deposition Father Guarino denied that he had ever talked with anyone about Patriarca's pardon or ever authorized the use of his name. Father Brambilla deposed that his signature had been obtained by fraud, since he had been told that Patriarca's record consisted merely of minor juvenile delinquencies. Father Fagen turned out to be completely nonexistent.

Former Governor Hurley appeared among the witnesses, moon-faced, cautiously defensive. He could not explain why he had given Patriarca's pardon such high priority. Coakley, he said, had presented the petition to him personally, stating that Patriarca had been persecuted by the Providence police.

At times Coakley and Bushnell seemed on the verge of blows. Taking the stand in his own defense, Coakley denied he had ever received money or anything of value to help convicts obtain pardons. In a voice that trembled, he told the senators that any charge that he knew the Patriarca petition contained untruths was "false as hell." He admitted he had invented the name Fagen, but that was only because he could not recall the actual name of Patriarca's pastor. In any case the whole episode was "trivial and insignificant," and he accused Bushnell of attempting to torture him. Bushnell took two hours for his summing-up, his voice at times rising in shrill anger. While he was speaking Coakley sat twiddling his thumbs.

After the dragging weeks of trial the senators reached their verdict in three hours. By a vote of thirty-three to six they found the Brighton councilor guilty on ten of the fourteen impeachment articles. As the voting progressed, the quiet of the almost silent chamber was broken by the sobbing of Coakley's daughter Eileen. He himself remained impassive. At the session's end he stood defiantly outside the chamber door to greet the die-hard six and glare silently at the others. Afterward he issued a statement to reporters, referring to himself—as he customarily did—in the third person. "Men are attacking Dan Coakley who know nothing about his good qualities," he lamented. "I can only say 'forgive them, Father, for they know not what they do.' "

Disbarred, forbidden to hold office, Coakley nonetheless continued to tread the well-trodden path between City Hall and the State House, as jaunty, brash and conspicuous as ever. Weekly he attended the Parker House luncheons of the Councilors Club, where present and former members of the council ate with the governor after each Wednesday morning council meeting. His finances remained mysterious. He claimed that he had used up all his funds and was now dependent on his children, yet he still kept his suite in the Parker House, his town house in Brighton and a country estate at Buzzards Bay on Cape Cod.

In 1942 Coakley appeared at the State House to take out nomination papers as a candidate for the United States Senate. Several pals came up to congratulate him on his healthy appearance. "It's because I have a clear and good conscience," he told them. But his career was over. He dropped out of the senate race—young Senator Henry Cabot Lodge, overseas in a major's uniform, was in any case unbeatable.

By the war's end Coakley had given up his Brighton house and was spending most of his time at Buzzards Bay. When he was eighty-one, he announced that he was writing his memoirs, "The Sparkling Past," and had already signed a contract with a well-known publisher. He was setting down the unvarnished truth about Massachusetts leaders "from the Supreme Court down, in all their stark nakedness and Jacob's robes—the most famous and infamous in the long and glorious history of the Commonwealth of Massachusetts." According to Coakley, prominent national, state, county and city officials had already read extracts and had "predicted this book will be the classic of the century." It would, he said, enable him to move for reinstatement to the bar. He did not plan to practice again, "but reinstatement will mean exoneration for me, and I want that before I reach the end of my road."

"The Sparkling Past" never did appear. Nor did Coakley realize his dream of reinstatement. He lived on in his Cape Cod quiet for another five years, dying in 1952 at the age of eighty-six. If he did not die in the odor of sanctity, he at least died in the bosom of the Church, being buried from St. Margaret's, Buzzards Bay. In him the Boston Irish were dealt their knave. This would probably have amused him as an epitaph.

Honey Fitz at a football game in 1913, having shed his derby—the politician's trademark—for a cap.

JOHN THE BOLD: BOSTON'S
JOHN F. "HONEY FITZ" FITZGERALD

THE THREE-ACT PLAY RUNS A CENTURY: SIXTY YEARS FROM THE GREAT Hunger in Ireland to the election of John Francis Fitzgerald— "Honey Fitz" to Massachusetts—as mayor of Boston; forty more years to see his namesake grandson, the twenty-nine-year-old John Fitzgerald Kennedy, elected to Congress from Honey Fitz's old district as the first planned step to the Presidency. Those three dates, cut so deeply in Boston's history, mark the beginning, middle and end of a phenomenon as old as history itself—the superseding of one class by another. Seventy years before the Potato Famine the seaport peninsula had seen it all happen before when on a blustery March day in 1775, Admiral Lord Howe embarked the Boston garrison, and the provincial aristocracy sailed away with the redcoats into exile. Those proudly armigerous Brattles and Vassalls and Dudleys and Hutchinsons abandoned the town to the nonarmigerous class below them.

As Boston resumed its pace after the Revolution, the old mansions had new faces in them. "Fellows who would have cleaned my shoes five years ago now ride in chariots," a disgruntled relative of General Joseph Warren observed. The emergents were the sober, hard-faced merchants, men who would never dream of giving up their new counting houses for moth-eaten loyalties. Inheriting the town by default, they—within the limits of their bourgeois sobriety—came to adopt the behavior pattern of their predecessors. One can mark the two eras by comparing the Palladian sophistication of Governor Shirley's Roxbury mansion (1745) with the naivety of Bulfinch's State House (1795), just as one can mark the next emergence in the contrast of the brick Federalist town houses of Beacon Hill with the Hyannis compound.

It takes about three generations for a new class to consolidate itself, and it took the grandsons of the Federalist merchants to give Boston its provincial label of the Athens of North America. That moment of flowering was not so much fruition as the pause before the end. And the end came to the self-contained brick town with the waves of Irish immigrants fleeing the Famine.

Between 1846 and 1854 over a million and a half people left Ireland for North America. They were driven out, dispossessed, without hope. Because the Cunard Line terminus was then in Boston, most of them landed there. Sunk in their defeat, they came over like cattle. Five percent of them died aboard the "coffin ships" on the way. The stench of those ships brought back memories of the old slavers; the Boston harbor master could recognize the odor of an immigrant vessel when it was still off Deer Island. Often there would be thirty or forty deaths in the course of a voyage on a ship containing five hundred to six hundred passengers.

The immigrants' memory of that flight and that passage and the desolation of their arrival remained green and bitter for generations. Over half the immigrants were illiterate; three-quarters had no trade. In Boston their life span averaged fourteen years. An able-bodied Irish laborer in the city could not in the 1850s earn enough by himself to keep his family. During the first-year depression of the Civil War the newcomers in their Paddyvilles and Mick Alleys starved. With their arrival they became the solid core of the new urban proletariat, alien in temperament, tradition and belief to that Yankee plutocracy for whom they were to furnish the cheap labor and from whom later—to the outraged astonishment and moral indignation of the latter—they were to take over Boston.

They were the base of the social pyramid, the unfailing source of exploitable labor: ditchdiggers, stevedores, hod carriers and stableboys. Construction bosses from all over America sent to Boston for fresh supplies of Irish workers. The Paddies went as contract laborers in coaches with sealed doors, the curtains nailed across the windows. Along the Erie Canal and the new railroad lines they died like flies.

These unassimilable foreigners with their uncouth solidarity more than doubled the population of static Boston, turning it from a coherent and comprehensive town to an incoherent and incomprehensible metropolis. From the padded perspective of the welfare state, it is easy to condemn the callousness of the Yankee Bostonians toward the newcomers, but the tremendous forced migration had no precedent; there was no mechanism for dealing with it. Beacon Hill felt no sense of responsibility for what was happening in East Boston. Rather, the Yankee epigoni, appalled by the Celtic locust-swarm, withdrew to the Beacon Hill–Back Bay redoubt. Unlike their Tory predecessors they did not quit the fort. For decades yet they would manage to keep political control of what they felt was their city. Its financial structure was and would remain in their hands—the industries, the banks, the stores, the investment houses. It was in reaction to these untouchable newcomers that the tradition of Boston *hauteur* came into being, the proper Bostonian, the myth of the Brahmin—that term the kindly Dr. Oliver Wendell Holmes coined originally to mean no more than a bread-and-water intellectual asceticism and that would now come to mean a class-conscious membership in the Yankee State Street financial oligarchy.

Though exploitable, the Irish seemed to the newly proper Bostonians (in the words of Mayor Lyman) ''a race that will never be infused with our own, but on the contrary will always remain distinct and hostile.'' In the harsh atmosphere of Boston, alienated from the common life of the community both by their background and their religion, the Irish formed a society within a society, an emerging Catholic political bloc of their own against the Protestant Yankee oligarchs. The younger immigrants formed gangs in the spirit of the old Irish Whiteboys. During the seventies and eighties, these gangs and barroom associations controlled the politics of their street and block, gradually spreading out, precinct by precinct, ward by ward, until it was clear that in a matter of time the Irish would capture the city. Politics came naturally to the temperament of the Celts, particularly when all other avenues of mobility were barred to them.

Following the pattern of almost all ethnic groups, the transplanted Irish began by electing their best. Hugh O'Brien was the first Irish immigrant to become mayor. With the support of dissident Yankee Democrats, he was elected in 1884 for the first of four one-year terms. Six years previously he had been chairman of the Board of Aldermen, and this date marks the first break in the Yankee political structure of the city, although the Irish position was not consolidated for another generation. Not until 1902 did Boston receive its second Irish-born mayor, Patrick Collins. Both O'Brien and Collins were outstanding men, able and honest, the type one might expect to find as lord mayor of Dublin or Cork or Limerick. Collins, whose widowed mother had brought him over as a child in the Famine years, started out in life as an upholsterer. After years of struggle he managed to enter the Harvard Law School and received his degree at twenty-seven. As first president of the American branch of the Irish Land League he became a friend of Parnell. In 1880 he was elected to Congress from the newly reapportioned and overwhelmingly Democratic district that included Boston's North and West Ends, and East and South Boston. He served three terms. In 1893 President Cleveland appointed him consul general in London.

Like his poet-friend John Boyle O'Reilly, Collins in his innate mobility tried to pretend away the caste barriers erected against the proletarian Irish. He denied that there was any such thing as an Irish vote, and declaimed passionately: "Americans we are; Americans we will remain." He hoped for the future of the Boston Irish in the light of his own development as a process of accommodation and acceptance, with the Irish conforming to the respectable pattern of their Yankee neighbors. But in the hard emergence of the Fitzgeralds and the Curleys and the Coakleys he saw this hopeful dream dissolve. In his later years, disillusioned, Collins turned to drink, even as O'Reilly in his disillusionment finally ended his own life.

Collins, on his return from England, was urged by Boston Democrats to help reunite the quarreling factions in the party by running for mayor. Reluctantly, he agreed. He was elected in 1901 and re-elected in 1903. Unbribably honest, he disliked the political atmosphere of City Hall. The practical necessities of patronage he detested. While managing to thwart the City Council's periodic raids on the treasury, he preached "caution, prudence and economy" to deaf-eared politicians. In 1905 he died in office.

After him the practical men took over. The Irish-American politicians, more and more of them now second-generation, felt no obligation to observe rules made by the Back Bay ascendancy who had exploited them. The way was open and the trough full. In the autumn of 1905, John F. Fitzgerald was elected mayor of Boston.

Honey Fitz, he was called, for his mellifluous rendering of "Sweet Adeline" on the hustings and on all possible social occasions except funerals. The song became his trademark. The taking over of City Hall by this dynamic little political buccaneer was as decisive a date in the history of Boston as General Howe's evacuation of the town.

John Francis Fitzgerald was not born with a silver spoon in his mouth, but he was born with a spoon—and this was much in the Irish North End in 1863. His father Thomas had come from Wexford, and like most immigrant Irishmen had worked first as a laborer, but by the time his third son Johnny came into the world he had become the proprietor of a North End grocery and liquor store. Four more sons were to follow.

A hundred years before, the North End had been a fashionable residential section with an eighteenth-century unsegregated mixture of stout artisan houses like Paul Revere's scattered between the mansions of the aristocracy. Governor Thomas Hutchinson had his elegant town house there, with the English Crown carved on the lintels, where he had written his history of Massachusetts until the house was sacked by the Stamp Act mob in 1765. Encroached on by the business district, the neighborhood had managed to preserve a faded respectability until it was overwhelmed by the Famine immigrants. These ragged illiterates swarmed up from the waterfront to pack the partitioned rooms of decayed mansions, to overflow into the hulls and gutters of the dock alleys and rot away in basement warrens. Copp's Hill with its ancient burying ground was renamed Connemara Hill, Donegal Square's earlier name was forgotten, and Kerry Village came into being. The North End became and stayed a slum.

The Fitzgeralds lived in a four-story, eight-family, red-brick tenement near the Old North Church. Their flat had no bath, no modern gas lighting, but no other family shared the few rooms and there was always food on the table. By the standards of the Irish North End the Fitzgeralds were well-off, and the boys did not think otherwise. Young Johnny came to love the narrow streets and never developed the bitter sense of alienation that his more savage rival, James Michael Curley, did.

"Johnny Fitz" the gang called him. He was smaller than the other boys, quicker with his feet than his fists. The teeming streets, littered with horse droppings, crowded with pushcarts and hucksters, were all he at first knew. He tagged after the older boys in their games along the docks. Masts and spars were part of his horizon. On winter days fog would often blanket the North End. In the hot, breathless summer nights the boy, lying in bed with his brothers, listened to the long-drawn wail of steamship whistles, the clang of the East Boston ferry bell. Johnny Fitz felt the sea in his bones. He never forgot it. "My playgrounds," he said years later, "were the streets and wharves busy with ships from every part of the world."

Early he showed that somewhat officious enterprise that is the mark of the embyro politician. The Fitzgerald brood were of course regular attenders at the North End's St. Stephen's, and Johnny was equally regular in attending all the parish social functions. As he grew older he helped the priests run picnics, minstrel shows, suppers, fairs and dances. At outings he usually won the sprints and always the potato race. So involved did he become in neighborhood affairs, so reliable was he in getting things done, that he was elected president of the Neptune Associates when most of the members were old enough to be his father. The club was the strongest social and athletic organization in the North End.

Yet no one could say that Johnny Fitz was Alger all the way. At a time when most North End boys were considered fitted for life with a grammar school diploma, he attended the Boston Latin School where, as a contemporary of Santayana and Berenson, he received a reasonably classical education. During those years he lost his mother. On graduating from Boston Latin he entered the Harvard Medical School, but at the end of his first year his father died, and he had to turn to and help keep the family together. He left Harvard—still a heretical institution to most of the Boston Irish—and took the examination for a job in the Custom House. "I had to take care of all six of my brothers," he liked to relate tremulously at political rallies in after years, neglecting to add that he was then eighteen and that two of his brothers were several years older. "I washed dishes, scrubbed floors, sifted ashes and brought up scuttles of coal and firewood, climbing three flights of creaky stairs. For some reason it was my trust to boss the family. I even washed the faces of the younger boys every day, and oftentimes dressed them."

He came out near the top of the list on his examination, and for the next three years served as a clerk in the Custom House, where he took the measure of the civil service. Then he resigned to set up an insurance office in the North End, specializing in fire insurance. In those willow years he joined every organization that came his way and made his way to others: the Massachusetts Order of Foresters, the Ancient Order of Hibernians, the Knights of St. Rose, the Red Berry Club, the Heptasophs, the Royal Arcanum, the Charitable Irish Society, the Dorchester Catholic Club, the St. Alphonsus Association, the

Catholic Union of Boston, the Young Men's Catholic Association of Boston College, the Franklin Typographical Association, the Knights of Columbus and still others. He was glib and persuasive in casual talk, he was noddingly acquainted with almost all the North End families, and he knew every voter by name. Although nothing like a generation before, the North End was still a slum. Johnny Fitz sentimentalized it even as he flattered its inhabitants. "Dear old North End" tripped so easily and so frequently from his tongue that his supporters there came to be known as "Dearos." To those who were not his supporters, young Johnny became Fitzblarney. When he was twenty-six he married Mary Josephine Hannon, a young woman whose good looks became one of the inherited characteristics of the Kennedy clan. She had been Johnny Fitz's "girl" for eight years. After their marriage some of the Fitzgerald brothers moved in with them.

Johnny Fitz, with his flourishing insurance business and his face amiably familiar from one end of the North End to the other, was now as ready for politics as a duckling for a pond. Outwardly he suggested more a bantam rooster than a duckling, diminutive and cocky. He was a bouncing, dapper man, so much so that one tended to overlook at first the narrow mouth, the eyes a little too close together, the ready voice pitched just a little too high.

Democratic Boston in the nineties had no consolidating and controlling Tammany Hall as in New York. Power was split among the ward bosses: in the West End, Martin Lomasney—the Ward 8 Mahatma—the most picturesque, the most notorious, yet also the best of the bosses; in East Boston, Patrick Joseph Kennedy, a genial saloon-keeper and liquor dealer (he would become the paternal grandfather of a future president); in the North End's Ward 6, Matthew Keany; in the South End, at a later date, James Michael Curley.

Keany, attracted to the assertive, quick-tongued Johnny Fitz, had taken him into his organization and soon made him one of his trusted heelers. Being a ward-heeler was an education in the rudiments of political control. In was an education that Johnny absorbed so zealously that a few years later when Keany died he managed to elbow his way into place as boss of the North End.

In 1892 Fitzgerald—not yet boss and not yet Honey Fitz—got himself elected to the Boston Common Council. It is true there were seventy-four other members in this haphazardly disreputable assembly, but it was a beginning. He hired a secretary and turned over most of his insurance business to his brother Henry. The upstairs office became the Jefferson Club, where anyone in the North End was free to drop in at any time. He was at every dance and caper, expanding the Catholic socials, introducing the first "sunlight dances" to Boston. He kept a card index of everyone in his district who needed a job. At Thanksgiving and Christmas he was on hand with turkey baskets. No wedding took place in the North End without a prominently displayed present from him. Each morning he scanned the death notices in the *Globe*, and he never missed a wake. He had the actor's gift of easy tears. In the summer of 1892 he announced that he was running for the state senate. The old-time leader of Ward 6 died at this time, leaving the young councilor undisputed boss. "The North End Napoleon," the reporters ticketed him, and Johnny Fitz delightedly began to read up on Napoleon and even adopted some of his mannerisms.

Lomasney's announcement from neighboring Ward 8 that he was supporting Fitzgerald made the latter's election certain. It was politician's luck that the Mahatma had an old grudge against Honey Fitz's opponent.

All the political, historical and sociological strands that make up the Boston ward boss were to be seen in the career of Martin Lomasney. Yet of all the bosses, he profited least from his position. An orphan bootblack, he started out in manhood as a lamplighter. Eventually he managed to become a city health inspector, and then, as the first step to controlling his ward, he founded the Hendricks Club (named after Cleveland's Vice President, Thomas A. Hendricks, who had once made a speech defending the Irish). It did not take long before Lomasney was master of the West End. His formula was basic: know every family in the West End; help everyone who needs help. The Mahatma's iron paternalism came to dominate the narrow slum streets. There should be a place, he maintained, where a man could come when he was in trouble, no matter what he had done. That place was for Lomasney the Hendricks Club.

> From the standpoint of politics [Lomasney wrote], the great mass of people are interested in only three things—food, clothing and shelter. A politician in a district such as mine sees to it that his people get these things. If he does, he hasn't got to worry about their loyalty and support.

Lomasney's cohorts were on hand to meet each immigrant ship as it arrived. The newcomers were welcomed, given lodgings and jobs, and their names entered permanently in the Hendricks Club's files.

For Johnny Fitz and Jim Curley, being a ward boss was a somewhat slippery steppingstone to something else. For Lomasney it was an end in itself. Day after day he held court in the nondescript hall that was the Hendricks Club. His familiar place was behind a battered rolltop desk, a straw hat, yellow with age, tilted over the baldness of his long head. A drooping handlebar mustache framed the jutting eminence of his pugnacious jaw. One by one the supplicants came to him, and his appraising blue eyes measured them through narrow gold-rimmed spectacles. No one would ever have dared lie to the Mahatma.

Ward 8 was a clean ward in the sense that there was no vice, no gambling, no rough stuff, no trouble about votes. Lomasney, with his filing system, saw to that. The little streets voted to his order. So did former residents who returned in droves as overnight lodgers to vote in old Ward 8. The Mahatma did not take graft. Money to run the Hendricks Club services came from two sources. Those who got jobs, although it was never mentioned, understood that something was expected in return. Lomasney also accepted donations from all concerns that did business in the West End. The firms made their donations voluntarily, even cheerfully, but they might have found reason to regret it if they had not. Whatever money Lomasney had personally he made in real estate. He was shrewd and he was strategically located. It often happened that when the City of Boston needed to acquire a parcel of land for a school or public building, Martin Lomasney was found to have title to that parcel.

There was surprise among the pols when the Mahatma decreed that he was backing Fitzgerald. "Johnny Fitz must have hypnotized Martin," was the ward-heeler's verdict, and indeed Lomasney would live to regret the leg-up he had given to the North End Napoleon. Fitzgerald was almost unanimously elected. He spent two unspectacular years in the senate quietly building up his machine for the next leap forward, using his State House opportunities to settle relatives and strategic supporters in plush jobs. With exemplary patriotism he sponsored the April 19 anniversary of the battle of Concord and Lexington as a local holiday, and with an eye to the Italians now appearing on the waterfront he wangled the same favor for Columbus's birthday in October.

In 1894, moving crabwise but with his eye permanently fixed on
City Hall, Fitzgerald announced his candidacy for Congress. The
congressional district was made up of the first nine wards of Boston,
and was the only sure Democratic district in the state. Again Lomasney
backed him, opposing Congressman Joseph O'Neil, who was supported
by most of the other ward bosses. It was a rough election as the Irish
wards knew elections, with slugfests, mattress voters and sudden
darkness in the occasional close-vote polling place as enthusiasts cut
the gas pipes while others rushed in to stuff or steal the ballot boxes.
But with the solid support of Wards 6 and 8 Johnny Fitz, "the boy
candidate," was not to be beaten.

Three terms Fitzgerald served as congressman. In his first term he
was the only Catholic in the House. He made no name for himself,
achieving scarcely more than a whimsical reputation as a jack-in-the-
box for his insistence on popping up in irrelevant debate. He did
sponsor a bill to purchase the frigate *Constitution*, "Old Ironsides,"
then rotting away at a pier in Portsmouth, New Hampshire. He
managed to get the Charlestown Navy Yard reopened, and helped
obtain several million-dollar appropriations for Boston harbor. His love
for the sea and for Boston the seaport was real and would last him
all his days, but he also knew how to turn this love to his own ends.
His chief concern in Congress was to expand his political power. Brother
Henry in the North End kept the machine oiled and saw that supplies
of oil were forthcoming. Johnny, during the Washington years, bought
a house in rural Concord, but he still kept his legal address in the dear
old North End.

In the 1895 election the time was not yet for another Irish mayor.
Boston's ward bosses had to go outside the city to Quincy for the Yankee
Democrat necessary to defeat Republican Mayor Edwin U. Curtis. The
man they picked and elected was Josiah Quincy, after whose ancestors
the town had been named. Three bosses—no friends of Lomasney's—
did the picking: Smiling Jim Donovan, the chairman of the Democratic
City Committee; Judge Joseph J. Corbett, the election commissioner;
and East Boston's Patrick "P.J." Kennedy. Impressed by the rise of
Fitzgerald, they were willing—if he would turn his back on the
Mahatma—to admit the congressman to their circle as the fourth mayor-
maker. Honey Fitz was willing.

Then in 1901 the Big Four, still biding their time, managed to
persuade the austerely respectable Patrick Collins to be their candidate.

Collins was easily if reluctantly elected. He always found the job of mayor distasteful. Smiling Jim he made superintendent of streets, but he refused most other patronage demands. Johnny Fitz galled him.

Meanwhile Fitzgerald had bought a moribund neigborhood paper, *The Republic,* for five hundred dollars. This he turned into an Irish-American social weekly which he both edited and published. Nothing in it was of any great interest, nor did readers flock to it. Nevertheless department stores, public utilities, and contractors hurried to buy half- and full-page advertisements. Despite its small circulation and stiff rates, *The Republic* somehow seemed a desirable advertising medium. Soon it was netting its new publisher $25,000 a year.

In 1903 Fitzgerald moved back from Concord to dearer old Dorchester. The house he bought on Welles Avenue was an ornamental wooden chateau in beer-baronial style, with a scrollwork porch, blank plateglass windows and a mansard turret. On the stair landing he had a stained-glass window installed with a Fitzgerald coat of arms and the Gaelic motto *Shawn A Boo* (John the Bold).

John the Bold, full of bounce and pugnacious confidence, knew that the municipal election year of 1905 was his year, that he was on the crest of his political wave, and that the tide was coming in. Every ward-heeler and precinct worker sensed instinctively that Johnny Fitz would be a candidate, would be indeed *the* candidate for mayor. Collins had died that September, and the question for the bosses was: whom should they run against this dynamic challenger they had built up so casually a decade before? Smiling Jim and Kennedy turned to the Mahatma, and the three of them decided on City Clerk Edward Donovan.

Impelled from the clerk's office to the hustings, Donovan scarcely knew what hit him. Johnny Fitz was off like a whirlwind on the most spectacular campaign Boston's twenty-four wards had ever seen. Vacant walls were pasted with his posters twice as fast as opponents could tear them down. Bigger, Better, Busier John was emblazoned under the smiling Fitzgerald phiz, retouched to benignity by the photographer. The city, long used to pre-election free-for-alls with brickbats and "alley roses" sailing past a speaker's platform, marveled at the roar of its first political motorcade. Honey Fitz toured the wards in a large red car followed by flying squads of what the reporters described as "Napoleon's lancers," to be met in each precinct by crowds of militant Dearos. Ward 8 itself was invaded and here a zealous Dearo at one point pulled a pistol on several Hendricks Clubbers. Secretly, Fitzgerald solicited the help of younger Democratic hopefuls, the bosses-yet-to-be—and secretly they gave help. Even James Michael Curley, soon to be Fitzgerald's most durable enemy, now planned to back him.

For weeks Johnny Fitz made ten speeches a night denouncing the bosses of the "machine," and on the evening before the primaries he reached the almost breathless climax of thirty. But for Lomasney he would have buried Donovan. Fitzgerald won the nomination, carrying twenty of the city's wards, although it took a dozen wards to make up for what happened to him in Ward 8.

The reform Republicans and the Good Government Association—a civic organization founded two years before by the Chamber of Commerce, the Merchants Association, the Associated Board of Trade, the Fruit and Produce Association and the Bar Association—had succeeded in nominating the highly respected speaker of the Massachusetts House of Representatives, Louis Frothingham. Unreformed Republicans, with the concealed moral and financial encouragement of Fitzgerald, ran Judge Henry Dewey—already beaten by Frothingham in the primaries—as an independent Republican. The split Republican ticket made Fitzgerald's election a certainty, as wily old Martin Lomasney at once realized. Nevertheless the Mahatma preferred defeat with Frothingham. "That gun play," he remarked, "on top of all the stuff they had been springing on the stump, made me determined to fight."

Frothingham represented all the things that Fitzgerald could ring the sour changes on—Harvard, blue blood, inherited wealth. Honey Fitz also spread the rumor thickly (and unjustifiably) that his opponent was anti-Catholic and anti-Irish. He kept up his whirlwind campaign with variations, visiting department stores and glad-handing the salespeople, even inaugurating a "soda water campaign" with refreshments provided for women's groups in critical wards. Honey Fitz had always been—with prudent impartiality—a ladies' man, and women always thought more of him than did men. They were his most solid supporters, from the days when he used to waltz with the wallflowers at the Irish social clubs.

The battle cost Fitzgerald $120,000—twice as much as it did Frothingham. "But it was not money which won," George Kibbe Turner wrote in *Collier's,* "it was action, ingenuity, and boundless, cheerful effrontery. For thirteen years Johnny Fitz had held Ward 6 obedient and cheerful by public jobs. He extended that one basic system of ward politics over all the city."

The new mayor took possession of the gray mock-renaissance City Hall on School Street like a conqueror exacting the submission of a taken town. *Enrichissez-vous!* Perhaps Johnny Fitz had read the Napoleonic maxim. His cohorts did not need to read it. The mayor himself kept control of all the city departments except the schools and the police. He replaced physicians on the board of health with saloonkeepers, he appointed another saloonkeeper superintendent of public buildings, a whitewasher superintendent of sewers, a bartender who had been expelled from the legislature superintendent of streets. For deserving Dearos he created such new offices as that of city dermatologist. Eight additional deputy sealers were added to the Department of Weights and Measures—a department soon to erupt in open scandal. The vestiges of civil service were circumvented by the invention of novel job categories—tea warmers, tree climbers, wipers, rubber-boot repairers, watchmen to watch other watchmen. Brother Henry was given charge of patronage and payments. "See Henry!" was the edict from the mayor's office.

During Johnny Fitz's first administration, graft was blatant in all departments. "Thieves in the House," John Cutler entitled the chapter on that period in his discreet Fitzgerald biography. During these two years the city lost $200,000 in dealings with a single coal company, whose manager later absconded. In subsequent investigations the Finance Commission discovered that Boston had been paying sixty cents a barrel more than the going rate for cement—a $240,000 annual loss. "Bills and vouchers could not be found," Leslie Ainley wrote in his life of Lomasney. "City work was contracted and bids often accepted verbally." There were dozens of strange land deals where the city ended up paying three times more than anyone had imagined a given property was worth. The Finance Commission reported "a steady deterioration in the technical competency and moral strength of the heads of executive departments, until administrative business of this great city was, with few notable exceptions, in the hands either of men without education, training, experience, or technical qualifications of any sort, or of men who had become so demoralized by the conditions which surrounded them as to be unwilling to protest against the most obvious extravagance or graft, if favored by the mayor. For the first time," the commission went on to say, "a man was elected to the office of mayor whose aim was not merely to use or perfect the political machine then in existence, but to become that machine itself."

Meanwhile, *The Republic* continued to flourish and expand—its advertising rates were perhaps the highest in the nation in ratio to its circulation. The Boston Elevated Street Railway Company and the American Telephone and Telegraph Company bought up pages, as did the New England Telephone Company, Edison Electric, New England Gas and Coke, Boston Consolidated Gas, the Boston and Maine Railroad and any number of contracting companies. A list of the paper's advertisers read like a summary of the Boston Stock Exchange. In one special issue the city's banks took fourteen pages.

For most of the time the accumulating scandals seemed secondary to the dynamic ubiquitousness of the little man in the mayor's chair, who might suddenly appear at his office in a black-and-brown checked suit, blue striped tie and bluestone scarf pin. During his first term, he is estimated to have attended 1200 dinners, 1500 dances, 200 picnics and 1000 meetings; made 3000 speeches; and danced with 5000 girls. He thought up Old Home Week and applied it first to Boston—even though Beacon Street held aloof. With his entourage he liked to drop in for a sudden meal, amidst the flattering bustle of the staff, at the various city hotels—the Adams House and the Parker House, Young's, the Democratic politicians' eyrie of the Quincy House on the fringe of the North End, the Winter Palace and the South End's naughtily Edwardian Woodcock. He excelled as a greeter, entertaining personally such varied visitors as Prince Wilhelm of Sweden and the magician Houdini. Between 1905 and 1907 Johnny Fitz made himself a city institution.

Two years of Fitzgerald, however, brought an inevitable reaction. There were still transplanted Irish in Boston who felt that Patrick Collins was a worthier representative than Johnny Fitz and his Dearos. They could still remember how Collins, as mayor, had welcomed the delegates of the National Municipal League and asked them to report to him if they found anything shady in his administration. What the delegates might have found in the Fitzgerald administration did not bear thinking about.

For the 1907 elections anti-Fitzgerald Democrats nominated Representative John Coulthurst. Coulthurst also had the backing of Hearst's *American* and of all the bosses except Lomasney, who this time returned to Johnny Fitz. The Republicans picked their own variety of boss, George A. Hibbard, the Boston postmaster. Hibbard was a parrot-nosed, thrifty Yankee who announced he was running for one term only for the purpose of "cleaning up the mess." Fitzgerald conducted his usual bouncing, badgering campaign, adding such bizarreries as circulars in Yiddish to persuade the newly arrived Jewish voters. Most Jewish leaders as well as the more responsible Catholic leaders repudiated him. In a narrow election Coulthurst swung enough Democrats from Fitzgerald so that Hibbard was able to win with a plurality of the voters.

Mayor Hibbard, while looking after needy Republicans, did much of what he had promised. He cut down on municipal workers, halved the cost of street maintenance and reduced the city's debt. Through departmental efficiencies he managed to save about a million dollars. Toward the end of his administration, and in the hope of more reform mayors to come, the Good Government Association maneuvered the adoption of a new city charter. According to its terms party designations were to be dropped from the municipal ballot. There were to be no more primaries, and nominations for mayor could be made by the petition of five thousand voters. A nine-member council would replace the thirteen aldermen and seventy-five councilors.

Electorates soon weary of reform interludes, and those who are barred from the trough weary even sooner. By 1909 it seemed that the wheel had turned and that the colorless Hibbard would be replaced by the pied Johnny Fitz. To avoid four entrenched Fitzgerald years, Republicans and reformers united on the bluest blood of Beacon Street, James Jackson Storrow. A predestined Harvard man, Storrow had been captain of a crew that had beaten Yale, and now, as New England's wealthiest banker, he was an overseer of Harvard College. With far more civic conscience than most of his kind, he had served as chairman of the Boston School Committee, had been a president of the Boy Scouts, had founded the West End Club for newsboys and had given much for playgrounds and amenities in the slums. A lean, imposing figure, he was a poor speaker. This was offset, however, by his being that atavistic anomaly, a Yankee Democrat.

Smiling Jim Donovan threw in his lot early with Storrow, impressing on the banker the truism that political campaigns cost money. Storrow was impressed—to the extent of half a million dollars before he got through. Storrow money was loosely plentiful, and Smiling Jim understood its application. Curley, then the visibly rising boss of the South End's Ward 17, said later that he had refused $60,000 to side with Storrow. Fitzgerald knew that without the support of Curley and

Lomasney he could not win. The three came to an agreement. The thirty-five-year-old Curley, as junior partner, was to take over Fitzgerald's old congressional seat and bide his time in Washington until the next municipal election. What Lomasney was offered remains a secret, but in spite of personal distaste he stuck with Johnny Fitz.

"Take Storrow's money, but vote for Fitzgerald," was the word the Dearos passed round. Storrow tried to argue about corruption and the issues of municipal government. Johnny Fitz simplified the election to a contest between an Irish-Catholic boy from the slums and a wealth-encrusted Harvard blueblood who was anti-Catholic, anti-labor, anti-black and anti-anything else Fitzgerald could think of between speeches. He papered the walls with large photographs of City Hall on which was inscribed:

NOT FOR SALE MR. $TORROW

"Manhood against Money" was another Fitzgerald slogan that was used under a touchingly domestic photograph of Johnny Fitz, his wife and their three boys and three girls. The Storrow forces countered with a photograph of Fitzgerald alone, the word GRAFTER lettered across his forehead. That stung enough to bring tears. Storrow even coined the term *Fitzgeraldism* to describe the antics of Johnny Fitz's administration, but when *Fitzgeraldism* appeared in newspaper advertisments, Fitzgerald countered by running parallel advertisements with slogans: "For Better Streets!...For Better Schools!"

In a day when a political meeting was for many the most entertaining event of the year, when the catharsis of a campaign could purge the emotions, as in later years films and television never could, when partisans packed the hall for hours to wait for their chosen candidate, Johnny Fitz was a circus and a prophet combined. His campaign is said to have cost somebody, if not him, a quarter of a million dollars. During the frenzied weeks before the election, he led his motorcade through several thousand miles of back streets, shouting his tenor voice hoarse at halls and corners. Storrow, trying in his unfortunate Harvard accent to emulate him, was driven out of South Boston by a mob swinging torches and throwing chunks of ice. Fitzgerald even managed to persuade Hibbard, mortally stricken with tuberculosis of the throat, to run as a token candidate in order to draw votes from Storrow.

The Saturday night before the election Fitzgerald staged his biggest and most bumptious rally in Faneuil Hall in the dear old North End.

As an added attraction he had hired a brass band, instructing the leader
to play "The Star-Spangled Banner" at his entrance and follow it up
with "The Wearing of the Green." The latter song concluded before
Fitzgerald and his entourage could manage to handshake their way
to the platform. Because it was a popular song of the moment, and
with nothing more in mind, the bandleader had his men strike up
"Sweet Adeline." Everybody joined in the chorus. When it came time
for the second verse, Johnny Fitz, with deft spontaneity, capered down
the platform and sang it solo, then led the crowd again in the chorus.
And in that bellowing moment of beaming fair faces, the Honey Fitz
legend was born. Ever after that the tenor voice and the treacly song
would be harmoniously linked, and whenever at a Democratic meeting
the speeches began to run dry, the cry would go up for Honey Fitz
to sing "Sweet Adeline."

It was generally admitted by politicians afterward that Honey Fitz's
demonic gusto in the last few days of the campaign won him the
election. On the final night he spoke at thirty-five rallies and topped
it off by singing "Sweet Adeline" from the roof of a hack. Even so,
in the largest vote in Boston's history, he barely squeaked through with
47,177 votes to 45,775 for Storrow. The ailing Hibbard, repudiated
by the Republicans, received only 1,614 votes—but enough to have
swung the election if they had gone to Storrow.

Not much could be said about Honey Fitz's second term as mayor
that was not said about his first, except that Boston grew accustomed
to the shenanigans. After four more years of Fitzgerald in City Hall
no Storrow would have a ghost of a chance of being elected mayor—
or would want to take that ghost's chance. And there were the solid
accomplishments, whatever their price tag. Honey Fitz built the City
Hall Annex, the City Point Aquarium, numberless public convenience
stations memorialized with his name and the Franklin Park Zoo. He
founded the High School of Commerce to prepare boys directly for
the business world who could not go to college. One of his more original
minor inspirations was the painting of white traffic lines, for which
he was accused by proper Bostonians of disfiguring the city's historic
streets. With appropriate regard for sentiment he established the local
sanctity of Mother's Day and began the custom of having a Christmas
tree on Boston Common. He also inaugurated the banned-in-Boston
tradition by forbidding the Turkey Trot and the tango as immoral,
the opera *Salomé* as sacrilegious and the red flag in parades as both.

The mayor's official car was now the *Sweet Adeline II*. In 1911, as he sailed for a tour of Europe on the *Franconia*, he sang his theme song from the bridge. For the voyage he had packed a supply of rockets and other fireworks to set off at the first sight of the Irish coast, with the result that the Irish Coast Guard finally signaled: "Do you need help?"

Greeting and entertaining were his official delight. He welcomed such assorted figures at City Hall as the French actress Gaby Deslys, New Jersey's Governor Woodrow Wilson, William Jennings Bryan, Theodore Roosevelt, Lady Gregory and the lord mayors of Dublin and London. Sir Thomas Lipton relaxed in his company, visiting him not only in Dorchester but in the wooden-gingerbread ark of Fitzgerald's summer house in Hull, overlooking Boston harbor. In 1914 Honey Fitz's oldest daughter, Rose, married a brash, up-and-coming young Harvard graduate, Joseph Patrick Kennedy, the son of East Boston's P. J.

Honey Fitz had made a bosses' agreement to leave City Hall at the end of his term. He toyed briefly with the quixotic notion of running for governor or even for United States senator, but as his pleasant and profitable months in the gray School Street building narrowed he began to feel that his earlier renunciation was premature. Meanwhile, Congressman Curley, rounding out his second term in Washington, was regarding the gilt edge on top of City Hall with an increasingly calculating eye. "You are an old man," he told the fifty-year-old mayor by way of a Curley-type hint. "Get your slippers and pipe and stretch out in your hammock and read *The Ladies' Home Journal*."

The lone wolf of Ward 17 was the one opponent whom Honey Fitz feared. Unlike most politicians, Curley never developed a nickname. Even though he had begun by imitating the Ward-6 Napoleon, he had been brought up in a harder school. He had a more commanding presence and a more resonant voice, a crueler tongue and a quicker fist. Honey Fitz may have been meaner, but Curley was tougher, and he had the instinct for the jugular.

In November 1913 Curley let it be known, officially, that he would be a candidate for mayor in the January election. A few weeks later Honey Fitz came out with the announcement that he had decided to run for a third term. Next day the *Post* quoted Curley's comment: "Fitzgerald wants a licking, and he will get it." The two were now archenemies, and in spite of intermittent superficial political gestures of good will, they were to remain enemies the rest of their long lives. A few days after Honey Fitz's announcement Curley told reporters:

I am preparing three addresses which, if necessary, I shall deliver, and which, if a certain individual had the right to restrict free speech, I would not be permitted to deliver.

One of these addresses is entitled: "Graft, Ancient and Modern"; another, "Great Lovers: From Cleopatra to Toodles"; and last, but not least, "Libertines: From Henry VIII to the Present Day."

Curley gave his speech on graft wth comparisons between the Rome of the Caesars and Boston of the Dearos, at the Dorchester High School. But before he could deliver his Toodles address on Boston Common, Honey Fitz, "on grounds of ill health," had withdrawn his candidacy.

The Ferncroft Inn was one of Honey Fitz's ports of call, and it was at a large party there that he had met Toodles Ryan, later Dan Coakley's client. Subsequently she became his close companion, queen of the revels at the South End's Woodcock Hotel on Washington Street, his favored hostelry with its intimate private dining rooms. A blur of talk followed the mayor and the over-bosomed blonde, their names becoming more permanently linked in a jingle repeated *sotto voce* by local politicians:

A whiskey glass
And Toodle's ass
made a horse's ass
of Honey Fitz.

In later years Honey Fitz self-righteously insisted in a statement to the *Post* that he had never done more than kiss Toodles casually and publicly at the Ferncroft party, with his wife present. Those close to Honey Fitz have tried to argue away the Toodles stories as no more than malicious jokes. Curley insisted that they and similar Honey Fitz tales long current in Boston were true, and he always maintained that his threat to tell what he knew about Toodles drove Fitzgerald from public life.

After his withdrawal, Honey Fitz and the ward bosses—with the exception of Lomasney—united incongruously with the Good Government Association on an anti-Curley candidate, City Councilor Thomas J. Kenney, an honest but uninspired budget expert who had once served on the School Committee. At the last moment P. J.

Kennedy shifted his support to Curley. In spite of the opposition of the rest of the bosses—whom Curley now swore to destroy—the young man from the South End was unbeatable.

Winning inspired no charitable thoughts in Curley. When at his inaugural he had to shake hands with his predecessor, he stared coldly away. Then, with Honey Fitz sitting a few feet from him, he attacked the ex-mayor so bitingly that the latter's face twitched and reddened. Six hundred of Honey Fitz's supporters employed at City Hall had to walk out the back door the day Curley walked in the front.

With Curley's election, Honey Fitz's political career came to an end. Though he would live on for a third of a century, though he would several times be a candidate, he would never again occupy public office.

For some time he enjoyed his leisure. He could now indulge in his passion for long auto rides, for cruising in Boston harbor and for sporting events—baseball, football and prize fights. With the approach of winter, he sunned himself in Florida. His social life buzzed much as ever. He dined and he danced, he spoke and sang. In 1915 he received an honorary doctorate of laws from Notre Dame University, and liked afterward to have himself referred to as Dr. Fitzgerald. But by 1916 he could feel the old political stirrings in his blood.

That year was the first in Massachusetts for direct election to the United States Senate, and Senator Henry Cabot Lodge, who had served three terms by vote of the Massachusetts legislature, was now forced to take his chances with the electorate. The chill autocratic Yankee with the gray curls and the gray spade beard was not an endearing personality. Disaffected Republicans and old Roosevelt Bull Moosers would have no part of him. Harvard's President Lawrence Lowell was later to refer to him as "a degenerate son of the University." A Yankee Democrat, in the wake of Wilson's Presidential victory, could probably have defeated Lodge that year. Not, however, Honey Fitz. With Curley occupied at City Hall, Fitzgerald managed to grasp the brass ring of the Democratic nomination. Only his Celtic optimism kept him from seeing that the ring was worthless. *The New York Times* could not understand why Massachusetts Democrats had not put up a worthier candidate against the "gentleman from Massachusetts." From the perspective of New York, Honey Fitz was "an amiable kisser of the Blarney Stone, warbler of 'Sweet Adeline,' rider of Florida sharks, butterfly flitting unconcerned around the solid men of Boston."

The following year brought with it another municipal election, but

Honey Fitz had no intention of tangling with Curley again. He preferred to take a temporary step down the political ladder and run for Congress from his old district. The present congressman, Peter Tague, was under a cloud in Boston, or at least in Ward 8. Lomasney had originally given Tague the support that elected him, but turned furiously against him when Tague failed to propose in Congress that the entry of the United States into the war be contingent on England's granting Ireland independence. In spite of the Mahatma's backing, Fitzgerald won the nomination by only fifty votes in a contest memorable even in Boston for the numbers of false registrations, mattress voters, repeaters, burnt ballots and stolen ballot boxes. Tague refused to accept the result and announced defiantly that he was running on stickers. To counter this, Honey Fitz had blocks of stickers printed without the gum on the back. On election day dozens of his supporters, pretending to be Tague workers, handed out these stickers at the polls. When the ballots were placed in the box the ungummed stickers fell off, leaving blank ballots. Fitzgerald won by 238 votes. At once Joseph Kane, Tague's tough professional manager, complained to Washington that the election was a fraud. A congressional committee came to Boston to investigate Kane's charges. They found enough evidence of fraudulent voting and "padded returns of alleged residents in cheap lodging houses" to unseat Fitzgerald and replace him by Tague.

In January 1922 Honey Fitz announced that he was again a candidate to oppose Lodge for the United States Senate. As a token of party unity he and Curley shook hands at the Elks Club and then, to prove their harmony, sang duets of "Sweet Adeline" and "Tammany." But when the Republicans took to quarreling among themselves like so many Democrats about a candidate for governor, Honey Fitz decided he would rather take advantage of their dissension than confront the frosty Lodge. Not for another decade would the Irish Democrats take over the state, and Honey Fitz's challenge to Republican Governor Channing Cox failed by 60,000 votes. Nevertheless, the *Post* paid tribute to Fitzgerald's coruscating effort: "Nothing like it has ever been seen in Massachusetts. He is the superman of campaigners, and he is greater in defeat than he ever was in victory."

Honey Fitz, now in his sixties, was grayer, plumper, his jowls deeper, his face puffier, but still with the old outrageous bounce. Late in 1925 he let it be known that he was once more a candidate for mayor. Then, four days later, he changed his mind, to the relief of his son-in-law

Joe Kennedy, who was getting a little tired of the Toodles stories that were revived with each Honey Fitz candidacy. Instead of becoming a candidate, the ex-mayor celebrated his birthday by singing "Sweet Adeline" over the radio. The mayoralty contest boiled up with six others, but somehow a Boston campaign without Honey Fitz lost half its savor. A reporter wrote nostalgically: "Lovers of the spectacular may regret that this most colorful personality will not be seen charging up and down the municipal gridiron, going through for gains, being thrown for losses, smearing his opponents or being smeared. The battle will not be the same with the 'doctor' out."

Some time in the mid-twenties Fitzgerald sold the Dorchester chateau and moved to a rent-free suite in the Bellevue Hotel, the politicians' Valhalla beside the State House. The summer house in Hull he exchanged for one in Wareham on Cape Cod, near the Kennedy compound. For an antidote to restlessness he took long rides in h.· chauffeur-driven Locomobile. As he grew older, that mellowing process took over by which politicians and other wayward characters become fixtures, so that in the end even their old enemies are glad to see them. In 1927, when the Adams House with its memories of so many political figures closed, it seemed fitting that Honey Fitz should ring down the curtain with "Sweet Adeline."

The year 1930 marked his last real political battle. He announced that he was a candidate for governor. Massachusetts Republicans were never to recover from that second Depression year. Boston had been a Democratic city for a generation, and now it was the turn of Massachusetts to become a Democratic state. If Honey Fitz had won the nomination that year, he would have been elected. But two weeks before the primaries he collapsed, and from his hospital bed he sent word that he was withdrawing from the contest. In one of the strange turnabouts of Boston politics, Curley, who had become his most impassioned supporter and speechmaker, refused to accept the withdrawal—not from any belated affection for Honey Fitz but out of blind hatred for the leading candidate, Yankee Democrat Joseph Ely.

In the 1932 Roosevelt year, Curley was the first Massachusetts politician to sense the swing of the tide and to shift his mercurial allegiance from Al Smith to Franklin Roosevelt, a shift so unpopular among local Democrats that he was dropped from the Ancient Order of Hibernians. Honey Fitz remained an Al Smith man right down to the Democratic Convention, even though his astute son-in-law had become a member of the strategy group, "the Silent Six," touring the country in Roosevelt's campaign train. Nevertheless, the old Dearo was granted the innocuous postelection honor of the presidency of the Massachusetts delegation to the electoral college.

The mellowing process continued, but now to a point of isolation. P. J. Kennedy had died in 1929. Lomasney followed him shortly after Roosevelt's inauguration. Only the indestructable Curley remained, alternately winning and losing elections. In 1936 Honey Fitz became president of the Clover Club, a local Celtic variation of Washington's Gridiron Club, and took the chair for the first time, dressed as Napoleon. The next year, with wry pride, he saw his son-in-law appointed ambassador to England. On Honey Fitz's seventy-fifth birthday, 750 guests attended a party for him at the Boston Chamber of Commerce, and he noted with content that the patrician ex-secretary of the navy, Charles Francis Adams, was among them. He was on hand to meet Roosevelt's train when it arrived in Boston in 1940, and the younger charmer greeted the old with: "Welcome, Dulce Adelina!"

One of the few Republican survivors of the 1936 landslide had been Henry Cabot Lodge, Jr., the grandson of the "gentleman from Massachusetts," who had managed to capitalize sufficiently on the accumulated resentments against Curley to defeat him in the contest for his grandfather's old senatorial seat. Senator Lodge came up for re-election in 1942, and Roosevelt picked Democratic Joseph Casey to run against him. Honey Fitz, though now eighty years old and in failing health, decided to have his last political fling by contesting the nomination. For a few weeks he staged a radio counter-campaign with ghost-written speeches and a ghostly voice signing off with "Sweet Adeline." Son-in-law Kennedy consulted with Tague's old secretary, Joe Kane, wise in the ways of pols. Kane was sure that Honey Fitz, in spite of his age, could, by spending a few hundred thousand dollars, beat Roosevelt's dictated candidate. Kennedy wanted to know if the old man could beat young Lodge in the election. Kane said that he could not. Kennedy reached for his hat. "I don't know where you're going," he told Kane, "but I'm going back to the Ritz."

Although no one admitted it openly, it was obvious by the forties that the last of the Dearos was slipping. On his eighty-first birthday party at the Parker House, a congratulatory message came from the White House addressed to Boston's Number One Booster. Charles Francis Adams was again present. The climax of the party came just as Honey Fitz was singing "Sweet Adeline," when his grandson Jack—now Naval Lieutenant John Kennedy—whom he had not seen for over a year, suddenly walked into the room, lean and yellow but buoyantly alive after surviving the loss of his P.T. boat and an attack of malaria.

There were bewilderments and there was sadness as well in Honey Fitz's closing years. In the spring of 1944 gossip columns spread the report that his granddaughter Kathleen Kennedy, then in London with the American Red Cross, was about to marry the Marquess of Hartington, the eldest son of the Duke of Devonshire. "Impossible," her grandfather told reporters at the Bellevue. "No grandchild of mine would ever marry outside the Catholic Church." But a few days later Kathleen Kennedy and Lord Hartington, a captain in the Coldstream Guards, were married at a registry office. The best man was Kathleen's brother Joseph, then serving in England as a Navy pilot. Young Joe was to die that August when his plane blew up over the Channel on a bombing mission. Lord Hartington was killed in action a month later. If he and his wife had lived, she would have become the first duchess of England, but she herself died in the crash of a private plane in 1948.

Jack Kennedy, after his discharge from the Navy, came to Boston, took an apartment round the corner from the Bellevue to establish his legal residence, and let it be known that in 1946 he would run for Congress from his grandfather's old district. He set up headquarters in the Bellevue and began to build his organization. Ironically, his chief strategist became that same hard professional, Joe Kane, who had unseated Honey Fitz twenty-seven years before. Grandfather and grandson spent hours together, the Dearo retelling his old political sagas, giving his shrewd old advice. But Jack, with his wealth and his Harvard background and his clipped speech, represented a new breed of Irish-Americans for whom the Dearos and the Smiling Jims and the mahatmas had become crudely and quaintly obsolete, like gas lighting. The young supporters and strategists who gathered around Jack Kennedy in the Bellevue were Democrats in the liberal New Deal image: lean young men, college-educated, most of them ex-officers, many from private schools, with only their surnames to show kinship with the old.

Ten candidates filed for the Democatic nomination—equivalent in that district to the election. Joe Kane saw to it that there were enough to fragment the vote. He paid one candidate $7500 "to stay in or get out," whichever Kane might decide was more useful. When one Joseph

Russo threatened to monopolize the Italian vote, Kane dug up a second Joseph Russo to run against him. Kennedy won easily with 43 percent of the vote.

At the Bellevue, Honey Fitz danced a jig on top of a table to celebrate his grandson's victory and followed it with a quavering "Sweet Adeline." Then, with the pride of a grandfather, and perhaps with the prescience of an old pol, he predicted that Jack would be President of the United States.

Honey Fitz lived long enough to celebrate his diamond wedding and to see Jack overwhelmingly renominated for Congress, but not quite long enough to see him triumph over Senator Henry Cabot Lodge, Jr., the grandson of his old Brahmin adversary.

I remember first seeing grandson Jack, Congressman Kennedy, in 1952 when he was running against Senator Lodge. He was on the platform at Springfield, with the members of the Democratic State Committee, welcoming Adlai Stevenson to Massachusetts. Those assembled machine politicians were of the second generation: heavy-jowled, heavy-paunched Neanderthal types. The shoulders of their suits were vast and padded, their ties were handpainted in rainbow tints, and their eyes had that curiously beady look that one finds only in politicians, undertakers and professional baseball players. Stevenson, the mutely dressed academic Hamlet, and the third-generation congressman in his narrow-shouldered suit and regimental-striped tie seemed from another world. Kennedy looked like what indeed he would become, the youngest member of the Harvard Board of Overseers. Curiously enough, he had come to look much as Harvard overseers had always looked in their younger days. Watching him, I suddenly realized that, in this young man moving rather elegantly among the slobs, the consolidation of a new class had reached its conclusion.

Mayor Curley at seventy-two, escorted by U.S. marshals, on his way to Danbury to serve a jail sentence for mail fraud. Note the collar two sizes too large.

THE LAST OF THE BOSSES:
JAMES MICHAEL CURLEY

OR THE FIRST HALF OF THIS CENTURY AND BEYOND, JAMES MICHAEL CURLEY was the most flamboyant and durable figure on Boston's political scene. Mayor off and on for a total of sixteen years, he spent four terms in Congress and two in jail, and for two Depression years he was governor of Massachusetts. At his death he lay in state for two days in the State House Hall of Flags, the fourth person in the history of the Commonwealth to be so honored. His seventeen-room neo-Georgian mansion on Jamaicaway, with shamrocks cut in its shutters, was both a landmark of the rise of the immigrant Irish and a nose-thumbing in the direction of Yankee Beacon Hill. He was hated by proper Bostonians with a proper and ultimate hatred, and held in mindless affection by the slums. His Irish-American political associates alternately embraced and knifed him. Counted out a score of times, he always bounced back. On several occasions and long before his death, he received the last rites of the Catholic Church.

Like his old enemy Honey Fitz, Curley was a transitional figure, a symbol of the emergence of the famine Irish from their proletarian status to political dominance. His father, Michael, came to Boston from Galway in 1865 at the age of fourteen. Sarah Clancy, his mother, arrived that same year—a meager-boned Connemara girl of the type the Irish wit Dr. Gogarty called Firbolg. She was twelve years old and worked first as a maid on Beacon Hill. Michael Curley became a hod carrier at ten cents an hour by the grace of Patrick "Pea Jacket" Maguire, boss of Ward 17, where Galway men clustered. Michael Curley was good-looking in a stumpy, plodding, impassive way. At twenty-one he married Sarah and took her to a tiny flat in one of the rotting three-deckers off Northampton Street. Along Roxbury Neck there were hundreds of those fetid wooden tenements that had been run up by jerry-builders for the shanty Irish. Beyond Northampton Street lay the North Bay, and at low tide the marsh gas sifting in across the mud mixed with the sour permanent stench of the Southampton Street dump. It was said that in Ward 17 children came into the world with clenched fists. In that Roxbury flat James Michael Curley, the second son, was born in 1874.

The boy's horizon was the waterfront slum. By the time he was five he ran with an urchin gang, pilfering, dodging the cops, wandering along the edge of the Roxbury flats while the herring gulls wheeled overhead, scaling stones at the wharf rats that scuttled across the dumps, selling old whiskey bottles they found there to Jakie the Junkie. Daily they would see the cargo schooners coming up the Fort Hill channel from far-off places like Maine or Nova Scotia. In the summer they played about the old Roxbury canal or swam in the murky South Bay. Evenings they could hear the bullfrogs croaking from the marshes. Sometimes, though rarely, they wandered outside the ward. Only a little over a mile to the north was the newly filled area of the Back Bay with its wide avenues and brownstone-front town houses. To tenement boys, these opulent mansions with their turrets and gablings seemed like castles.

By the time Jim reached grammar school he was peddling papers. Afternoons he worked as a delivery boy at the Washington Market. When he was ten his father died. Mike Curley had always been proud of his strength. A workman challenged him to lift a 400-pound edgestone onto a wagon. He managed to raise it but then collapsed. Three days later he was dead.

The Curleys were then living in an alley tenement in Fellows Court. Pea Jacket Maguire's point of view was limited—no votes, no help. And there was no help for the Curleys.

Sarah kept the family together by scrubbing floors in a downtown office building. Jim and his brother John, two years older, wrapped bundles and served customers at the Washington Market in their free time until the end of grammar school. At twelve, Jim was working in a drugstore an hour and a half before he went to school, and from half past four until eleven after school.

Reared in poverty, corroded with hatred of the Beacon Hill Brahmins, young Jim Curley formed his hard, unwavering, egocentric determination to succeed. Success, the road up from the Fellows Court flat to the imagined great house, was through politics. He knew that when he was still in short trousers. There was no other road for an Irish slum boy. Politics, then, was a game he would play as he found it, not to change the game or reform it, but to win. In the harshness of his own few years he grasped instinctively Boss Martin Lomasney's neoplatonic axiom, that, politically speaking, the mass of people are interested mainly in food, clothing and shelter. For these they would barter their votes.

At fifteen, after a series of small jobs, he settled for the next eight years as a deliveryman, driving a wagon for C. S. Johnson, Grocers. He was strong like his father, wily and wiry, and except for his somewhat vulpine nose, handsome. He had a resonant voice and soon learned to modify the harshness of his gutter speech. From time to time he would drop in at Curran's livery stable, where the ward-heelers gathered, or at One-armed Peter Whalen's tobacco store, another political hangout of the district.

Meanwhile, he attended the Boston Evening High School two nights a week. In the public library he read Dickens and Thackeray and Shakespeare, and the Boston *Transcript*. He taught Sunday school, ushered and passed the plate at St. Philip's on Harrison Avenue and joined the Ancient Order of Hibernians. He became chairman of committees for picnics, outings, minstrel shows and church supper dances. For his straight purpose, games and girls and conviviality had no meaning. Time was too short; life too dear.

He knew the families on his grocery route as if they were his own family; he talked with people—after church, at the Hibernians, at Whalen's, on committees. Always he was obliging and always available. By the time he reached his majority he showed the indefinable air of future success that a sixth-sense pol like One-armed Peter Whalen could spot at once. In 1898 Whalen tipped him to run for the Boston Common Council against Pea Jacket's organization, and staked him to his first contribution. Curley won by several hundred votes, but by the time Pea Jacket's henchmen had finished with the ballot boxes, he found himself counted out. The next year he organized his own strong-arms, and after weeks of pre-election gang fights and corner brawls, he won—

too handily for Pea Jacket to challenge him. So at twenty-six he formally entered political life as one of the three council members from
Ward 17.

With his defeat of the aging Pea Jacket, Curley consolidated himself
as the new boss, organizing Ward 17 on the Tammany model of tribute
and social services, and even calling his organization the Tammany Club.
There was, however, this difference: Curley's organization was personal
rather than self-perpetuating. In politics he would always be a lone wolf.

From that time on Curley never lacked for money. Merchants and
others who did business in Ward 17 now paid to him on a more
regulated basis what they had paid to Pea Jacket. But from the ordinary
people of the ward, deserving and otherwise, whose needs and requests
Curley took care of quickly and efficiently, he expected nothing in
gratitude but their votes.

The core of his support would always come from the slums. There
he was given an allegiance that the Pea Jackets could never command.
But Curley never had a political philosophy beyond that of taking care
of himself and his own. With equal ease he would at various times
support Al Smith, Franklin Roosevelt, Mussolini, Father Coughlin and
Senator McCarthy. If he had had the vision, he might have become
to Boston and Massachusetts what Al Smith was to New York. But his
vision was limited to his own drive for power.

With Ward 17 in his pocket, Curley moved on to the Massachusetts
legislature, where he spent one term, more as an observer of the political
passing show than as a participant. He was still learning. At the Staley
College of the Spoken Word he took elocution lessons, modifying his
speech still further to its final form. The Curley accent was unique,
with grandiloquent overtones, impressive and at once identifiable, yet
underneath synthetic. It achieved the desired effect, but it never rang
wholly true. And in an election pinch, it could always be dropped for
something more primitive.

In 1903 Curley met his first reverse. He was caught impersonating
one of his less talented ward workers at a civil service examination and
sentenced to sixty days in the Charles Street Jail. Yet, far from being
disconcerted by this lapse, he capitalized on it. In later years he often
planted stooges in his audience to get up and ask: "How about the
time you went to jail?" Curley then liked to draw himself up and announce floridly: "I did it for a friend." Ward 17 understood. While
in jail, where he spent a not unpleasant two months reading all the

books in the library, he was elected to the Board of Aldermen, the upper chamber of Boston's city government.

Curley remained an alderman until 1909, when he became a member of the new City Council. And all the time he was laying his lines carefully toward his own clear though unexpressed goal—to be mayor and boss of Boston. His retentive mind had the city and its departments catalogued for future use. No one would ever be able to fool Curley.

Established in his thirty-second year, he now found time to marry Mary Herlihy, whom he had met at a St. Philip's minstrel show. With a background much like his own, she was a woman of grace and character, and she became a permanently steadying influence on him. It was a happy marriage for them both and a fortunate one for him. The boys in the back room might make up limericks about Honey Fitz and Toodles Ryan, but no enemy could ever touch Jim Curley that way. His private life was always beyond reproach, though it was to end sadly—only two of his nine children survived him.

In 1880 Mayor Frederick O. Prince had said: "No allegation of municipal corruption has ever been made against any Boston official." By Honey Fitz's time such a remark could be considered a flat, cynical joke. When Honey Fitz was elected to his four-year term in 1909, Curley, willing to wait for the next round, let himself be persuaded to run for Congress by the district incumbent, Bill McNary, who counted on insuring his own re-election by having Curley split his opponent's vote. For the first time Curley stumped outside Ward 17. In a day when political rallies were still a prime source of entertainment, Curley put on a campaign that was a combination of vaudeville, Chautauqua and the prize ring. No one, his opponents realized too late, could equal him as a showman; no one could talk him down. There was the usual torchlight parade with the bands blaring "Tammany" to celebrate his victory.

He spent two undistinguished terms in the House and his weekends back in Roxbury. In Washington he and his wife mixed in a more sophisticated society than they had known before. They took instruction in etiquette, and this became a source of later jokes in Boston. In his autobiography, Curley maintained that he liked Washington. But Boston—the hard core of the city, the massed wards of the South End—these were his roots, and he never really functioned outside them. Before his second term was up, he resigned to enter the 1913 mayoralty contest.

Young Jim Curley—back from Washington, aggressive and domi-
nating—was like a tidal wave. Honey Fitz, recognizing both the wave
and the tide, retreated from the beach. He and the ward bosses finally
produced a nonentity as token opposition to the Curley flood.

Curley's campaign for mayor dwarfed his congressional campaign
four years before. He stormed the autumn city in racoon coat, "iron
mike" on his head and the gilded voice booming. He promised to
clean out City Hall and give it back to the people—whatever that might
mean. He savaged the ward bosses and invited the voters to call on
him personally at City Hall. He promised more schools and playgrounds
and beaches and parks and jobs. Politicians can hear the grass grow,
and there was the underground feeling that he was unbeatable.

Incongruous as it might seem in later years, or even months, the
newly elected Curley was at first hailed as a reform mayor. Hundreds
of Honey Fitz's officeholders were ousted. True to his promise, Curley
opened up City Hall. Those who wanted to see him about jobs, favors
or assistance, he received without appointment. A squad of secretaries
catalogued each visitor before he was taken to the mayor. Decisions
were made on the spot. If a request could not be granted, Curley said
so and why. He was the superboss. Ward bosses became obsolete: Curley
had destroyed their power, even in Ward 17. He talked to an average
of two hundred persons a day.

The financial and business community's satisfaction with the new
mayor was brutally short-lived. Curley, they soon discovered, had lost
none of his old resentments. Assessments were raised all round. A vast
construction program such as Boston had never seen before was begun.
Streets were ripped up, transit lines extended, beaches and playgrounds
laid out, hospitals built and services expanded. There was a job for
every jobless man in the city. Here lay Curley's basic formula, then
and in all his administrations: a juggler's act of public works without
regard for cost. When the city treasury was empty he would borrow.
The outraged Yankees could pay for it all through taxes.

Yet much of what he did needed to be done. The cost would be
excessive, the payrolls padded, a percentage of the contractors' fees
would always find its way into Curley's pocket—but without him most
of these projects would never have been undertaken. By the end of
his first term he had altered the face of the city; by the end of his fourth
term the tax rate had quintupled.

Though with him money went as easily as it came, though he liked to be known as the mayor of the poor, he enjoyed lush living. Midway in his first term he built himself the house overlooking Jamaica Pond that would be known as the House with the Shamrock Shutters. It was better than anything on Beacon Street. Some of the trimmings, including the mahogany-paneled dining room and the winding staircase, came from the recently demolished Fairhaven house of Henry H. Rogers, the Standard Oil executive. The Finance Commission and others were to ask in vain how anyone could build a $60,000 house on a $15,000 lot on a salary of $10,000 a year. Such questions never bothered Curley. In his autobiography he maintained—archly and without expecting to be believed—that he had made the money for his house on a stock market tip. Almost everyone in Boston knew that the house had been a donation from a contractor. The Curley wards felt he deserved it.

In 1917, when Curley ran for re-election, a curious amalgam of businessmen and bosses took the field against him. Martin Lomasney, the only ward boss to survive unscathed, entered two congressmen with Celtic names as pseudocandidates to cut into Curley's Irish-Democratic vote. It was an old gambit, used many times by Curley himself, and it worked well enough to defeat Curley.

After several ludicrously unfortunate business ventures—in such matters Curley would always be both gullible and inept—he became president of the Hibernia National Bank, within wistful sight of City Hall. But this was for him only an interlude. His real life was always politics.

The 1921 mayoralty campaign was one of the closest and meanest in the history of Boston, and Curley fought alone. No political pro in the city was for him, and the betting against him ran over two to one. But his opponent, a respected Catholic lawyer named John R. Murphy, was not prepared for what he now had to face. It was said commiseratingly of him afterward that he was too much of a gentleman. Among other things, Curley sent some of his workers to Charlestown dressed in clerical black and carrying prayer books. There they let it be known that turncoat Murphy had joined the Masons and that he was divorcing his wife to marry a sixteen-year-old girl. Other Curley supporters rang doorbells through Catholic South Boston, posing as members of the Hawes Baptist Club and soliciting votes for John R. Murphy. Curley even gave a Ku Klux Klan organizer known as the Black Pope two thousand dollars to campaign against him.

Against all odds and predictions Curley won, with 74,200 votes to Murphy's 71,180. For the first time in a Boston election women could vote, and it was generally felt that Mary Curley's "Personal Appeal to Women Voters," an open letter circulated at the last minute, gave her husband the extra votes that elected him.

Before anyone quite knew what was happening—anyone except Curley—there were twenty-four million dollars' worth of building projects under way. Several times the city treasury gave out. Curley merely borrowed more money against future taxes. If a banker showed reluctance to lend, Curley would threaten to start a run on his bank "a mile long." Taxes and assessments, as well as buildings, went up.

During Curley's second administration, and with Curley pointedly in mind, the Republican state legislature passed a law that no mayor of Boston might succeed himself. Instead, in 1924 Curley ran as Democratic candidate for governor against Alvan T. Fuller, who would later become widely known in connection with the Sacco-Vanzetti case. It was a Republican year, and in any case, Massachusetts would not be ready for Curley until after the transvaluations of the Depression. Curley tried to make an issue of the Ku Klux Klan and his own opposition to it. Wherever he spoke in the rural sections of the state, fiery crosses would suddenly blaze out on nearby hills just in time for him to point to them and say, voice resonant with emotion: "There it burns, the cross of hatred upon which Our Lord, Jesus Christ, was crucified." Later he admitted that the crosses had been touched off by his boys. Fuller won—but the size of Curley's vote gave the state party leaders, whose enthusiasm for Curley was at best limited, something to think about.

In the Presidential election of 1928 the Commonwealth of Massachusetts was one of the eight states carried by Al Smith. To the Irish Democrats of the Commonwealth, Smith was the most creditable man from Irish ranks who had yet appeared in politics. Before the national convention the Massachusetts leaders were solidly for Smith. All of them were at odds with Curley, and they took care that the ex-mayor would have no part in the convention or in the subsequent Smith campaign. They reckoned, however, without Curley.

Shortly after Smith's nomination, Curley opened what he called his Bull Pen in the vacant Young's Hotel near City Hall. He had the walls plastered with Smith signs and photographs. There were loudspeakers in the windows blaring a raucous mixture of speeches and music. Every day was open house in the Bull Pen. Inside it was like an amateur night. Anyone who felt like walking in and speaking his piece about Smith was welcome to use the microphone. And when Al Smith arrived in Boston to ride through the city in a whirl of ticker tape, the excluded Curley was somehow there in the car beside him, to the chagrin of the official members of the party. In the election, when Smith was trailing Hoover by 83,000 votes outside Boston, and the city's roaring majority gave him the state by 17,000, it was Curley's desperate drumming up of the last few thousand votes that made the difference.

After the Hoover sweep, Curley was astute enough to realize that Smith would not have another chance, no matter what Massachusetts Democrats thought. Four years later Curley was the first and in fact the only politician in the state to come out for Franklin Roosevelt before the convention. Massachusetts Democrats, still solidly and emotionally for Smith, were shocked and furious. Curley was a traitor. The wilderness was where he belonged.

The Massachusetts delegation to the 1932 Democratic Convention was headed by Governor Joseph B. Ely, an old Curley enemy. Curley was not to be a delegate to this convention; in fact, if Ely had anything to say about it, he would not even be a spectator. But, as the event again showed, one had better not count Curley out too soon. For directly behind the Massachusetts delegation in the convention hall sat the Puerto Ricans with their chairman—none other than Alcalde Jaime Miguel Curleo. The Alcalde, in a familiarly florid accent, cast the six Puerto Rican votes for Roosevelt; though even after the Roosevelt stampede the Massachusetts delegation glumly and stubbornly held out to the end for Smith. Behind the scenes, Curley had helped arrange with Hearst and Garner the deal that finally gave Roosevelt the nomination.

Public opinion in Massachusetts veered quickly. The emotions that for four years had been bound up with the fortunes of Al Smith were transferred overnight to Roosevelt. Having left Boston as an outcast, Curley came back from Chicago a hero. He arrived in North Station to find that a crowd of 250,000 had turned out to meet him. Streets were jammed all the way to the Common. Inside the station twenty-one bands were blaring at one another. It took a hundred reserve policemen to clear a path for Curley to his car.

From that night until the election all Curley's efforts went into the campaign. He reopened his Bull Pen, this time decorating it with

Roosevelt motifs. He mortgaged the House with the Shamrock Shutters. He traveled 10,000 miles through twenty-three western and midwestern states to deliver 140 speeches. For the election he spent a quarter of a million dollars of his own money. With James Roosevelt as an assistant, he was the Roosevelt ringmaster in Massachusetts.

All this activity had not been undertaken just for the Forgotten Man. What Curley now wanted was to set the seal of respectability on his career by becoming Secretary of the Navy. After all, it was a job held recently by a Boston Adams. Shortly after the election, Curley, with his daughter Mary, called on Roosevelt at Warm Springs. There, according to Curley, Roosevelt told him, "Well, Jim, if that's what you want, the job is yours." A few weeks later, however, at Calvin Coolidge's funeral in Northampton, James Roosevelt took Curley aside and told him that a cabinet post was not possible. James went on to tell him that he might instead become ambassador to France or Italy, and suggested that he drop in at the White House to talk it over.

On that visit the President mentioned Italy. Curley asked for a few days to think it over. Whether Roosevelt ever intended to send the boss of Boston to Rome, whether Boston's William Cardinal O'Connell vetoed the idea, or whether Curley was simply being given the Roosevelt run-around, will never be clear. In any event, at Curley's next interview, the smiling President said there were difficulties about Italy and offered him instead the post of ambassador to Poland, remarking that Poland was one of the most interesting places in the world. "If it is such a goddam interesting place," Curley is said to have replied, "why don't you resign the Presidency and take it yourself?" To the newsmen who crowded around him outside the White House, he used a quick term to describe Roosevelt that Truman later reserved for music critics. In Boston a witticism went the rounds that if he had accepted, he would have paved the Polish Corridor.

Between the two conventions Curley had been elected mayor for the third time by a clear majority, and once more with the odds against him. His principal opponent was another respectable Democratic lawyer, Frederick W. Mansfield, silently endorsed by Cardinal O'Connell himself, who had long felt that Curley was a discredit both to the Irish and his Church. The Cardinal, from a slum background similar to Curley's, was of the cast of a Renaissance prelate. He spoke Italian like an Italian, English like a cultivated Englishman. An urbane and aristocratic man, he wanted to see the emergent Irish become respect able and accepted. Politically, the cardinal was an innocent.

Curley, in his inaugural address, attacked the Republican Good Government Association and the "select and exclusive body of social bounders in the Back Bay." His new administration began with the usual Curley public works projects, the need for which was accentuated now by the onset of the Depression.

Even before his election he knew that his wife was doomed by cancer. She died the following June. Mary Curley's influence on her husband had been stabilizing and restraining. Without her he seemed to lose his balance. He drank too much, he coarsened physically, he grew bombastic and careless, he had less control over his quick temper. Opposing Ely's nomination for governor, he got into a fistfight with the chairman of the Democratic State Committee at radio station WNAC.

The older, less careful Curley now made the political blunder of appointing his friend Edmund L. Dolan city treasurer. Dolan was the legal owner of Curley's ninety-three-foot yacht, punningly named *Maicaway*. As Curley's understudy, Dolan headed the Mohawk Packing Company and the Legal Securities Corporation. Mohawk was organized to provide meat for city institutions—at a third above the usual cost. Through the Legal Securities Corporation, Dolan managed to sell bonds to the city and also buy them from the city to sell to brokers, collecting commissions at both ends. The state-appointed Finance Commission uncovered these and certain aspects of land-takings and other facts sufficient, so it seemed for a while, to send both Curley and Dolan to jail. The younger Curley would never have left himself so vulnerable.

Eventually Dolan was charged with the theft of more than $170,000 from the city. When the case came to trial, he was caught trying to bribe the jury and received two-and-a-half years in jail. At the same time a bill in equity was brought against Curley, and after three years and thirty-four continuances, he was ordered to pay back $42,629 to the city treasury.

Now that he had no more Washington ambitions he badgered Roosevelt for more aid and more money for Boston. He devised new projects for the Civil Works Administration. After all, a CWA was what he had been occupied with all his political life. With Governor Ely, still a disgruntled Smith man, retiring in 1934, Curley had little trouble in getting the Democratic nomination for governor. That election, the second New Deal wave, swept almost the complete Democratic state ticket into office. Boston had taken over Massachusetts at last. The crowd from City Hall moved up Beacon Hill to the State House.

Curley's two-year term as governor marked both the height and depth of his career. No such turmoil had occurred on Beacon Hill since cynical Ben Butler had been governor fifty years earlier. Curley would now use the greater resources of the Commonwealth as he had previously used those of the city, but this time with a recklessness and an arrogance he had not shown before. Work there was, projects useful and otherwise, feverishly undertaken from the Berkshires to Cape Cod, and where there was no work there were at least jobs. The State House offices bulged with idle incompetents, the governor's anterooms swarmed with old City Hall petitioners. When the Finance Commission again threatened to dig up old Curley City Hall scandals, its members were bribed or dismissed. Curley rode roughshod over the Governor's Council, courts and department heads, his energy as boundless as his activities were unregulated.

Insolence of office trailed him through the state as he scorched the roads in his limousine with its S-1 license plates, preceded by state police motorcycle escorts with sirens wailing and followed by carloads of his military aides, bright in incongruous blue-and-gold-braid uniforms. S-1 was in a series of accidents. One state trooper was killed, another badly injured. Curley moved across the Massachusetts landscape like a Latin dictator. For the 1936 Harvard Tercentenary, he arrived at the Yard escorted by scarlet-coated National Lancers, drums beating and trumpets sounding, to move ostentatiously past a stony-faced President Roosevelt, while a few Harvard die-hards booed.

Just before he took the oath of office, Curley had swung a parting punch at Governor Ely. That outrageous brawl within the State House became symbolic of his administration. The inauguration ball, held at the Commonwealth Armory, was a monstrous affair to which 14,000 people were invited. During his first year in office the governor spent $85,206 for taxis, flowers, dinners, luncheons, cigars, refreshments and trips for himself, his guests and secretaries. The following winter he moved his entire staff to Florida. In those Depression times his daughter Mary's wedding to Edward C. Donnelly, Jr., of the Donnelly Advertising Company, was the gaudiest ever held in Massachusetts. The bride's trousseau cost $10,000—paid for, and not donated, as anti-Curleyites had hinted. At the packed Cathedral of the Holy Cross, under the dismayed eyes of Cardinal O'Connell, many of those present stood on the pews as the bride and her father came down the aisle. There were 2,300 guests at the Copley Plaza reception afterward. They downed two tons of lobster at thirteen dollars a plate.

Financially buttressed at the end of his governor's term, Curley determined to revenge himself on Roosevelt. The President had not liked him as governor, and he would like still less to find him in the United States Senate. For Governor Curley the senatorial nomination was easy to manipulate; the election seemed equally so. His Republican opponent was Henry Cabot Lodge, Jr., the grandson of the old anti-League senator, whose political experience was contained in two terms in the Massachusetts legislature. Curley liked to refer to him as "Little Boy Blue." Yet in the New Deal landslide of 1936, when every other major Democratic candidate in the Commonwealth was overwhelmingly elected, Curley lost to Lodge by 136,000 votes. All the states except Maine and Vermont went for Roosevelt, but Massachusetts had had enough of James Michael Curley.

In a sense, however, Curley had the last word, for on that day when the cannon boomed across the Common to announce a new governor, he stole the whole show by marrying again. His second wife, Gertrude Casey Dennis, was a widow, a quiet woman without political or social ambitions, who would give him again the domestic stability he had found with his first wife.

The following year he again ran for mayor. He found himself opposed by a "reform" candidate, Maurice Tobin, a handsome and hardy young Democrat from his own district, who in the wheel-spins of politics would twice become mayor, then governor, and finally figurehead Secretary of Labor in Truman's cabinet. Curley accurately described him as "a protégé of mine who learned too fast." It was to Curley's mind an easy election, but on election morning there appeared on the masthead of the Boston *Post*, whose editorials generally reflected the views of the archdiocese, a brief notice to the voters of Boston that read:

Cardinal O'Connell, in speaking to the Catholic Alumni Association, said, "The walls are raised against honest men in civic life." You can break down these walls by voting for an honest, clean, competent young man, Maurice Tobin, today.

Thousands of copies of the *Post* were distributed free in front of all the churches. The quotation was from an address the cardinal had made six years before, but few readers noticed that the quotation marks ended before Tobin was mentioned. To the faithful, it seemed that

His Eminence had endorsed Curley's opponent. Curley furiously tried to get a retraction broadcast, but the cardinal could not be reached. It was a maneuver worthy of Curley himself. Enough pious votes were swung to Tobin for him to win.

In 1938 Curley was strong enough to take the nomination away from the Democratic governor, but he was still unable to win the election. His opponent was the long-jawed speaker of the Massachusetts House of Representatives, Leverett Saltonstall, who as a Republican, a Harvard man and a Brahmin combined the three things that Curley was best at excoriating. Yet Saltonstall was a new type of Old Yankee who represented a *rapprochement* with what Curley liked to call "the newer races." The growing numbers of middle-class Irish liked him. In later years, when he and young Senator Kennedy were colleagues in Washington, they became so friendly that Kennedy refused to endorse Saltonstall's next Democratic opponent. Saltonstall also had the advantage of owning one of the most agreeably ugly mugs in politics. Curley made the mistake of quipping that Saltonstall might have a South Boston face but he would never dare show it in South Boston. Of course Saltonstall walked through the South Boston streets the next day, talking with everyone he met and dropping in at the innumerable bars. He overwhelmed Curley at the polls.

By the time of Boston's next municipal election Mayor Tobin had built a tight political machine of his own. Curley ran against him nevertheless and suffered his fourth defeat in a row. At sixty-seven, after a generation in politics, it looked as if he had come to the end of the road. But that was not the way Curley saw it. He turned again to his solid core of supporters in the close wards of Roxbury, South Boston and Charlestown. As if he were now going down the ladder he had once climbed, he asked them to send him back to Congress in 1942.

These days he was short of funds, and every week there was the $500 installment on the $42,629 he had been ordered to pay the city. A few months before Pearl Harbor, unlucky as usual in his private ventures, he had run into a Washington promoter named James G. Fuller, who was organizing a five-percenter corporation to mediate between manufacturers looking for war contracts and the appropriate heads of government agencies. Fuller offered to make Curley president of this organization, to be known as the Engineers' Group, Inc. Later, Fuller was shown to be a confidence man and ex-convict. Curley, in spite

CURLEY THE THUG

In 1924, when Curley was the Democratic candidate for governor, he was attacked with malicious persistence by the Boston *Telegraph*, a tabloid that had once supported him. On meeting the *Telegraph*'s publisher, Frederick W. Enright, on State Street Curley knocked him into the gutter. Enright riposted by publishing this cartoon for which he was later convicted of criminal libel and sentenced to several months in jail.

When I looked for the cartoon in the Boston Public Library's newspaper collection, I discovered that it had disappeared from the files. I hoped for better luck in the State House library but was told that its old newpaper files had been sent on to the New England Deposit Library. That vault of a building behind the stadium, although shared by various institutions, is controlled by Harvard. There, after some time searching through the dusty canvasbound *Telegraph* volumes, I at last uncovered the missing cartoon. But when I asked the curator about photographing it, he said I must first get permission from the Harvard librarian.

That permission, I assumed, would be no more than a formality. I was wrong. When I told the librarian about the cartoon he said that, much to his regret, he could not allow it to be photographed.

Once outside, I telephoned an accident photographer I knew, offering him double rates if he would meet me in front of the Deposit Library at nine the next morning. He was there. "Just stand by the door with your equipment," I told him. "Then when I wave, charge in!"

I rang the bell, and after some delay the curator opened the door. He was amiable enough. "I guessed you'd be back," he said. "I left the stuff on the table for you." Stepping inside, I beckoned to my photographer, who followed me with an armful of cameras and lights. We spread the still-open volume on the floor. He focussed while I plugged in the lights. In less than two minutes we were done. I thanked the curator. He didn't even bother to ask about permission.

of his title, had little to do with Fuller's corporation except to appear on its letterhead. Curley resigned from the company before being elected to Congress.

Two years later the Engineers' Group was one of the concerns investigated by the Truman Committee, and Curley was indicted because of his connection with it. He always maintained that the case against him was directed from the White House. His trial was postponed to allow him to run for mayor of Boston in November, 1945.

Tobin had moved on to become governor. The acting mayor was an obscurity, as were the other four candidates. Postwar Boston itself seemed derelict, a fading seaport as drab as the blackout paint that covered the gilt dome of the State House. So much needed doing, from street repairs to housing for veterans, and "Curley gets things done." That, at least, was the campaign slogan spread casually in public by his paid workers and taken up by others. Looking back to the prewar days, it seemed true enough. What if Curley was under indictment for some contract swindle? If he was guilty he hadn't done very much, no more than the rest of them. Anyhow, he got things done!

On election day Curley beat his closest opponent by two to one. For the fourth time he became mayor of Boston, thirty-one years after his first inaugural. Two months later he was convicted by a Washington jury of using the mails to defraud.

His appeal to the Supreme Court was rejected in 1947. As the date neared for his sentencing he took to his bed. He received the last rites of the Church, and then unexpectedly his health picked up. Finally, the postponed but inevitable day came. He appeared in court in a wheelchair and wearing a collar a size too large. His lawyer produced a certified list of nine ailments from which he was suffering, any one of which might prove fatal. Unimpressed, the judge sentenced him to six to eighteen months at the Federal Correctional Institute at Danbury, Connecticut. "You are sentencing me to die," Curley croaked at him as they wheeled him away. Democratic House Leader John W. McCormack circulated a petition for Curley's release and it was signed by all the Massachusetts delegation in Washington except Senator Kennedy. After five months, President Truman pardoned Curley—because, as the President said later, "he was innocent."

Although it was not known at the time, Curley was shattered by his Danbury experience. There was nothing left of the young man who could shrug off a few months behind bars by reading all the books in the prison library. He now felt his age and a sense of failure, and for the first time he knew self-doubt. On his release, according to his daughter, he was hesitant about facing people again.

It warmed him to be met by a great milling crowd in front of the House with the Shamrock Shutters, welcoming him with "Hail to the Chief." Inside he found familiar faces and a huge cake inscribed HAPPY BIRTHDAY TO OUR BELOVED BOSS. In a few days he was back at City Hall at his old desk, looking fifteen years younger and running the city in his old way.

Yet the city was not the same. His personal openhandedness as boss of old Ward 17, and in his many years as mayor had now become a more impersonal function of government. Voters were no longer gratefully held in line by a job shoveling snow, by the odd ton of coal, by the perennial Thanksgiving turkey and Christmas basket. Social security and unemployment insurance and the psychiatric social worker had taken over. The Irish were becoming middle class. One couldn't even soak the rich any more. In an almost bankrupt city the tax rate could go no higher. What Boston mostly needed now was an efficient receiver.

In the 1949 election, Curley, to his derisive surprise, was opposed by John B. Hynes, who had served as mayor while Curley was in prison. "A little city clerk," Curley called him contemptuously, but when the ballots were counted, Hynes, the administrator, had won by 15,000 votes. It was the end of Curley's political career.

The next year, by a twist of fate, his daughter Mary and his son Leo both died on the same day.* Mary, who had been closest to him, had led an unhappy life; her marriage had ended in divorce in 1943. Leo was, at the time of his death, a lieutenant in the Navy. In Curley's loss, even his enemies could feel pity for him.

After Curley got out of Danbury, he had complained to a Boston newspaperman, Joseph Dinneen, that the press had always been unfair to him. Dinneen thereupon offered to write Curley's life story honestly and objectively. Curley agreed, and with his collaboration *The Purple Shamrock* was written. It appeared in 1949. Curley was proud of the book and used to give away autographed copies to City Hall visitors.

---

*Officially it was given out that they died of "cerebral hemorrhages," but the more informed have considered them suicides.

Curley lying in state in the Hall of Flags, Massachusetts State House. At the lower right his sons George and Fr. Francis are shown greeting those coming to pay their respects.

The Purple Shamrock, the first attempt to put Curley's career in perspective, was the beginning of the Curley legend. What it told was true and often amazingly frank. Dinneen admitted that money was never a problem for Curley, although Curley could never quite explain where he got it, how his income skyrocketed when he was in office and shrank to a trickle when he was not, or how "there wasn't a contract awarded that did not have a cut for Curley." Yet Dinneen felt that even so, Curley's accomplishments justified the cuts.

Now that Curley was no longer to be feared politically, he began to seem a kind of institution. He had been around for so long. Even the Bostonians who had fought him hardest in the pugnacious City Hall days, now, in the nostalgia for their greener years, felt a certain left-handed affection for him. He in turn was pleased and flattered by the occasional courtesy from a Lowell or a Lodge. Every political figure from Senator Saltonstall to the last South Boston ward-heeler would drop in on the way past the House with the Shamrock Shutters. Curley in his old age could still charm the birds out of the trees.

When Edwin O'Connor's novel *The Last Hurrah* was scheduled to appear in 1956, it was carefully let out in advance that here was a novel about James Michael Curley. The editor of the *Globe* sent Curley a copy with the suggestion that he review it. The next day the book was returned with a note from Curley to the effect that he was consulting his lawyers.

Frank Skeffington, the politician-hero of the book, is undoubtedly Curley, even to his feud with the cardinal, but he is a retouched Curley, less violent, more urbane. After Curley's first resentment had worn off, he began to see the Skeffington portrait as an asset. The book had toned down his ruthlessness, emphasized his benevolence. The various hints of fraud and peculation were, after all, no more than the admissions of *The Purple Shamrock*. For a while Curley took jokingly to calling and signing himself Skeffington. From originally intending to sue O'Connor, he ended up by congratulating him. As an aftermath he decided to write his autobiography, to out-Skeffington Skeffington by putting into a book what Dinneen had either not known or discreetly omitted.

In the final section of *The Last Hurrah*, when Skeffington is on his deathbed, someone standing by the apparently unconscious figure remarks unctuously that if Skeffington had it all to do over again, he'd no doubt do it very differently. The dying man then manages to rouse himself and whisper: "The hell I would!" It was from this episode that Curley took the title of his own book, *I'd Do It Again*.

It is a rambling and uneven book, often dulled by the memory of obscure and forgotten ward-heelers, but on the other hand enlivened by the brazen candor of Curley's admissions. Though actually written by Honey Fitz's biographer, John Cutler, after conversations with Curley, it preserves Curley's own style of the informal cliché. What runs through the pages as an undercurrent, sensed even when not visible, is the after-feeling of the Famine years, the old Celtic bitterness against the chill Yankee. *I'd Do It Again* is more reticent about Curley's financial background than is *The Purple Shamrock*. There is no mention of his income tax irregularities, and nothing is said of his connection with the Mishawum Manor blackmail scandal.

The summer after *The Last Hurrah* was published, Curley sold his Jamaicaway house to the Oblate Fathers. Those shamrock shutters, once a gesture of defiance, had become a familiar landmark. The massive furniture, the library, the Georgian silver, the Waterford glass and Crown Derby china, the jade and ivory *bibelots* and pious statuary had been purchased for the most part from auction rooms. Now to auction rooms they would return.

Curley moved to a small suburban Colonial house the other side of Jamaica Pond. He settled down there with his governor's chair and his mayor's chair and a selection of his smaller belongings. Governor Foster Furcolo appointed him to a sinecure job, for Curley was hard up again. The Boston papers always seemed to be printing little human-interest stories about him: photos of him fishing, or being shaved by Sal, the Huntington Avenue barber. Edward R. Murrow ran his Person-to-Person television show from the new house, and on it Curley announced that he was going to live to be 125 years old so that he could bury all his enemies.

Though Curley belittled it, from the time he moved his health began to fail. He was in and out of the hospital for checkups. His face grew gray and flabby. Yet his right hand had not forgotten its cunning. When Columbia Pictures was about to release its film version of *The Last Hurrah*, Curley, after he had viewed the picture privately, filed suit for "irreparable damage to a valuable property"—that is, his life story. Columbia paid $25,000 for the damage. Then it was discovered that the lawyer to whom the check was made out was nonexistent and that the stamp on the release form was that of a nonexistent notary. Curley claimed that his signature was a forgery. Officially, no one knows yet who got the money. When Curley renewed his threat of a suit, Columbia settled for an additional $15,000. The picture was running at a Boston theater when Curley died.

He entered the City Hospital for an intestinal operation on November 4, 1958, election day. Just another campaign, he remarked. For the first few days he seemed to be mending. He was able to walk about and to talk of the great Democratic victory. A week later he had a relapse. The end came quickly.

He lay on a bier in the State House in the great hall where the battle flags of Massachusetts regiments are kept, and in two days 100,000 people filed past. Then, on a warm morning like an aftermath of September, he was buried from Holy Cross Cathedral. It was the largest funeral ever seen in Boston.

According to the Boston papers, Archbishop (later Cardinal) Richard J. Cushing had flown from Washington to deliver the eulogy. The late Cardinal O'Connell had spoken one when Curley's first wife died; the archbishop himself had eulogized Mary and Leo eight years before. Now he sat silent and dominant in the sanctuary. The celebrant was Curley's youngest son, Father Francis X. Curley, S.J.

The coffin of polished mahogany glittered in the candlelight that was reflected again on the scabbards of the Knights of Columbus, Fourth Degree, who formed the guard of honor. They stood there, plump and middle-aged, in silk capes, their hands on their sword hilts, white plumes covering their heads. As the requiem mass reached its conclusion, the archbishop approached the coffin. Then he prayed, in the grating, honest, South Boston voice that was his inheritance and that he was too proud to change. High overhead, suspended by a wire from the Reconstruction-Gothic dome and directly over the coffin, Cardinal O'Connell's red hat swung slightly in the air currents.

The prayer ended, and everyone watched the archbishop's seamed face under its white miter, waiting for him to mount the steps to the pulpit. But the archbishop did not move. There was no eulogy.*

---

*According to a Jesuit acquaintance of mine, Archbishop Cushing on entering the sanctuary looked around the cathedral and remarked *sotto voce*, "I see we're playing to a full house today."

Courtesy of the Boston Public Library, Print Department

Mayor Peters and General Clarence Edwards at the mustering out parade of the Yankee Division in April 1919. General Edwards is wearing a British warm, a type of greatcoat worn only by British officers of field rank and above.

THE MAYOR AND THE NYMPHET

FOR DANIEL MORIARTY, A BEACHCOMBER POKING HIS WAY ALONG THE HIGH-tide mark of Long Beach, Long Island, just after sunrise, that 8 June, 1931, promised to be nothing more than a casual, hot summer day. Then suddenly in the curled line of seaweed he came across the body of a young woman lying face-up, left there by the night tide. She was wearing a silk dress, a black coat and stockings. Her mouth was open, her hair a tangle of rockweed and sand, and she stared at Moriarty with brown unseeing eyes. He stumbled up the beach and across the road to call the Long Island police.

Within the hour the young woman's body was taken to the morgue and within the day she was identified. She was Starr Faithfull, twenty-four years old, who had been living with her mother and her step-father, Stanley Faithfull, at 12 St. Luke's Place in New York's Green-wich Village. Faithfull had already notified the Missing Persons Bureau and had been telephoning friends and acquaintances to ask if they had seen Starr. An autopsy showed her body had been in the water two days. She had not been drinking, but she had taken several grains of Veronal. Although there were some bruises on her body the cor-oner concluded that she had drowned either by accident or self-intent.

Long Beach is in Nassau County. Its District Attorney Elvin Edwards, a man for whom publicity was its own reward, decided that Starr had been murdered. It was a view he usually took in such cases, and at times he had even been right. After several days of investigation he interrupted her funeral to demand a further autopsy and to announce:

"I know the identity of the two men who killed Starr Faithfull. One of them is a prominent New York politician. They took her to Long Beach, drugged her, and held her head under the water until she was drowned. I will arrest both of them within thirty-six hours." No one was arrested.

Starr Faithfull's end with its hints of murder was a news sensation for several weeks. Her name itself added glamor to the mystery. Reporters and photographers competed with the police for space in the Faithfulls' small walk-up apartment. Faithfull was garrulous, willing to talk with anyone and everyone. A police detective fingering through the books on Starr's bookshelf came across a mem book and a diary. Morris Markey—later to become a reporter-at-large for *The New Yorker*—was one of those early on the scene who were allowed to read the diary.

> It was written in a kind of shorthand [he noted]—no names of anybody, only initials—but even its fragmentary nature told clearly enough of a bitter, and frustrated, and indeed ruined life. Its most interesting feature, to the tabloids, was that it contained passages of eroticism which even they did not feel disposed to print. But a set of initials cropped up persistently: AJP. Sometimes she hated AJP and sometimes she was affectionate in her references, but always she was frightened sick of him . . . .The villain of the piece was identified by Faithfull in his story of "Mr. X." But it did not take long for those who had read the girl's diary to associate this individual with the "AJP" so often referred to in its pages. And almost as quickly a man was located whose name fitted the initials. He was Andrew J. Peters, former Congressman, former Mayor of Boston, a distant relative of Mrs. Faithfull's.

Andrew James Peters. The name had an apostolic ring that James Michael Curley liked to mock. In 1918, at forty-six, Peters had become an interlude-mayor between Curley's first and second terms. Andrew James was, Curley wrote in his autobiography, "a part-time mayor with a passionate addiction for golf, yachting, hammock duty and other leisurely pursuits." But for the Boston Police Strike that occurred while he was in office and, a dozen years later, the enigmatic death of Starr Faithfull, Peters would have faded into the oblivion of such earlier twentieth-century mayors as Thomas Hart, Daniel Whelton, George Hibbard; their accomplishments—if any—beyond recall.

In then rock-ribbed Republican Massachusetts Peters remained a Yankee Democrat. Those pre-Irish Famine Democrats came mostly from the western part of the state with its folk memories of Shay's Rebellion. But some, such as Colonel William Gaston of the law firm bearing his name, whose father had been Boston's mayor in 1870, and Mayor Richard Russell of Cambridge, kept the anti-Whig tradition alive in the Boston area. President Eliot of Harvard was a Democrat, as were the Quincys, the Brockton shoe manufacturer William Douglas, President Cleveland's Secretary of War William Endicott and Winslow Warren, descendant of the Bunker Hill general and president of the Cincinnati.

The first Peters, a distiller—also named Andrew—arrived in Boston in 1657. Though the Peters endured locally, they were not noted in the history of the province, the Revolution or even the Civil War. Wealth came to the family early in the nineteenth century through Edward Dyer Peters, who in 1811 founded Boston's first wholesale lumber firm, one that exists to this day. An astute merchant trader, he sent his ships to and from the chief ports of the world. The Peters lived in Jamaica Plain on a butte overlooking the flatlands of Forest Hills. Their eighteenth-century house had been modified and enlarged until it looked more Regency than Colonial. Andrew James was born there in 1872 and would live there all his life.

Jamaica Plain was on a higher social, as well as geological level than the Roxbury Highlands, but considerably lower than the Beacon Hill benchmark. The Peters remained on the fringe of the Brahmin world. Not until Andrew James's marriage in 1910 to the twenty-eight-year-old Martha Phillips of the more formidably elite Boston tribe did his name appear in the Social Register. Like many a dissenting Yankee family the Peters, under the influence of Phillips Brooks, had drifted into Episcopalianism. Andrew James was sent to St. Paul's School, not, indeed, as fashionable as Groton or St. Mark's, but fashionable enough. He entered Harvard with the Class of 1895.

At Harvard he left no notable scholastic or athletic record behind him. As a freshman he played football, but gave up the game after he had been injured. In his sophomore year he "ran for the Dickey," the club within a club comprising the first forty-five of those taken into the Institute of 1770. Members of the Institute generally became members of the Hasty Pudding Club the following year. (Some years later the two clubs would merge.) Those belonging to these threshold clubs—about a quarter of each class—were winnowed into the final clubs, the ultimate goal of socially minded undergraduates. Peters failed to survive the winnowing.

From the college he went on to the law school, and after receiving his degree joined Colonel Gaston's law firm. In 1904 and again in 1905 he was elected to the Massachusetts House of Representatives, and after two terms there graduated to two terms in the state senate. His Republican Jamaica Plain district was of singular advantage to him. The minority Democrats voted for him because he was a Democrat; the Yankee Republicans crossed party lines out of ethnic allegiance to his Puritan descent. Politics was nothing he took very seriously, certainly not as seriously as his recreations and club life. He was a member of the Eastern Yacht Club, the Country Club, the Tennis and Racquet, the Somerset, the Exchange, the Tavern and the New York Harvard Club. He had a cottage on Vinal Haven Island in Maine and spent much of his summers cruising along the coast in his schooner yacht. Sailing and riding were his chief diversions. Besides his Vinal Haven cottage he owned a farm and stables in Dover, an easy distance from Jamaica Plain.

In 1906 he took the larger step of running for Congress from an expanded district that included the anonymous streets and massed three-deckers of Forest Hills. "An abhorrent combination of Harvard and the slums," Curley called it. In those prewelfare days it was a district amenable to a candidate of judicious means. Peters was elected and three times re-elected. Though he did not make any political mark in Washington, he enjoyed its social life. But in the 1914 election year, threatened with defeat from a pugnacious Irish-American candidate, Francis Horgan, he quietly resigned from Congress to accept an appointment from President Wilson—always considerate of Yankee Democrats—as assistant secretary of the treasury in charge of customs at Boston. There he remained until 1917.

In that year Curley, finishing out his four-year term as mayor, determined to succeed himself. Equally determined that he would not were Martin Lomasney and Curley's archenemy Honey Fitz. Peters had been chosen as a reform candidate by the Good Government Association (derisively labeled the Goo-Goos by Curley), and was backed by the minority Republicans, proper Bostonians and various real estate and business interests alarmed by tax increases brought about by the free-spending Curley. Behind the curtain the real scenarists were Honey Fitz and Lomasney, the Ward 8 Mahatma. In a straight election, as they were well aware, Curley would overwhelm the lackluster Peters. But it would not be a straight election. Of this Fitzgerald and Lomasney made certain.

As boss of the West End's Ward 8 Lomasney held a crucial position in the Democratic city. If not a kingmaker, he was at least a Congress-manipulator. James Gallivan of South Boston and Charlestown's Peter Tague owed their congressional seats to him. At his "suggestion" they entered the mayoralty race. Though they knew they had no chance of winning, his suggestion was their command. Curley in a fury stormed up to Lomasney's Hendricks Club to demand that he remove his "decoy" candidates. "Why do you think I put them in?" the Mahatma asked him blandly. "I put them in to lick you."

From still farther behind the curtain Honey Fitz could rub his hands together in vengeful spite. His actions, the frustrated Curley announced, were "characteristic of his usual yellow tactics—tactics embracing all that is low, mean, contemptible and unmanly." But the Fitzgerald-Lomasney arithmetic was correct. "Vote for Gallivan and elect Peters," Curley had warned the crowds at his rallies. This is just what happened. Peters received 37,923 votes, Curley 28,848, Gallivan—"the jitney messiah from South Boston," Curley called him—19,427 and Tague a negligible 1,751. But for Gallivan, who dominated his district, Curley would have swept South Boston to gain a city majority of over 10,000.

Peters in his four years as mayor never managed to familiarize himself with the intricacies of City Hall. He enjoyed the prestige of office but was never really in control. Finding himself beyond his depth, he turned to the ward bosses who had helped elect him. He filled his staff with the men they suggested, allowing them to assume the bothersome details of administrative work. Subtly, and in some cases not so subtly, the underlings took over. While he leaned back in his mayor's chair, they did business in the anterooms. Greenbacks passed routinely in the corridors. Under Honey Fitz contractors had had the habit of charging the city for each side of a granite paving block. Under Peters they sold the foundations of City Hall. "Peters' administration," John Cutler wrote in his Fitzgerald biography *Honey Fitz,* "because of his inability to cope with a rapacious palace guard who sold jobs and promotions flagrantly, proved to be one of the most graft-ridden in Boston's history." He was, said Curley, "an innocent dupe for a conscienceless corps of bandits." Joseph Dinneen's *The Purple Shamrock* tells how in an anteroom adjoining Peters's office

> there was a "bagman" who would deal, dicker or negotiate for almost anything. For an agreed price a play would not be

banned. . . . Jobs and promotions had price tags on them. Political affiliation meant nothing. Anybody could buy almost anything at the bargain counter. All that was needed was the price. . . . Peters was one of the most trusting souls ever placed in a job that required the quick eyes, ears and instincts of an honest poker player among cardsharps. He believed implicitly everything he was told. He signed his name to documents without reading them, and even repeated into a telephone acknowledgements and commitments which his secretariat called to him. . . . He never took a wrong nickel while in office and a time came when he looked around blinking, bewildered and uncomprehending, not knowing what had happened. He never did figure it out.

In his mid-forties the new mayor was developing an alderman's paunch and losing his hair. His domed forehead with its rufous fringe gave him the spurious look of a thinker. He had petulant, too-full lips, and his singularly tufted eyebrows arched out to a point. Though a Yankee of Yankees, he resembled more an aberrant Scot. His rather high-pitched voice had a precise Boston accent, the exaggerated broad *a* that is not quite English and not quite anything else.

Three Boston events of note marked his unnotable term: the mustering-out parade in April, 1919, of the Yankee Division—Massachusetts's own, returning from France—which Peters reviewed standing beside Major General Clarence Edwards; the strike of the Boston Elevated Railway workers several months later that for four days stopped the city's streetcars and subway and El trains; finally, the Boston Police Strike in September.

Peters was not on hand for the El strike or its settlement, having conveniently left Boston several days earlier for a Maine cruise. At sea, caught in a fog, he could not be reached. As a wit in the City Law Department noted:

> Our Andy is out on the ocean
> Our Andy is befogged at sea
> Our Andy has just got the notion
> It's a damn good place to be.

Nineteen-nineteen was a year of strikes, in part a visceral reaction to the High Cost of Living—as inflation was then known. The 1914 dollar had in five years sunk to forty-seven cents. Wages, except in war industries, had lagged far behind. A policeman who at the beginning of the war had thought himself reasonably well off with a thousand dollars a year, felt himself impoverished at the war's end. So it was with the Boston police, aggrieved as well by a ten-hour day and a seven-day week.

The ingredients of the police strike were a fated mixture. There were the policemen themselves—mostly of Irish descent—angry and belligerent, preparing to form a union affiliated with the American Federation of Labor. There was an intransigent police commissioner of the Yankee epigone, Edward Curtis, who forbade the police any such affiliation, insisting with tight-lipped righteousness that a policeman was not an employee but a government official whose impartiality would be compromised by his joining a union. There was a Republican governor, Calvin Coolidge, determined not to act unless he had to, though it was the governor and not the mayor who held the appointment of the police commissioner. And finally there was Mayor Peters, unaware of the extent of his own powers, spending most of the crisis period aboard his yacht.

When, defying Curtis's order, the police organized their union, the commissioner charged the new union's leaders with insubordination and ordered eighteen of them to stand trial. The union countered by warning him that if these men were disciplined the police would strike. Faced with this threat Peters appointed a Citizens Committee of Thirty-Four to try to find a way out of the impasse, then left for Maine. The committee recommended granting the police a union independent of the American Federation of Labor, with no action to be taken against the union officers. With some reluctance the policemen would probably have accepted the compromise. But Curtis would not. The eighteen had acted in direct violation of his orders. He suspended them. And as he did so almost the whole Boston police force walked out.

A night of riots, looting and mob violence followed. Before the disturbances ended eight persons had been killed, twenty-one wounded and at least fifty injured. A third of a million dollars worth of property was either stolen or destroyed, downtown Boston left a shambles.

The violence could have been averted if, as the policemen prepared to leave their posts, the state guard had been sent in to take over. Peters, although he was unaware of the fact, had the authority to call out the state guard units within the Boston area "if tumult, riot or mob is threatened." But even when on his quick return from Maine he was informed of this he hesitated. How could he know for sure whether tumult, riot or mob threatened? First it had to happen.

Governor Coolidge could have called out the state guard before the rioting started. But, as he was cannily aware, any governor who calls out the militia prematurely commits political suicide. As a boy in a Vermont boarding school Coolidge had gone to bed one night just before several prankish boys in the dormitory pitched an old iron stove downstairs. He heard the crash but stayed in bed. When next morning a master asked him why he had not done anything, he told him, "It wa'n't my stove." The police strike wa'n't his strike.

Only after a night of riot and destruction did Coolidge act. He then called out the six regiments of the state guard. As the guardsmen moved into Boston another turbulent evening ensued, but by morning the guard was in unchallenged control of the city. Peters, assuming the guard to be his auxiliary police force, was still prepared to negotiate with the union. At this point Coolidge, as the guard's commander-in-chief, brushed Peters aside and took over the Boston Police Department. While guardsmen were moving into the Commonwealth Armory, the governor and the mayor happened to meet there on the stairs. At the sight of Coolidge Peters lunged at him in impotent rage, punching him in the eye. Coolidge did not respond, but for several days he nursed a shiner.

As the head of the American Federation of Labor, Samuel Gompers sent Coolidge a long telegram on behalf of the police, appealing to him "to honorably adjust a mutually unsatisfactory situation." Coolidge replied tersely, concluding: "There is no right to strike against the public safety by anybody, anywhere, any time." The strike had become a national event, and that blunt sparse sentence burned itself into public awareness. Overnight Coolidge became a hero. The strike, in its aftermath, would make him President.

In his annual message on February 2, 1920, Peters attacked Curtis and Coolidge, blaming the commissioner for the strike and the governor for the disturbances that followed. The mayor's remaining two years in office were inconspicuous enough. He did consolidate a number of departments, and by reassessing the property of six of Boston's largest corporations replaced the city's debt of four-and-half million dollars by a surplus. This would have occurred under almost any mayor in the immediate postwar expansion as would the construction of several hundred miles of streets. In his valedictory address he claimed that his four years as mayor were the most satisfactory of his life. Although he served for a time on the Democratic State Committee, he never again held public office. Occasionally visions of political sugarplums still danced in his head, as he admitted in a little poem, "Reflections Upon Running for Office," which he dashed off a few months after leaving City Hall:

> I've done my job as Mayor
> And they say I've done it well,
> So I'll give up public life
> And rest and play a spell. . . .
>
> And of course I've done my bit
> To keep the Nation going—
> So I've no interest at all
> In political winds a-blowing—
>
> No none at all—and yet—
> There's the Gold Dome on the hill,
> Perhaps a couple of years up there
> Would really fill the bill.

The bill would never be filled, though his party still thought well enough of him to send him as a delegate to the Democratic national convention in Houston in 1928. There he made one of the seconding speeches nominating Al Smith. A year later the Democratic State Committee was even considering him as a candidate for governor, but when the chairman called him up he happened to be taking a nap and could not be disturbed.

Locally he became head of the Chamber of Commerce, a director of the First National Bank and of the Federal Reserve and president of Jamaica Plain's Faulkner Hospital. In 1928 he formed a law firm with Harold L. Clark and Richard E. Keating. He died on June 26, 1938. According to the Boston *Post*, "not since the funeral of former Senator William M. Butler in March 1937 has such a throng of notables entered Trinity Church in final tribute to one of the city's most illustrious citizens."

Peters had five sons: Andrew James, Jr., born in 1911; Alanson Tucker (1913); John Phillips (1914); Bradford (1917); and Robeson (1919). But his private life, serene on the surface, was shadowed by his relations with Starr Faithfull.

Starr had been born Starr Wyman. When her father Frank, a Beacon

Hill ne'er-do-well, abandoned his family, his wife turned to Peters for help. He raised money among various relatives and became the guardian of Starr and her younger sister Tucker. It was all very proper, even generous. Yet beneath Peters's brownstone exterior lurked a perverse personality known only to a select few. For in spite of his affection of his family, he had an uncontrolled and apparently uncontrollable passion for pubescent girls. The Wyman sisters often played with Peters's boys, and sometimes Starr visited him alone. Just before he announced his candidacy for mayor and when he was forty-five he managed to seduce her. She was eleven. It began with his reading her tidbits from Havelock Ellis's *Studies in the Psychology of Sex.* At the same time he taught her to sniff ether. She became something of an ether addict. It was while she was in a dreamy half-sleep that he initiated her sexually. From that time on he continued his anesthetic advances.

The Wyman girls went to Park School, a small private school in Brookline, before going on to Brookline High. Starr was then sent to Rogers Hall, a fashionable boarding school in Lowell. Often Peters would drive over with his chauffeur to pick her up. During vacations he would take her on trips across New England, sometimes for several weeks at a time. His wife knew and was as angry as she was troubled. Once when she came home and found them together she ordered Peters to take Starr out of the house. "Get this Bambi creature out of here!" she shouted at him.

On July 2, 1923, Starr recorded in her mem book:
    Left with AJP for North Haven in the car.
    Stayed at Portland overnight in the Lafayette Hotel. Arrived at
    North Haven next day. Stayed at North Haven next day. Stayed
    at North Haven about two weeks and four days.
From there, she wrote, they drove to Quebec and spent two nights at the Chateau Frontenac, came back by way of the White Mountains and ended up in Marblehead.

At seventeen Starr looked a woman, and Peters took to signing her in as his wife. However dark her moods, she continued to submit to him. After they had spent a rainy night at the Biltmore in Providence, she wrote in her mem book: "Spent night AJP Providence. Oh, Horror, Horror, Horror!!!" Finally in the summer of 1926, after two nights with him in New York's Astor Hotel, she broke down and told her mother.

The year before her mother had married Faithfull, an eccentric and impecunious inventor, and had gone to live with him in Greenwich Village. Later Starr and Tucker moved in with them. For all his fecklessness, Faithfull showed himself a caring stepfather. The two girls adopted his surname.

In the wake of what Starr told her mother Peters hurriedly sailed for Europe aboard the *Leviathan*. "Mr. Peters would be very relieved to find me dead," Starr jotted down. What then happened has been obscured. All that is known is that Peters on his return was approached and a sizable sum of money settled on the Faithfulls through his lawyers. After Starr's body was found, Faithfull told the reporters who had swarmed on on him that

> in order to correct any impressions that I or any member of my family thought to "profit" or to "blackmail" as the result of the experience suffered by Starr Faithfull in her childhood, I am pointing out the following circumstances in connection with the $20,000 made to us in 1927 after the story had been given to a Boston attorney without our solicitation.... This friend told him in confidence the story of how Starr had been mistreated in her childhood by a certain man whose name I possess.

According to Faithfull, the friend brought the story to F.W. Rowley of the Boston firm of Peabody, Brown, Rowley & Story, who handled the negotiations. Rowley admitted that he had "effected a full settlement for Starr Faithfull and her family as a result of the story she told me in the presence of her mother, her sister and her adopted father." He added that the man was related to the family and that Starr had played with his children. But Rowley refused to reveal his name. Subsequently he told persistent reporters that "the man who paid the money was not concerned with Starr Faithfull in any way. I don't intend to bring his name to public attention."

Rumor had it that the settlement had gone as high as eighty thousand dollars and that an additional forty thousand had been paid to Starr's mother. When questioned, Rowley merely replied that "if Faithfull said it was twenty thousand, or any other sum, I'll leave it at that." Faithfull explained that the money had been used for Starr's psychiatric treatment. But in the years until her death he and his family seemed to have had no other source of income.

At Rogers Hall Starr had shared in school activities. She made friends. She was a good swimmer, a sprinter, on the field-hockey team. But she had times when she held herself apart, sometimes spending days alone in her room. Her family could not understand her periods of "queerness." She would refuse to go swimming for fear of exposing herself in a bathing suit. In a day when women's skirts were creeping up to the knee-line, she wore hers at ankle length. Sometimes she even wore men's clothes. Later on, living in New York with her mother and stepfather, she neither worked nor concerned herself with a career. Most of what she did remains a blank. She numbed herself with Veronal and Allonal. She drank. At one point she spent nine days in a mental hospital. The men in her life were often pick-ups.

A year before her death she and a Joseph Collins registered as husband and wife in uptown Manhattan's St. Paul Hotel. When shouts and screams came from their room, the management sent for the police. A patrolman found her naked on the floor, bleeding and barely conscious. On the table was a half-empty gin bottle. Collins, in his undershirt, showed the patrolman his army discharge and then, oddly enough, was allowed to slip away. Starr was taken to Bellevue, recorded there as "noisy and unsteady. Acute alcoholism. Contusions face, jaw and upper lip. Given medication. Went to sleep. Next A.M. noisy, crying. People came. Discharged."

From 1926 on the Faithfulls had money to travel. Starr made several trips to England, the first time spending several months with her mother and sister in London, living in one of the innumerable small Knightsbridge hotels. Starr passed much of her days and most of her nights in neighboring Chelsea. Smart and attractive, she mixed easily in the bohemian life in and about the King's Road, becoming a familiar face in such pubs as The Goat in Boots, the Six Bells, the Cadogan. Her diary filled with the names of men she had met. She noted that "a man named Lord Brendan wanted me to go to Budapest with him." But on her second London visit she stayed alone in the isolation of the Greyfriars Hotel. There on one depressed evening she swallowed twenty-four grains of Allonal and might have died if the hallporter had not taken alarm and forced open the door of her room. Once she had recovered she was asked to leave.

In June 1927, sailing from Montreal to Glasgow on the Cunarder *Aurania*, she had stopped in several times at the sick bay to consult with the ship's surgeon, George Jameson-Carr, a forty-two-year-old bachelor. Consultation led to friendship. Soon they were on a first-name basis, seeing much of each other. In the enforced intimacy of the voyage he became a confidant with whom she shared her darker secrets. She fell in love with him, importunately. From London she wrote to her mother that they were engaged. When the mother wrote him a letter of congratulations, he replied that there was some mistake. He was not engaged to anyone. Nevertheless Starr continued to pursue him. Her unbridled attentions soon embarrassed him professionally. She wrote him long, ardent letters. She rushed to see him whenever his ship was in port. If she had had the money she would have sailed with him.

On May 29, 1931, the Cunard liner *Franconia* was to leave New York on a round-the-world cruise with Jameson-Carr as the ship's surgeon. Starr had not seen him in seven months. The evening the *Franconia* sailed she, tipsy and distraught, slipped up the gangplank and made her way to his sitting room. Just before the sailing hour he sent her away. Instead of leaving, she mixed with the passengers until the *Franconia* was halfway down the harbor. Finally a purser spotted her. "Kill me! Throw me overboard!" she screamed as, struggling and kicking, she was put aboard a tugboat and returned to New York.

The next day she wrote Jameson-Carr soberly at some length:

I am going (definitely now—I've been thinking of it for a long time) to end my worthless, disorderly bore of an existence—before I ruin anyone else's life as well. I have certainly made a sordid, futureless mess of it all. I am dead, dead sick of it. It is no one's fault but my own—I hate everything so—life is horrible. Being a sane person you may not understand—I take dope to forget and drink to try and like people, but it is of no use.

I am mad and insane over you. I hold my breath to try to stand it—take Allonal in the hope of waking happier, but that homesick feeling never leaves me. I have, strangely enough, more of a feeling of peace or whatever you call it now that I know it will soon be over. The half hour before I die will, I imagine, be quite blissful.

You promised to come to see me. I realize that it will be the one and only time. There is no earthly reason why you should come. If you do it will be what I call an act of marvelous generosity and kindness. What I did yesterday was very horrible, although I don't see how you could lose your job, as it must have been clearly seen what a nuisance you thought me.

Three days later she wrote him a formal note of apology—obviously intended for any censorious Cunard official—in which she addressed

him as *Dear Sir* and signed herself *Yours sincerely*. On June 4, the
day she disappeared from her home, she wrote him once more:

Hello, Bill Old Thing:

It's all up with me now. This is something I am going to put
through. The only thing that bothers me about it—the only thing
I dread—is being outwitted and prevented from doing this, which
is the only possible thing for me to do. If one wants to get away
with murder one has to jolly well keep one's wits about one. It's
the same way with suicide. If I don't watch out I will wake up
in a psychopathic ward, but I intend to watch out and accomplish
my end this time. No ether, Allonal or window jumping. I don't
want to be maimed. I want oblivion. If there is an afterlife it
would be a dirty trick—but I am sure fifty million priests are
wrong. That is one of the things one knows. . . .

It's more than I can cope with—this feeling I have for you.
I have tried to pose as clever and intellectual, thereby to attract
you, but it was not successful, and I couldn't go on writing those
long, studied letters. I don't have to worry, because there are
no words in which to describe this feeling I have for you. The
words love, adore, worship have become meaningless. There is
nothing I can do but what I am going to do. I shall never see
you again. That is extraordinary. Although I cannot comprehend
the words "always"—or "time." They produce a merciful
numbness.

The following day she was seen at the New York docks boarding
and then leaving the *Mauretania* which was to sail that afternoon. It
is probable, though not certain, that she went aboard the *Ile de France*
berthed nearby and scheduled to sail at ten in the evening. She was
not seen leaving nor was she ever seen again.

Jameson-Carr demolished the murder theory when he arrived from
England with Starr's suicide letters. Just how she died could never be
exactly determined. It seems most likely that she secreted herself on
the *Ile de France* and jumped overboard in the darkness as the ship
was passing Long Island.

Starr's name first appeared in the New York papers. They quoted
District Attorney Edwards as saying she had been murdered and that
in clearing up her case he expected to subpoena several of the men
mentioned as having known her earlier, among them a Boston man,
Andrew J. Peters. Boston papers then played up Starr's death and her
link with Peters in banner headlines.

Alarmed, Peters engaged a senior corporation lawyer, John W. Davis—Democratic candidate for President in 1924—to act for him in New York. Davis informed a *Times* reporter that Peters would give any information he had about Starr Faithfull, but he had none. "My client," Davis concluded, "has seen no member of the Faithfull family for five years and knows nothing about the case."

In Boston, where rumors were revolving like spinning tops, Peters's former corporation counsel, Alexander Whiteside, acting "not as a counsel but as a friend," told the press that he was authorized by Peters to say that

> if he [Peters] had any information or evidence which would be of the slightest assistance to District Attorney Edwards...he would gladly give it to him, but he has no evidence whatsoever....
> The girl was a distant cousin of Mr. Peters's wife. Mr. Peters has told me that never in his life did he have any improper relations with her in any way whatsoever.
>
> The foregoing is the only statement Mr. Peters cares to make.

Edwards's demand for Peters's appearance was much modified after he had received a call from Davis. He now said that "although some of the prominent residents mentioned in Starr Faithfull's diary may be called to tell what they know of her life, Andrew J. Peters will not be one of them."

Edwards had gone to Boston on his own, explaining that he wanted to question "a big Boston politician who held the secret of the Starr Faithfull mystery." Instead of answers, he faced a wall of silence. He told reporters: "I learned when I went to Boston to question the man on information given me by Stanley Faithfull that he was so highly placed it would be advisable to proceed with caution. Police Commissioner Hultman and Superintendent of Police Crowley told me that they would not summon the man to headquarters to be questioned because of his prominence." When asked by a reporter if pressure had been brought on him to keep the man's name secret, he replied: "I'll answer that by saying it is considered advisable by everyone concerned not to name him."

Edwards remained adamant. "I have good reason to refrain from answering any questions about the Boston angle of this case," he told reporters. "I refuse to talk about it." Angered by his evasions, a Boston *Post* reporter finally asked him: "Why are you protecting the Boston man like this? What reason have you for treating him differently than the others whose names you have so freely given out?'' According to the reporter, Edwards bit his lip, whitened and replied: ''I will not answer that question!''

By the month's end Starr Faithfull's name with whatever mystery it still contained had vanished from the newspapers. For Peters there was a similar unnaming. By agreement with the Faithfulls, Edwards had burned the diaries, and the AJP initials remained a fixed secret. Yet the implied questions endured. Who was Faithfull's wealthy and respected Mr. X? Who was the prominent politician, the older relative who had so damaged Starr's childhood? Who was Rowley's anonymous client? In Boston the answers seemed all too obvious.

In the half-dozen years that were left him Peters went his way as if nothing had happened. Yet everyone in his world knew, and he knew that they knew. At his clubs, when he walked down State Street, at Harvard reunions, at the public dinners he attended, in the Somerset Club dining room, whenever he sat at one of Thompson's Spa's square lunch counters, always there were whispers, like a faint breeze, sensed rather than heard.

In 1932, for some reason, he was elected a Fellow of the American Academy of Arts and Sciences. That same year tragedy struck his family when in an autumn polio epidemic his sons Alanson and John came down with the disease. Alanson died then. John lived out another year as an invalid at the Warm Springs Foundation. Peters continued on the boards of various local charity organizations. Three years before his death he served on President Roosevelt's Birthday Ball commission and was asked to dinner at the White House.

Ordinarily he would have sunk below the political horizon, a negligible politician, a one-term Boston mayor elected during the First World War, his role in the police strike all but forgotten, the El strike itself forgotten. Only because his name is linked with that of a dead girl is he remembered. The few elderly survivors of his generation so recall him. ''Peters?'' they say, ''Mayor Peters?—Oh yes, Starr Faithfull.''

INDIAN SUMMER IN HYANNIS PORT

ANOTHER SUMMER COMES TO CAPE COD; THE HERRING HAVE LONG FIN-
ished their run, the shadbush has lost its whiteness and the lilacs
are by. On Hyannis Port's high hill above the Kennedy compound they have taken down the wooden shutters from the little mock-
gothic Episcopal church, St. Mary's-by-the-Sea. Surrounded by a tangle
of broom, dominated by its square fieldstone tower with four eroded
gargoyles, St. Mary's at first glance looks real-gothic. Like the church,
most of Hyannis Port hibernates, but it is a classy somnolence unlike
the uneasy dormancy of honky-tonk Hyannis two miles or so away.
Almost as many blue-denim drifters converge on Hyannis as on Provincetown, to the disgust of the tourists many of whom have American
flag decals on their windshields. The latter throw coins into the reflecting pool of the John F. Kennedy Memorial, and twice a day a man
in rubber hip boots gathers up the take with a squeegee. The money
goes to charity. "I wish I made as much a year as I rake up," he remarked
morosely the last time I was there.

Looking down the hill on a July morning, I can just make out the
widow's walk and the sprouting television mast of Father Joe's house
in the Kennedy compound. The other houses are hidden by the interlacing greenery. But this year the compound no longer seems a focal
point. Father Joe is long gone, Jackie's house is empty, so is Bobby's
and even Ted's—or so they seem to be, except for the occasional weekend
when the local police block the road to St. Mary's. Rose, the matriarch,
may or may not be there. All except one of the sentry boxes that sur

rounded the compound when Jack was President have now been removed. It is not really a very private place, but Father Joe was still
emergent when he forsook the Irish summer enclave of Hull for Cape
Cod. Directly below St. Mary's is a spit of land running to an isolated
peninsula with three or four large houses on it. If he had been more
sophisticated at the time he would have bought the peninsula rather
than the piecemeal section that the tourists now flock to see. Ted would
not have had to get his second and more secluded house across the
bay at Squaw Island. But I suppose one had to start somewhere.

I notice they are building a new house on the edge of the peninsula, complete with fake windmill. Hyannis Port is full of fake wind-
mills, as if there were something of the wind's whim in the subtown's
opulence, its overly white houses and manicured lawns and too little
privacy. The bay on this bright morning is full of sails. Across the golf
course, beyond the marshes, I can see the outline of Falmouth and to
the left Martha's Vineyard almost as part of the mainland. Farther out
to sea is the brief low hump of Nantucket. Then a half-turn to the
left and I am looking at Hyannis harbor and the compound's conceal-
ing greenery. Here the two ends meet: Hyannis Port and Martha's
Vineyard.

It is over a decade and a half since Ted Kennedy drove his car off
the bridge at Chappaquiddick. The release of the inquest report that
spring wrote an official finis to the incident. On Cape Cod the scandal had the aspect of a palimpsest, with the May trial of a Provincetown
handyman and drug addict, Antone Costa, for the murder and dis-
memberment of two young women almost blotting out the report. Ted,
like any politician from Boss Platt to his own grandfather Honey Fitz,
trusted that time would blur if not obliterate; that the vague shadow
of the bridge would not darken the image of the peace candidate,
brother Bobby's successor, the unwearying spokesman for the war-weary,
the idol of the young and the university liberals, whose voice was a
clarion call to "stop the war. Stop the ABM. Stop the MIRV. Stop the
arms race." Politically that was long ago. Ted with his middle-aged
spread has become the bloated figure that Tom Wolfe caricatured so
cruelly, too aged now for any dynastic succession. His divorce was the
signal that he would not be a future Presidential candidate. The image of the bridge is always latent.

"If Ted had only told the truth," a Boston politician said to me,
"if he'd just admitted he was driving down to the beach with a pretty

girl to look at the moon, he'd have had every husband in the country solidly behind him.'' The whole sad incident was a simple one, and it seems extraordinary that it took a complication of legal experts and speechwriters headed by Theodore Sorensen to write the account that Ted gave on television a week later. Once he had given this face-saving version, it hung around his neck like a dead albatross. That was his story, and he was stuck with it. He could not change it without making himself out a calculating liar. He could not keep it without being exposed to its contradictions.

Could he, while driving Mary Jo Kopechne back to the Edgartown ferry from the party, have made the wrong turning from the macadam road to the bumpy dirt road and continued the three-quarters of a mile to the Dyke bridge? Judge Boyle at the inquest decided that ''Kennedy and Kopechne did not intend to return to Edgartown and that Kennedy did not intend to drive to the ferry slip and his turn into Dyke Road was intentional.'' Ted had driven over the bridge that afternoon to go swimming, as he admitted at the inquest. Several times that day he had driven up and down the macadam ferry road. How could he make a false turn under such circumstances? How could he help but be instantly aware of it if he had? I have tried to ask myself what I should have done in the event of such an accident. It seems to me I should have rushed to the nearest house, pounded on the door and shouted for help. Ted on the other hand trudged a mile and a quarter past several houses without making any attempt to summon anyone. Perhaps there were no lights, as he said, perhaps he was in a state of shock. Still, he was able to walk the distance and to talk coherently when he arrived at the cottage where his party was still going on. Then, as he told it, he drove back to the bridge with those two obscure figures, his cousin Joseph Gargan and Paul Markham. The water had risen, but the wheels of the overturned car were still visible. Markham and Gargan stripped and dove down, and Gargan claims he actually managed to get inside the car. But they, though in no state of shock, made no effort to summon help. Ted said he could not bear the thought of calling Mary Jo's parents, his mother and his wife in the middle of the night to tell them that she was dead. Yet he could have called the police or the fire department. In fact, as he walked back, he passed a red-lighted fire-alarm box. According to John Farrar, the fire department captain and scuba diver who had recovered Mary Jo's body, if Kennedy had pulled the fire-alarm switch, a Coast-

Guard helicopter would have been on the scene in fifteen minutes. At that point, he thought, Mary Jo was probably still alive and he could have saved her.

Yet neither Ted nor his hangers-on did anything. "Don't upset the girls," he told them, if one can believe his story. Gargan and Markham took him to the ferry slip and he swam across the channel to Edgartown. The other two drove back to the cottage where they spent the night, still silent, still doing nothing about the girl in the car. Ted, in his room at Edgartown's Shiretown Inn, changed his clothes. At 2:25 A.M. the proprietor noticed him in the courtyard, outwardly tranquil at least. He asked the time and complained that the loud party next door kept him from sleeping. Was this inner agitation, or was it an attempt to establish an alibi of having spent the night at Edgartown? Ted returned to his room, coming downstairs at 7:30 and stopping at the desk to ask the clerk to order him a copy of the *Times* and the *Boston Globe*. Then, according to his inquest story, he met a sailing competitor and talked with him for a half an hour about the race of the day before. One cannot look into people's hearts, but on the surface, at least, it seems coldblooded, with Mary Jo locked in the car underwater.

Gargan and Markham, still keeping their silence, left the cottage and came over on the ferry at about eight. On meeting Ted, they recrossed to use the telephone on the ferry slip. Ted's first call was neither to the police nor for any assistance, but to his family legal adviser Burke Marshall. By this time the news of the accident was out on the island although the names of those involved were not yet known. The rest of the story is too familiar to bear repeating. Yet, if one can make any final judgment it is this: The accident itself was one that might have happened to anyone driving over that bridge at night at twenty miles an hour. But the actions of Ted and his hangers-on after the accident seem motivated more by concern for the Kennedy legend than by any thought of a girl trapped underwater in a car. Ted admits that his not reporting the accident until the next morning was indefensible. What remains really indefensible is that no one attempted to summon help.

Deputy Sheriff Huck Look, driving home late that evening along the main Chappaquiddick road, noticed a large black sedan swing off onto the dirt road that leads to the bridge. Then he saw it turn a few yards up an overgrown sand road. He could see a man and a woman in the front seat and a person or bundle in the back. Thinking they were lost, he got out of his car to help. But as the driver caught sight of Look's uniform be backed up suddenly and sped down the bridge road. In his detailed study of the affair Jack Olson has evolved the theory that Ted, alarmed at the uniform, tried to escape.

Fearing he might be followed, he turned the car over to Mary Jo and hid in the bushes, telling her to drive on and pick him up when the coast was clear. She, diminutive and unused to such a large car, had driven away and off the bridge. After some waiting Ted returned to the party they had left without her and did not learn what had occurred until the next morning. To avoid admitting he had run off and hidden, he concocted his improbable explanation. There are a dozen other explanations. But what really happened at the bridge that night only he knows.

In a theatrical television gesture Ted offered to resign his Senate seat if the people of his state had lost confidence in him. He need not have worried. After his broadcast the outpourings of devotion to him in Massachusetts were maudlin, how maudlin one could best judge by listening to the radio talk shows. Outsiders expressed their doubts. John Marquand called Ted's apologia ''a masterly appeal to the Irish mother who abides in the core of the Kennedys' home constituency.'' But the Kennedy legend in Massachusetts remained unassailable. Ted was easily re-elected to the Senate though by a somewhat diminished majority.

The Kennedy compound below me in the morning sunshine now seems a part of the irrevocable past, on its way to becoming a national shrine. I find myself reflecting again on the historicity of the Kennedy legend, how differently it developed outside and inside Massachusetts. Nationwide it quickly grew to a myth of youth and martyrdom, of a vanished Camelot. One tends to forget that in the 1960 campaign both candidates received their nomination by political hocus-pocus with a minimum of popular demand, that a number of pre-election bumper stickers read: NEITHER ONE. And of course Jack Kennedy did have charm and wit and spontaneity—though after Eisenhower almost anyone in the White House would have seemed witty. In the days before Dallas, Kennedy's popularity was beginning to slip. If he had lived he would in all probability have foundered in the bog of Vietnam even as Johnson did. For his was the initial commitment. Jack Kennedy in his death gave an image and a legend to his country; in his native state he had created the image long before he was elected President.

What he represented in and to Massachusetts was that periodic phenomenon of history, the emergence of a new class. I realized that on the first and only occasion I ever saw him, in the autumn of 1952 when I was driven to Springfield to hear Adlai Stevenson about whom I was writing an article for an English paper. Young Congressman Kennedy was then on the platform with members of the Democratic State Committee to welcome Stevenson to Massachusetts, led by the waddling Governor Dever, a man so gross that the Parker House is said to have provided a special basement exit for the occasions when he had difficulty in maneuvering down the front steps. Among those political saurians the slender, easy-mannered Jack Kennedy moved with urbane detachment. They were of the ward-heeler past that had spawned the Mahatmas, the Diamond Joe Timiltys, the Honey Fitzes, the Dan Coakleys, the Jim Curleys. Jack represented the future, the merging of the old Celtic inheritance with the American mainstream.

It began of course with the Irish Famine years, that disaster of the 1840s that in less than a decade sent a million and a half Irish refugees to North America. Unlike the Jews who came later and rose quickly, the Irish were slow risers. They were not people of the book. Their native cohesiveness found its easiest outlet in politics, which became a way of life, perhaps the only way of life for them. The mean streets of East Boston and what had now become the proletarian Celtic matrix of South Boston did not need accommodation but jobs and handouts and unconsidered assistance in distress that the Yankees in their thrifty cash ethic would not provide—something for the faithful, something for the out-of-lucks, something for the boys. Those who followed where Mayors O'Brien and Collins had blazed the trails understood perfectly. Men like Honey Fitz and Curley felt no obligation to observe the rules made by those who had exploited them.

When Mayor Collins died in 1905, President Cleveland said of him: "In public life he was strictly honest and sincerely devoted to the responsibilities involved." With one accidental exception it was the last time this could be said of a Boston mayor for the next half-century. If anyone had said this of Honey Fitz, he would have had to cross his fingers and smile. Under the new mayor, City Hall became a place of high politics and low comedy. Honey Fitz of course was eclipsed by Curley, a tougher, cleverer, more relentless and certainly more flamboyantly entertaining political buccaneer, who would eventually drive him from public life. It was the era of Edwin O'Connor's "Hurrah" boys, of

Honey Fitz's Dearos, of Curley's transmogrified Tammany; clownish, disreputable, profitable, a good show and always one in the eye for Beacon Hill and "that place across the river"—as Harvard was known in South Boston. Looked at reminiscently the period becomes a kind of vaudeville: Honey Fitz as king of the revels with his blonde Toodles Ryan at the old Woodcock Hotel; Curley photographed *en smoking* or snapped in a coon coat and iron mike on St. Patrick's Day, meeting the scandal publisher of the *Telegraph*, Enright, on State Street and knocking him into the gutter, swaggering into the City Hall Barbershop with a pail of beer for all-comers; David I. Walsh and his "boys in the band" at the Lenox, his deviation never in all the years mentioned in print. So much was known, so much remained aural. I remember talking with the newspaperman who had written a journalistic life of John Boyle O'Reilly, and asking him why he had not said that O'Reilly committed suicide. "There are things you can't say in Boston," was his reply. I suppose there is not a politician in Massachusetts over forty who has not heard the jingle about Toodles.

Politics was at least exciting in those days of open-air rallies and limited alternate amusements. Second-generation Irish, still overwhelmingly proletarian, were satisfied with the antics of their leaders, not begrudging them their ambiguous fortunes. Not so the third generation. Until World War I there were indeed men of wealth among the Massachusetts Irish, but the great majority still roosted in South Boston's three-deckers. In the words of the bawdy, and also unrecorded song (except in a most bowdlerized form), "Southie is my home town." But after World War I, if slowly at first, the exodus began, from Southie to the middle-class suburbs of Milton and West Roxbury, from three-deckers to brick-veneered singles. "Two-toilet Irish," the deserters were called derisively by those who remained. In Milton and West Roxbury they went to local preparatory schools like Roxbury Latin rather than to the Jesuit Boston College High or Boston's Public Latin School, they continued on to that place across the river rather than to Boston College. And as they acquired the middle-class patina, they grew ashamed of Honey Fitz and "Sweet Adeline," of Southie's annual St. Patrick's Day parade enlivened by japers like Knocko McCormack; of deft operators and blackmailers like Dan Coakley; of silvercrossed younger pols like ex-mayor Tobin, the supernumerary secretary of labor in Truman's cabinet. As respectable taxpayers they did not want to be identified any longer with flamboyant houses on Jamaicaway display ing shamrocks on the shutters. Enough of them even voted Republican after World War II to elect a Mayflower descendant Governor Bradford over Curley, on the slogan "Had enough?"

When young Jack Kennedy appeared without forewarning on the Boston political scene in 1946, the middle-class suburban Irish hailed him with joy and relief. After half a century of oafishness, this attractive, well-spoken, graceful, witty, Celtic, Harvard-bred and very rich young man was what every suburban matron in Milton and West Roxbury would have liked her son to be. In fact many came to see Jack *as* their son. Whimsically enough, Jack in his first bid for office was a carpetbagger, establishing apartment residence on Beacon Hill to run for Congress from the district that had sent Curley four times to Washington and from where Honey Fitz had been elected congressman although subsequently barred from his seat because of election frauds. And in this campaign the Kennedy tribe, emerging for the first time into Massachusetts politics, left nothing to chance. The Kennedy women charmed the suburban housewives into ecstasy. Joe Kane ran enough additional candidates to split any opposition vote seven ways.

Jack Kennedy's walk-away election may have been the wish fulfillment of Democratic mothers in Massachusetts. But it was very much resented by the old-line pols who had come up the ladder rung by rung, often by knocking the feet from under the man just above them. Not the slow way for Jack, through the wards, into the legislature, to the state senate, with all the little wheels and deals along the way. This was, in the now banal term, "instant politics." Privately the pols expressed their outrage at being outflanked by a young whippersnapper who pronounced his *a*'s broad, and there was envenomed backroom talk of old scandals; Honey Fitz's caperings and Father Joe's diversions. I remember a neighbor of my aunt's in West Roxbury, the wife of City Councilor Joe White and mother of the future mayor, Kevin White. She, my aunt said, was ready to give me the real inside story about "those Kennedys." But as the Kennedy star (or stars) continued to rise, she grew distant, reticent, postponing our promised talk until I sensed that I should never get it. Backroom talk died too. The last outburst was in 1962 when Eddie McCormack, nephew of the Speaker of the House of Representatives, had the temerity to oppose the untried Ted in the Democratic state convention for Jack's vacant Senate seat. "Don't let them twist your arm!" was his slogan, but the twist was on. The doomed Eddie was certainly the more experienced and possibly the better man. But even beyond the twist there was the legend. As one political worker then explained it: "When they [the Boston Irish] hear Eddie McCormack speak they think of South Boston and their parents' lives. When they see Ted Kennedy they think of Palm Beach, Beacon Hill, the Virginia fox-hunting country and their children's future."

To a degree all of us live by legends. And it is within this Kennedy legend that the descendants of the Famine immigrants achieved respectability, asssurance, acceptance of themselves, their ancestors and their religion, not only in Massachusetts but across the continent. One thinks of the fate of Al Smith who, in 1928, arrived too soon.

As I turned down the hill toward the almost invisible compound, I found myself reflecting again on Hegel's thesis and antithesis. Every movement in its triumph contains the seeds of its own disintegration. After the Revolution the parvenu merchants of Boston, or at least their grandsons, gave the city a literary flowering. Very briefly. The Kennedys in their triumph brought in another ruling class. Once more the *maréchaux* became the kings. Ted in Massachusetts will be elected senator until his senescence, if he wishes. But the Irish Americans in their flowering have lost the pugnacious cohesiveness of Southie, they have lost much of their church-race identity and they are on their way to losing their dominance. It is no accident that recent Republican and Democratic governors in Massachusetts have had Italian names and the present governor a Greek one. *Plus ça change*—as Honey Fitz may have said to Jim Curley.

Governor Coolidge glumly inspects his State Guard.

CALVIN COOLIDGE'S VERMONT:
TWO PILGRIMAGES IN AN OFF-SEASON

C ALVIN COOLIDGE HAS VAGUELY PREOCCUPIED ME EVER SINCE, AS A SCHOOL-
boy, I first heard his nasal voice over my homemade radio crystal
set. My father, who was in the Massachusetts legislature when
Coolidge was governor, said one really had to know him to dislike him.
He considered Silent Cal the laziest governor in the history of the
Commonwealth, and used to tell how Coolidge came back from lunch
each day to spend two hours napping in the governor's chair with his
feet on the desk. My mother said that shaking hands with the governor
was like shaking hands with a codfish. But for me there was always
something poignant about that atavistic Yankee translated to the
Presidency almost in spite of himself, a man born out of his time, an
accidental and obscure Vice President who, on the sudden death of
President Harding and at 2:47 of an August morning in the Vermont
homestead, took the Presidential oath of office from his father, a local
justice of the peace. That simple ceremony in the front parlor, lit by
a kerosene lamp on the table next to the family Bible, with a grizzled
taciturn farmer facing the sharp-featured rufous little man he was then
to make President, was one of the dramatic incidental scenes of
American history. In the jazz-hot twenties it seemed a harking back
to a lost rural past, to the vanished decencies of a simpler way of life.

The tremendous impact of the Roosevelt era dwarfed the Coolidge
interlude, making most people forget there was ever such a thing as
a Coolidge myth. Coolidge has receded into a minor Presidential figure,

commemorated with the others on a postage stamp, a man of limited understanding and outlook, if with no blemish on his personal integrity. His twang is forgotten—he is supposed to have pronounced "cow" as a three-syllable word. His occasional acid remarks are no longer quoted. No one reads the adulatory books like *Coolidge Wit and Wisdom* or even the amusingly scurrilous *Rise of Saint Calvin,* subtitled *Merry Sidelights on the Career of Mr. Coolidge.*

In the normal course of events, Coolidge might have ended up as a state senator, a governor at most, but by a set of curious chances, by disaster and death, that inbred Yankee who was so aptly named Calvin, who always kept the copybook maxims of his school days in his mind and the Vermont hill country in his heart, became President of the United States in a period as opposite to his nature as his native Plymouth Notch, Vermont, was to Chicago. It was this contrast between the small man and his large destiny that appealed to me and when I was a Harvard undergraduate made me attempt an awkward verse play—fortunately long since destroyed—called *Calvin Coolidge,* that set me finally on the road to Plymouth Notch. Whatever his destiny, Coolidge had never moved beyond the hills of his birth. Only Vermont could break down his almost surly taciturnity. In 1928, toward the end of his Presidency, he made an impromptu speech from the train at Bennington, typically brief, in the somewhat archaic pattern of his boyhood, that for once reached the level of poetry. "Vermont is a state I love," he said, touched by the immediacy of his leaving it. "I could not look upon the peaks of Ascutney, Killington, Mansfield and Equinox, without being moved in a way that no other scene could move me. It was here that I first saw the light of day; here I received my bride; here my dead lie pillowed on the loving breast of our everlasting hills."

SPRING 1950

As I drove up from Ludlow the afterglow of the sunset was sallow against the hills in the fading metallic sky, and then the cloud-rack blotted it out and the wind buffeted my car halfway across the empty road and the rain pelted down. There were a few farmhouse lights, but the solitary filling station I passed was closed, and when I saw the sign ROUTE 103—RUTLAND wet and gleaming under my headlights, I knew I had lost the road. I turned back.

Mid-May seemed to bring no spring to this Vermont hill country. Driving north had been like driving back in time, for in suburban

Boston the elms arched over the road in all their light-feathered greenness and the lilacs were almost in flower. Here the elms tossed nakedly in the wind and the maples and hickories were a mass of interlacing bare branches. A dead landscape. Yet here and there my headlights picked out a solitary shadbush in blossom like a bridal dress of translucent shimmering whiteness. The roadside ditch held occasional clumps of marsh marigolds, and as I drove through a hollow and the wind died down temporarily, I could hear the iterant treble of spring peepers, a sound I had not heard for three weeks past in Massachusetts.

What with the weather, I decided to stay the night in Ludlow. Tomorrow would be time enough to take the back road to Plymouth. As I came down the hill on Route 103, the Ludlow streets were rain-sodden and deserted. I spent the night in a bathless, creaky room in Ye Olde Touriste Home.

Next morning was warm with the softness of spring, as if the season had relented, and the sun slanted lazily along the Ludlow pavements by the time I left the angular town and started again along the Rutland road. In the clearness of the morning I could see where I had missed the turn. Route 103 and Route 100 parted company in a wooded hollow, and the latter—a dirt road—veered right to Plymouth Union. The road funneled into the hills. There was ground mist in the valley as I jolted along a track glistening with puddles and still humped and broken by the winter's frost. In every swamp I could hear the red-winged blackbirds chattering with a sound like a rusty gate, and sometimes they would flutter upward, their orange and red wing-bands startling in the subdued morning colors. Bluebirds had come back too, and the sun caught the azure of their flight. The road wound ambiguously in and out, following the course of the Black River that connected Rescue Lake, Echo Lake and Lake Amherst like a thread. There seemed to be no far shore to these lakes. The hills plunged down to the water that spread out glaucous and reflective with streamers of mist wisping along the surface. Occasionally a fish would break and leap, and the hills would echo back even that brief sound, and the concentric ripples spread and spread like a silver tide until they dissolved against the shore. I saw two painted turtles on a log, just out of hibernation. The air held the scent of spruce and balsam in such crystal transparency that it was as if I could see each budding leaf and samara across the water. Always the road continued along the shore, past screens of speckled alder and aspen with the long catkins drooping from the lead-gray branches, past summer cottages and a jimcrack-ornamented summer hotel now all boarded up, and several abandoned farms with disintegrating stone boundary walls and empty cellar holes and lilac bushes grown dense to mark the old threshold.

The landscape turned from wild to derelict as I left the finger lakes behind under the shadow of Salt Ash Mountain. Abandoned farms clung to the edges of the overgrown fields, and there were other farms apparently on the point of being abandoned, banked with sawdust against the winter cold, their doors and windows sagging, the yards littered with rusty cans. As I approached Plymouth Union I came to a settlement of tarpaper shanties, where the rural jetsam holed up, workless, kept alive by the parsimonious assistance of town welfare. Here along the road, the decay of Yankeedom was inscribed in rotting farmhouse and squatter shack. The young and enterprising had gone away long ago. These harsh upland acres, scored by the northern winter, had nothing to hold a newer generation. There was no economy to sustain them—unless one counted the monstrous hooked-rug industry; the land was too poor even to be sold for taxes. Here lay the sweepings of an old tradition.

A man guiding a horse harnessed to a small sledge heaped with boulders moved the minimum distance in inches to let me pass without looking up at me, and some children playing in the dismantled tonneau of a Model T Ford before their front door stopped to stare. In front of one unpainted house I saw a sign: FRESH EGGS—FRESH COW.

One hundred years earlier, Plymouth Township had held 1,400 inhabitants. When Calvin Coolidge died in 1933 there were about 400. In 1949 there were less than 300. Yet when one penetrates the seedy outskirts to the old settlements of Plymouth Union and Plymouth Notch, the place is still intact, reminiscent, like an ancient soldier sitting in the sun.

I had no interest in stopping at Plymouth Union. The center of the village, composed of square white buildings with corrugated roofs— the usual meetinghouse, store, town hall and frame dwellings of the more substantial citizens—though in the New England tradition, was of no great charm. I drove past what had once been a small factory and then headed sharply uphill toward Plymouth Notch.

The road grew even more rutted as the gradient steepened; the trees encroached on the verges; then I came to a final crest and slipped down through masking trees, until at one last bend I could see the few buildings of Plymouth Notch ahead of me set in their bowl of hills. From my vantage point they had an air of coziness about them with nothing really identifiable in their grouping except the spire of the meetinghouse.

Plymouth Notch was a straggling collection of houses near the crossroad: what would usually be called a "corner" in rural New England. At the large white general store, with an obsolete Socony pump in front of it, the road turned left and up under a pale blur of elm buds into the background of the hills. Crows were cawing above the meadow hollow to the right. There were no other sounds in the morning quiet but the crows and the trickle of running water in the gulleys beside the road; no sign of any living being until a small boy in a checked lumberjacket appeared, trotted up the long steps of the store, and came out with a loaf of bread wrapped in wax paper. That was no doubt Miss Cilley's store, the one that once belonged to Coolidge's father. In its back room Calvin had been born. It was there, too, that the famous Moxie episode occurred the night he was sworn in as President. For on that sweltering evening, just before he took the oath of office, he had walked over to the store with Congressman Dale and a local newspaperman. "A hot night," he remarked laconically, and ordered himself a nickel glass of Moxie, a precola New England tonic. The other two did the same. When the three glasses appeared, the President-to-be downed his with quiet deliberateness, then took an old-fashioned purse with a snap clasp, laid a single five cent piece on the counter and walked out.

The Coolidge homestead lies along and parallel to the hill road about one hundred fifty yards beyond the general store. Originally it was a one-story Colonial-type building, a narrower adaptation of the Cape Cod cottage, with a later ell of smaller size added to connect it with the barn. The ell has a triangular gable in the roof and a porch running the length of the recessed front. Some time in the eighties, probably at the same time the old-fashioned window squares had been taken out and the glazing bars removed, a two-story bay was added that bulges out ludicrously, destroying the earlier symmetrical pattern. The large blank rectangles of window glass give the house an empty, almost desolate appearance. A barracklike two-story annex on the far side was added when Coolidge was President. The homestead looked squat, framed by billowing sugar maples that would nearly hide it under their summer foliage in another month, a nondescript place that no tourist would have glanced at twice if it hadn't been for Coolidge and that dramatic night in August 1923.

First I took a snapshot from across the road. Then I walked up to the porch and knocked on the side door that led to the main house. After a few seconds I heard shuffling, deliberate footsteps, and finally a bent old woman opened the door and looked me up and down without speaking. She had on a kind of tam-o'-shanter, and her leathery dessicated face with its thin set of mouth suggested the Indian blood that was part of many a rural Yankee inheritance. I asked if I could see the room where Calvin Coolidge was sworn in as President. She said it was pretty early, but she guessed I could come in. Her cracked voice had the overtones of the New England past that still suggested psalm-singing dissenters. Coolidge had had that same kind of voice. More than thirty-five years ago he had become President. In another generation there would be no solitary survivor, not even in waxworks Vermont, who would have kept that nasal twang.

"Right here's where Pres'dent Coolidge took his oath of office," she said with a snap of her jaw. "Look about."

The door opened directly into the room. It was small and mean. There was a rocking chair in the window bay, and empty cast-iron flowerpot holders fastened to either side of the molding. The wallpaper was a faded imitation brocade, and the gray floor paint had worn off in patches, especially around the black Glenwood parlor stove with its nickel trimmings. In an alcove near the window stood a cumbersome Victorian walnut secretary-desk. The old woman went over to it. In the light I could see the cords of her neck standing out like clotheslines and the bobble of her Adam's apple under the serrated skin as she began to speak.

"There's the table he took the oath on," she said pointing to the middle of the room. It was a splay-footed center table with a maple base and a cherrywood top. On it were postcards showing pictures of the homestead, and the meetinghouse down the road "where several generations of the Coolidge family have worshiped," and a blurred likeness of Coolidge in a cutaway. There were also little red-and-green felt banners price-tagged twenty-five cents, with PLYMOUTH, VT. stamped on them, for tourists to tie on their cars. Against the wall was set a horsehair sofa on which were displayed other souvenirs, pottery dishes, dolls, amateurish watercolors and similar bric-a-brac. Several yellowed newspaper photos hung on the wall in makeshift frames—one of Coolidge with his family when he was lieutenant governor of

CALVIN COOLIDGE'S VERMONT

Massachusetts, one of his first day as President, another showing his father welcoming him back for a visit. There was also a rather stilted letter of Calvin Jr.'s, the young boy who died in the White House.

I took two postcards, while the old woman watched me in silence, tapping her forefinger on the flat of the secretary; "Do many tourists— er, people—come here now?" I finally asked her.

The commonplace question seemed to thaw her out a little. She nodded and cleared her throat cords and seemed for the moment almost friendly.

"Not so many as used to," she said, rasping the words. "In the summer we get more visitors, of course. I guess it all fades into the past. They forget. But hist'ry was made in this room. An' some people say they wisht we had Coolidge President naow."

I waited for her to go on, but she was through.

"How much are the cards?" I asked.

"Ten cents," she said. "The money goes to help keep the place up. I hear down to Roosevelt's place they're chargin' folk to see it, makin' 'em pay just to get in—as if he hadn't cost the country enough as 'tis!"

"Did you know President Coolidge?"

"Lots of people ask me did I know him, but I say no one knew him. No one ever did. I was a hired girl when I came here. After he died they made me caretaker."

She broke off abruptly, shuffled out of the room and came back with a nickel in change for the quarter I had given her.

"What's the name of the mountain behind the crossroad?" I asked her finally.

"I don't know as it has a name," she said. "It's just a hill."

I turned away from the hill and the brown strip of road that receded into the distance, turned back and went down again to the Notch, past the one-room schoolhouse with its woodpile and the meetinghouse and the general store behind the red Socony pump, still farther down the slope and across the ridge to the old burying ground. There were more dead there under the knotted grasses than would ever live again in Plymouth Township. As I walked along the spongy, neglected paths, even the names on the slate and granite tombstones seemed remote shadows. No one would be likely to walk this earth again named Ichabod or Zeb, to say nothing of Lemuel, Ira, Achsa, Eli or Jabez. Calvin Coolidge's uncle had been named Julius Caesar Coolidge, and his grandfather, Galusha Coolidge—known locally as "Galoosh."

Most of the Coolidges were buried along the lower curve of the ridge, several members of the family often sharing the same stone. John Coolidge, the President's father, lay with his two wives, the date of his death—as one could tell by the freshness of the incised lettering—cut long after his name and birth date, a not uncommon practice in thrifty New England. It was cheaper to have all the family names, of the living as well as the dead, carved on a tombstone when it was ordered. The death dates could always be added with the event. Another Coolidge, the son of Sally N. (Billings) Coolidge who died in Quindaro, Kansas, was buried here at his last request, expressed in doggerel in the inscription:

> Carry me back to old Vermont
> Where the rills trickle down the hills,
> There is where I want to lie when I die.

There is a thin path to Calvin Coolidge's grave. The simple stone is of white marble rather than the prevailing granite or antique slate. It bears nothing but his name and the dates July 4, 1872—January 5, 1933. Carved above is the Great Seal of the United States. Near it is a smaller marble stone similar in design but without the Great Seal, marking the grave of his son Calvin, who died in his sixteenth year and of whom he wrote in his autobiography, "When he went, the power and the glory of the Presidency went with him."

Blue periwinkles were peering out of last year's leaves, and there were patches of moss pink in atrocious shades of mauve and magenta among the graves. The flags anticipating Memorial Day that marked the buried soldiers were still bright and unweathered. One could trace the decline of Plymouth there—the goodly scattering of Revolutionary graves, the numbers of red, white and blue cotton rectangles to mark men who had fought in the Civil War, Vermont Volunteers and the soldiers of the First Vermont Regiment, then the handful of veterans of the First World War. Close by, the State of Vermont had marked with a boulder the grave of Esther Sumner Damon, who had died in 1906, the last widow of a soldier of the American Revolution. Near the top of the ridge I found a solitary grave from World War II, that of Everett E. Blanchard, who was killed on the island of Guam and whose body was brought back after the war in one of those futile gestures that organized sentimentality makes toward the dead.

From his high grave I could see the sunlight bright against the marble of Calvin Coolidge's headstone flanked by dark yew shrubs on either side—the sunlight that even in the long days of summer faded here at four o'clock. Fate seemed a curious thing in the morning brightness, the power and the glory that had accrued to that sharp-faced Yankee with the harsh voice. Here in Plymouth he was born, here he lived— all the life that really mattered to him—here he lay under his Vermont hills. The cycle was complete. Even the Presidency had been merely an interlude.

AUTUMN 1975

How oddly isolated the sharp little hills are along Route 103, like miniature mountains on a Chinese scroll. Traffic is heavy on this mist-sodden Columbus Day morning, with tourists from southern New England up to see the leaves already several weeks beyond their high coloring. A quarter century has passed since I last drove to Ludlow on my way to Plymouth Notch. Then the road was narrow-crowned and winding. Now, as the Calvin Coolidge Memorial Highway, it is enlarged, graded, straightened as only federal funds can straighten. The landscape slips by in faded patches of red and yellow and green. I scarcely dare take my eyes off the scenic highway to glance at the scenery. Straight ahead in the mid-distance I manage to catch a glimpse of a meetinghouse spire, a graceful symbol of New England best seen from far away. There is rain in the air, and fingers of mist poke down through the gaps in the hills.

Gone are the swamp-Yankee shacks of my first visit. Rural poverty, wherever and however it exists, has been decently landscaped out of sight. Vermont has, of course, been industrialized in the last twenty-five years—the ski industry, the snowmobile industry, the hunting industry, the Swiss chalet industry, the second-house-in-the-country industry, the flight-from-the-city industry. Vermonters warned me I would find the state very different. Is a superhighway ever different? Or is it merely a knife blade severing a region from its past?

Now the roofs are slate again. That, at least, persists. A cluster of overly neat and overly extended wooden buildings painted chocolate I take for a sports center until I see the sign Revival Tabernacle. So the Pentecostal wave has touched the granite Yankee heart! Alleluia! Just down the road, however, a Citgo dealer remains unconverted, impenitently announcing himself a Highway Robber. "Buy, Sell, Trade

Almost Anything. Also Ice.'' The mist has turned to a thin drizzle. By the time I reach Ludlow it is raining hard, as it was on my first visit. On the outskirts I encounter an ornate wooden church, a formidable survivor of the McKinley-rococo when wood was cheap and carvers uninhibited. Such flamboyant ingenuity in these cusps and curlicues and dentations, all topped by a round tower that might have been designed by Maxfield Parrish for Walt Disney! Ludlow's Main Street is wider than I remembered, almost a boulevard. On the opposite side I see a small restaurant with the sign HOGANCAMP'S GOOD FOOD. Most unlikely, I think, but the rain is heavy and I go in. Oddly enough, the sign turns out to be true.

Beyond Ludlow, the ski areas and sports centers and motor lodges proliferate, hill-encompassing, magic-mountain transplants. There is no longer a rutted dirt road where Routes 103 and 100 part company, but a macadamized continuation of the memorial highway, slick and detached, impervious to the course of lakes and rivers. The boarded-up hotel of my first visit has been rejuvenated, glistening now in white paint and black shutters, proclaiming itself ''Open to the Public. Breakfast. Lunch. Dinner. Rooms. Pool. Beach. Dorms. Tennis. Boats. All Legal Beverages.'' The red deck chairs of summer are still on the porch, a tennis court in the rear, and across the way a graceless angular meetinghouse with red and green stained-glass windows glares at me, bleak as a Victorian Sunday afternoon. Echo Lake is scored with rain. The new little cottages on the opposite shore look as if they had been cut with a cookie cutter. At Lake Amherst, a brightly painted chalet stands out in uneasy contrast to the brown and russet foliage. Then a steep-pitched modern cottage that scorns paint, and beyond that the Ski-off Inn. Hospitality unlimited; hunters are not only accommodated but supplied with licenses. The highway veers right, continues its macadam progress over hill and hollow as Route 100-A. At Plymouth Notch there is a cutoff with a sign pointing to a fairly steep incline. I drive up to find myself in a large fenced parking lot. Before me the ground slips away to Plymouth Notch in diminished perspective, a clipped, trimmed, painted scene across which belated tourists walk like stage extras.

A new stone house similar to those in Chester guards the path to the village. This handsome if rather incongruous building is the Calvin Coolidge Memorial Center where one may buy a combination ticket to the Coolidge Homestead, the Coolidge Birthplace and the Wilder

Barn. To the right, one enters a large reception room with lounge chairs, an oversize fireplace and a grand piano. To the left, a shop sells pewter, wooden toys, scented candles, souvenir china, stained-glass plaques and other gewgawry. Kitsch it may be, but it is refined kitsch. The book counter has a fair selection of Vermont books and magazines and such minor reprintings as *Homespun Inaugural, The Boyhood of Calvin Coolidge* and the flag-entwined *Footprints of Calvin Coolidge.* A rear room is given over to a photographic panorama of Coolidge's life: his relatives, the sister who was so dear to him and died young, and the boy at school, the young man at college; then the newly elected president of the Massachusetts senate sitting with a cigar wedged in the corner of his grim smiling mouth, his wife laughing—perhaps at him—with her hand on his shoulder. A gracious woman, Grace Coolidge, witty, endearing and I suspect long-suffering. From governor to President, the photographs of the dour Yankee in the double-breasted suit that is always a bit too tight for him seem unvarying.

The porch of Cilley's store is bare except for a mailbox, the windows empty of goods. But a sign reassures the dubious: "Yes. This is a real working post office." I peer into the dusky interior where I can make out a counter with nothing on it, an old coffee grinder, and over the door in the back a Moxie sign. Another porch sign informs me that the offices of the Calvin Coolidge Memorial Association are upstairs.

Outwardly, the homestead across the way remains unaltered except that the barracklike annex has been moved down a dead-end road behind the house. Even from afar the annex keeps its ugliness. Large blank window panes have been replaced by small squares in an effort to make it look Colonial, but the chimney is too small and the whole building disproportioned beyond the reach of cosmetic carpentry. The attendant at the Wilder Barn told me that the place belongs to the living Coolidge son, John, who also owns the cheese factory down the road. Semiretired from the insurance business, he has now made the annex his new homestead.

However the Coolidge homestead may have preserved its outward appearance, inside it has been transformed, the rooms sealed off by glass walls past which one walks along a narrow corridor, peering through the glass as if one were in an aquarium. I surrender my ticket at the side door, ease down the corridor, gape as I go. On my right is the woodshed with an axe fixed in a stump. Beyond is a small room with carpenter's tools and beyond that a washroom with tub, washboard, hand-wringer and clothes boiler. Everything has been so carefully restored, re-olded, if there is such a word. The parlor where Coolidge was sworn in has long since been cleared of bric-a-brac, the horsehair sofa swept bare, the splay-footed table now holds a Bible, a pen, an inkwell and Calvin's father's notary seal. A shawl has been hung on the rocking chair; there are renewed lace curtains at the windows. Who can say it doesn't look exactly as it did that August night in 1923?

Axminster carpeting covers the floor of Coolidge's bedroom. On the wall is a sepia reproduction of "The Horse Fair." A pair of high-laced black shoes with hard rounded toes stands in the corner. A china pitcher squats in a china basin on the washstand. I did not think authenticity would go so far as to have a chamber pot under the bed, but there it peeps out, its lid matching the pattern of the pitcher and basin.

No sign of the rain letting up outside. I decide to skip the cheese factory and cross the street to the meetinghouse with the abbreviated tower. UNION CHRISTIAN CHURCH—1842 it says on the sign. A marble slab in the vestibule preserves the words that Coolidge spoke at Bennington, the one moment in his life when he was moved to poetry. Inside, the church is small with walls of stained deal, a chandelier of kerosene lamps. The pews, curved in like a miniature amphitheater, are of golden oak, as is the pulpit platform on which is a high-pointed Gothic chair flanked by two smaller chairs. The odor of old wood surrounds me, and that musty New England meetinghouse flavor that seems to embody remote Calvinism. I feel my claustrophobia creeping up on me and I flee.

I shall not bother about the Wilder Barn with its collection of stage coaches, sleighs, gigs, ornate hearses and assortments of obsolete farm implements. But there is still time, a few minutes left, to see that room in the back of the Cilley store where Coolidge was born. I go up the steps and into the anteroom that must have once been the kitchen. Muzak fills the air screechingly. A woman with a face as wrinkled as a winter apple sits in a rocking chair nodding in time to the rhythm. She punches my ticket and beckons me on to the little bedroom at the side. There is not much to see—a bed, towels, a chest, a kerosene lamp so cleverly electrified that it almost looks like kerosene burning, a few pictures. As I turn back I notice an oleograph of a small boy offering a small girl a basket of cherries. "A beautiful picture," the old woman remarks, "but you can't see it right in that light." There is also a framed, embroidered "Rock of Ages, Cleft for Me." She leans over and switches off the radio. It is obviously the sign for me to go.

Closing time at Plymouth Notch! The remaining tourists, I among them, head like homebound starlings for the parking lot. They carry limp packages of candles, pewter mugs, souvenir plates; or herb-flavored granular cheese, maple syrup, cans of baked beans, brown bread or corned beef hash from the cheese factory. The lights are beginning to wink out in the stone house. Another week and everything will close down. Plymouth Notch hibernates for the winter. I take one more backward glance at the village below me, laid out in miniature like one of those toy towns I used to have as a child. What brings people here? Not so much the blurred memory of an interlude President as the vogue for Victoriana and a wistfulness for lost rural simplicity. Thanks to the Vermont Division of Historic Sites, the whole area has become the Plymouth Notch Historic District, so neat, so authentic, so Williamsburged, so Sturbridgized. But the breath of life is gone, even the attenuated breath of a quarter of a century ago.

Ben Butler in 1874. His face, so often caricatured, seems a caricature in itself.

BUTLER THE BEAST:
BENJAMIN FRANKLIN BUTLER

THE GRASSY SLOPES IN FRONT OF BOSTON'S STATE HOUSE BOAST NO MONU-
ment to Ben Butler, former governor and Civil War general, though
another native son and conspicuously unsuccessful general, "Fight-
ing Joe" Hooker, bestrides his horse in front of the east wing. Butler
was not given equal statuary space because, it was felt, he was too well-
remembered in the flesh—and as a thorn in the flesh—to warrant a
reminder in bronze.

Massachusetts memories are long: when James M. Curley stormed
his way to the governor's chair in 1934, fifty-two years after Butler, and
proceeded to turn the State House and the state upside down, ex-
asperated Republicans proclaimed him "the worst Massachusetts governor since Ben Butler."

The comparison was as apt as it was bitter. Like Curley, Butler was
a tribune of the people, assailing and enraging the Beacon Hill
plutocracy. Both traded on their Irish ancestry (which in Butler's case
had to be invented), and both seemed to leave behind an odor of corruption. Like Curley, Butler had an acute intelligence unfettered by
any awkward ethical sense. Both made political hay by championing
the underdog. On Governors Butler and Curley, Harvard refused to
bestow its customary degree. Legends clustered around each: for Ben
Butler the most persistent—it is still believed in the South—is that
when he was recalled as military governor of New Orleans during the
Civil War he took with him a coffin filled with stolen silver spoons.

Nothing Curley ever did, however, made him as lastingly notorious as New Orleans General Order No. 28 made Butler. It said, "when any female shall, by word, gesture or movement, insult or show contempt for any officer or soldier of the United States, she shall be regarded and held liable as a woman of the town plying her avocation."

Butler was military governor of a conquered city, and the provocation had in fact been gross. Northern soldiers were repeatedly insulted by New Orleans women; some of the city's belles had taken to spitting on their uniforms or even in their faces. But Butler's "Woman Order," while it put a stop to such incidents, made him the most hated of Yankee generals.

The Confederacy's General P. G. T. Beauregard coined the phrase "Butler the Beast," and it stuck. Jefferson Davis, once Butler's friend, proclaimed him "an outlaw and common enemy of mankind," to be hanged on capture. Long after the war, Mississippi riverboats supplied their cabin passengers with chamber pots on the inside bottoms of which was painted the face of "Spoons Butler."

Benjamin Franklin Butler was a sixth-generation New Englander, born in 1818 in Deerfield Parade, New Hampshire. The youngest of three children by his father's second wife, Ben was a sickly child. He had reddish hair and a pasty face marred by a crossed left eye with a drooping lid, which would give him the unkind sobriquet Old Cock-Eye. He was only five months old when his father died; his mother worked days as a hired woman. She was a devout Baptist who knew her boy was intelligent and hoped he might become a preacher. For all his gnomish ugliness, Ben had a quick mind and a memory like a magnet. Before he entered school he had read *Robinson Crusoe* with his mother's help and could recite whole chapters from the Bible.

When Ben was nine a neighbor persuaded the head of Phillips Exeter Academy to give the boy a scholarship, but Ben's brief stay there was an unhappy, awkward time. He was not, a fellow student remembered, "particularly civil when his grain was crossed." After one term he left for Lowell, Massachusetts, the mill town where his mother now worked as a housekeeper in one of the factory workers' dormitories. Lowell was his home for the next sixty-five years.

Lowell was a model textile settlement, with central factories, company stores and a company burial lot, as well as employees' dormitories. The city was named after Francis Cabot Lowell, who on a sojourn in England had managed to filch the secrets of British power-loom construction. Although Lowell was their creation, the corporation owners never lived there, but filaments of gold ran from the mills to Boston pockets.

Compared with the "dark Satanic mills" of England's industrial cities, the large-windowed brick factories of Lowell were pleasant places. Most of the mill hands were New England country girls who earned from six to eight dollars a week, sufficient to sustain a single girl and to allow her to do her share in reducing the mortgage on the family farm. Whittier, who lived for a time in Lowell, called these buxom lasses "the flowers gathered from a thousand hillsides and green valleys of New England, fair unveiled Nuns of Industry."

Ben and his older brother, Andrew Jackson Butler, passed their adolescence in the vestal atmosphere of their mother's boardinghouse, attending the Lowell public school, whose master, Joshua Merrill, carried a leather strap to administer the Yankee blend of "licking and learning." Despite his crossed eye, Ben grew solid and tough, handy with his fists and impudent to authority. "Benj. F. Butler was a boy who might be led, but could never be driven," wrote his high school principal. In those early years Ben developed two enduring hatreds: of England, the country against which his grandfather had fought at Bunker Hill; and of the absentee plutocrats of Beacon Hill, the inheritors of British decorum who owned the mills of Lowell and the other spindle cities.

It was arranged for Ben to go to the Baptist college at Waterville, Maine, where he could fulfill his mother's dream of seeing him a preacher. But as a collegian his religiosity ebbed; he took keen interest in philosophy, history and chemistry, and developed sufficient aptitude for debate to become head of the Literary Society. In Whig New England he proclaimed himself a Jacksonian Democrat, scornful nevertheless of the abolitionists and their incendiary agitation. Politics intrigued him, and his interest in the law was aroused when he attended a murder trial and watched the deft maneuverings of the lawyers before the jury. At the end of his sophomore year he applied for an appointment to the United States Military Academy; his rejection left him with a lasting bias against West Pointers. He graduated from Waterville (later Colby) College in 1838 and that fall returned to Lowell eager to become a lawyer.

He began to read law, in the self-educating legal-political pattern of Clay and Webster and Lincoln, in the office of William Smith; in exchange for doing clerical chores he was given access to Blackstone and Kent.

For two years he spent over twelve hours a day on his law books. Whenever he grew too restless in his confinement he would borrow a horse and gallop over country roads reciting snatches of Byron, Moore or Scott to the evening sky. Since the small fees that he picked up handling Smith's debt-collection cases were not enough to live on, he taught school for a term in 1839. Like schoolmaster Merrill, he believed in the strap. While teaching, he became friends with Fisher Ames Hildreth, the son of a local doctor and well-known patriotic orator. Hildreth took Ben home for Thanksgiving dinner.

Dr. Hildreth was a widower with five daughters; the eldest, Sarah, acted as his hostess. She was three years older than Ben, more graceful than handsome, yet witty, animated and self-possessed. She fascinated him, and within days the two were keeping steady company. At first it went no further than that; Sarah, though promised an adequate dowry, had no intention of marrying until Ben's as yet nonexistent law practice could support them. She would not say yes to him, although she would not say no, either.

In 1840 Butler took his bar examination, using the occasion to differ with a decision the examining judge had made earlier that very day. Nevertheless, he was admitted to the bar the following day, and to cap it, the judge reversed his finding. The road lay open: Butler was ready to turn Blackstone into gold. He set up his own office in Lowell, where he was soon working eighteen hours a day. Factory girls, ignored by other attorneys, came to him with their petty cases and two- or three-dollar fees. From the first, he disrupted the still-colonial decorum of Massachusetts legal circles; he once spent a week in the Lowell jail after a judge had found him in contempt. Daring, astute, methodical and unscrupulous, Butler, with his grotesque, rufous exterior, was unforgettable. His manner of speech and easily summoned tears were convincing to juries. The plea of insanity in murder trials was his innovation. He became noted for finding flaws in indictments; he once managed to free a burglar by claiming that a key the man had stolen was not personal property but real estate. When a reporter for the Whig Lowell *Courier* denounced Butler's courtroom tactics as ''very scaly and disreputable,'' Butler stormed into the newspaper office and pulled the reporter's nose.

Butler inspected the letter of the law with his good eye, its spirit with his bad one. When the Lowell City Council passed an ordinance that all dogs must be muzzled, Butler walked his dog with a muzzle attached to its tail. He knew how to court popular favor by belittling Harvard's aristocratic pretensions. Once when asked in court to be more respectful because the witness was a Harvard professor, he told the judge, "I am well aware of that. We hung one of them the other day."

Soon it was being said that the cross-eyed young attorney with the rasping, staccato voice was the man to win hard cases. Special reporters were assigned to cover his sensational courtroom conduct. "He liked audacious surprises," said one of his enemies. "He was seldom content to try a simple case in a simple way." Clients flocked to him. To the mill owners he said, "If I am not for you, I shall be against you; and you can take your choice." Their choice was to hire him, even though he and they remained enemies. By the end of a decade of practice, Butler had become the most spectacular criminal lawyer in New England.

Ben and Sarah were finally married in 1844, and it turned out to be a serene and happy partnership. They had four children, three sons and a daughter (the first born, Paul, died before he was five). As Butler prospered, he invested in land, mills and other ventures. When Lowell's first woolen mill, the Middlesex Corporation, found itself in straits, he bought the controlling interest. With the mill came Belvidere, a graceful mansion in the Regency style. Situated in the select hill section above the city, Belvidere overlooked the Merrimack River; from its cupola one could gaze north to the hills of New Hampshire. Butler installed central steam heat—then an astonishing novelty—and a "Russian bath" in his bedroom. Though a lawyer of the people, he led the private life of a country squire.

As Lowell grew, its aspect and character changed. The Nuns of Industry were being replaced by the shanty Irish, the pallid and beaten refugees of the Famine. Faced with an abundance of labor, the operators cut wages. The neat boardinghouses disintegrated into slums, whole families inhabiting rooms where single girls had once lived, while other poor Paddies lived in mudwalled shacks along a common known as the Acre.

Partly out of genuine sympathy and partly from a shrewd realization of their political potential, Butler became the champion of the Lowell workers. He denounced wage reductions, comparing Lowell to a beehive from which the Boston proprietors extracted honey without

caring "whether the bees were smoked out or not." He advocated a
ten-hour day in the interest of the workers' health. The Whig legislature
was as unmoved as the mill owners, who insisted that the fourteen-
hour day was competitive, and that in any case their job was "to give
people as cheap calico as can be made."

In 1844 Butler was a delegate to the Democratic national convention in Baltimore that nominated James K. Polk. On his return to Lowell
he made his first political speech, against Henry Clay, the Whig candidate. His influence as a Hunker Democrat* grew. By 1850 he was
one of the state leaders instrumental in forming a coalition with the
Free-Soil party. Campaigning for the ten-hour day, the secret ballot
and the popular election of judges, the coalitionists swept the state
and elected Democrat George Boutwell governor. By agreement, the
Democratic representatives then voted with the Free-Soilers in the
legislature to elect the Radical Republican Charles Sumner to the United
States Senate. The coalitionists managed to pass a secret ballot law,
but Whig maneuvering delayed action on the ten-hour day.

In 1852, another Presidential election year, Butler was a Democratic
nominee for state representative. In a special run-off election he won
a seat and arrived in Beacon Hill in January 1853. With the Whigs
back in the majority position, however, he was unable to effect much
legislation. A ten-hour-day bill died in committee, but Butler scored
an indirect victory when the corporations, faced with the growing weight
of public opinion against them, voluntarily reduced the mill day to
eleven hours.

The fifties found Butler an emergent Democrat on the national scene,
a wealthy lawyer with the largest criminal practice in New England,
the head of a corporation owning three mills, the owner of the finest
house in Lowell and a full colonel in the volunteer militia. He was not
yet forty years old.

In 1855 the "Know-Nothing" governor, Henry J. Gardner, who had
been elected on an antiforeigner, anti-Catholic platform, disbanded
Butler's Irish militia company and removed Butler from his colonelcy.
Surprisingly, the cashiered colonel did not fight back. Secretly, however,
he campaigned among his militia comrades, and soon Gardner, much
to his chagrin, was forced to sign the commission of the newly elected

---

*They were called Hunkers because they were said to be "hunkering" after jobs. The Hunkers,
drawing their support from mill workers (who wanted no competition from freed blacks), had
little use for the abolitionists.

Brigadier General Butler, commander of the 3rd Brigade, 2nd Division, of the state volunteers. Two years later Secretary of War Jefferson Davis appointed "the youngest general in the United States" to the Board of Visitors of the United States Military Academy. Martial in sword and general's sash—if not in features—Butler appeared annually at West Point with the predictable pride of a civilian in uniform.

Butler was the only Democrat elected to the state senate in 1859. There he reorganized the state judiciary, but most of his time was taken up with local and ephemeral matters, with indirect digs at Harvard and with measures to please the foreigners who formed the core of his support.

The following year he accepted the Democratic nomination for governor, the first of his seven campaigns for that office. But men who, like Butler, sought to straddle the slavery question had become increasingly repugnant to New England opinion that was more and more solidly abolitionist. Butler received only a third of the 108,000 votes cast.

In the summer of 1860 Butler was a delegate to the Democratic national convention in Charleston, South Carolina. At that stalemated assembly he voted with his delegation seven times for Stephen Douglas and then gave his solitary vote fifty-seven times to Jefferson Davis, a friend whom he considered a moderate compromise between the intractable Southerners and the smoke-breathing abolitionists.

Massachusetts felt otherwise about the slave-owning Davis, and Butler was hanged in effigy on Lowell's South Common. His attempts at defending himself at a public meeting were booed and hissed. A rump Democratic convention at Baltimore had finally nominated Douglas, the Southern delegates having walked out to nominate Kentucky's John C. Breckinridge. When the anti-Douglas Democrats of Massachusetts nominated Butler for governor on a "Breckinridge" ticket, he received only 6,000 of the 169,534 votes cast. It looked as though Butler were on the wrong ship, and a sinking ship at that. He held intimate talks with Davis and other Southern leaders; long before most Northern politicians, he realized that secession and war were inevitable. Privately he urged Governor John Andrew to prepare the state militia for war, pointing out, among other things, that the volunteers lacked winter overcoats. Coats were ordered, and by curious coincidence, Butler's were the only mills able to produce the cloth immediately.

Three days after Fort Sumter was fired upon, Secretary of War Simon Cameron, alarmed at Washington's isolation, begged Governor Andrew to send him 1,500 militiamen for the capital's defense. Butler realized that if the men were dispatched in a unit, in a brigade instead of three regiments, they would need a brigadier general to command them. Butler wired Cameron, "You have called for a brigade of Massachusetts troops; why not call for a brigadier general and staff?" Butler also knew that the state treasury lacked the money to mobilize and transport the troops; he influenced a number of Boston banks to advance the funds—on condition that he lead the brigade. Andrew had no option but to place the Lowell lawyer in command. President Lincoln was not displeased to see so prominent a Hunker Democrat in a general's uniform rallying to support the Union, and Butler, in sash and gilt epaulettes, recalled that Presidencies were often won on the battlefield.

Washington lay like a beleaguered island in a Southern sea, and Massachusetts was the first to respond to Lincoln's appeal for troops. Butler dispatched his 6th Regiment ahead as an advance guard. In Philadelphia, Butler learned that the 6th had been attacked as it crossed through Baltimore en route to Washington. Three militiamen had been killed, and eight wounded. The mob had seized control of the city. No more troops could pass through.

Butler acted with vigor and dispatch. He sent the rest of his brigade to Annapolis by sea; he converted the Naval Academy into his base while readying himself to commandeer the railroad line to the capital. The governor of Maryland called a special session of the legislature, and Butler announced that if the members passed an ordinance of secession he would arrest every last man of them. He sent a squad of soldiers to impound the state's Great Seal, without which no legislative act would be legal. With Butler's firm measures and his opening of the railroad to Washington, secessionist sentiment in Maryland abated. In circumventing disloyal Baltimore and in providing Washington with troops, Butler was the first Northern general to make his mark.

Even New England Whigs thought him a hero, and he seemed even more heroic when, on May 13, 1861, he and the Massachusetts 6th seized Baltimore without a casualty. But in so doing Butler had disregarded the operations plan of Winfield Scott, the crusty, ancient General in Chief; Scott demoted Butler to the command of Fortress Monroe, a squat bastion on the Yorktown Peninsula. But to salve the sting, Secretary of War Cameron promoted Butler to major general.

Now Butler had twelve regiments in his command. As an organizer he was efficient and ingenious, and he was determined to make his fortress a model garrison. One of his problems was how to deal with slaves who had escaped to his lines. The property of those in rebellion could be taken as contraband of war; Butler declared that slaves were property, hence "contrabands" and subject to confiscation. Since human contrabands could no longer be held captive, they were free. The General's adroit legalism became a practical means of destroying slavery long before President Lincoln felt able to issue his formal proclamation. "Contraband of war" became a Northern catch phrase, bringing Butler the hearty applause of the abolitionists.

Butler's military reputation had reached its highwater mark, but his first operation out of Fortress Monroe turned into the North's first rout. In a promising beginning, he took the military post of Newport News, but in mid-June he sent two regiments under the command of another Massachusetts political general, Ebenezer Pierce, up the Peninsula against the Confederate stronghold at Big Bethel. Marching in the darkness, the two units fired upon each other; then, neglecting to send out scouts, they wandered within point-blank range of Rebel batteries. Butler's troops broke and ran. Big Bethel shattered Northern visions of a quickly-put-down rebellion. Butler blamed Pierce. The country blamed Butler.

Later that summer, Butler engineered a minor amphibious success at Pamlico Sound; this, in the dismal aftermath of Bull Run, was magnified into a great Union victory. Lincoln gratefully gave Butler a leave of absence to raise more troops in New England for Flag Officer David Farragut's amphibious expedition against New Orleans.

The South considered New Orleans, its largest and wealthiest city, to be impregnable. Seventy miles to the south of it lay Forts Jackson and St. Philip, guarding the approaches along the Mississippi. Nevertheless, Farragut and Commander David Porter sailed past the forts by night in April of 1862; New Orleans fell. Butler's army of occupation arrived without firing a shot.

The general rode through sullen streets and heard jeers that he would never see his home again. He proclaimed martial law, promising "to restore order, maintain public tranquillity and enforce peace and quiet under the laws and conditions of the United States." When the mayor refused to cooperate as Butler wanted, he took over complete civil administration.

It was Butler the military governor that produced his legendary infamy. His image as the scoundrel in uniform, the grafter, looter, thief, murderer, degrader of women and pilferer of spoons was one the South would never relinquish. But Butler was less a headlong sinner than a victim of bad publicity, albeit self-generated. What he did, typically, was to challenge the gentry, the leaders of the community, by appealing to the artisans and mechanics to make a common cause against the mercantile aristocracy. It was Butler the sans-culotte that the South never forgave.

Butler was still the able administrator. Even his most ardent enemies admitted that the white workers employed by his sanitary commission had cleaned up the city as it had never been cleaned up before. He opened stores, set prices and established a program of relief for the poor. As for his notorious Woman Order, it was so effective that it never had to be acted upon. Once General Order No. 28 was proclaimed, the tiny Confederate flags vanished from Rebel bosoms; no longer did young ladies dash to the piano to play "The Bonnie Blue Flag" when Yankee officers passed their houses; nor did they do any more spitting.

For poor-relief monies Butler assessed wealthy individuals and corporations, some of whom saw their possessions sold at auction. Relentlessly, skillfully, Butler ferreted out hidden bank assets and recovered funds taken from the United States mint. Southerners who concealed their wealth in European consulates found no lasting protection in foreign flags; Butler did not hesitate to break into the house of a liquor dealer who doubled as the Netherlands consul to seize 800,000 Mexican dollars. He easily persuaded the poor, the Northern-born and the half-castes to take the oath of allegiance to the federal government. Officials of the old governing class who refused to take the oath were forced from office. When an obscure gambler named Mumford pulled down the American flag from the roof of the mint and tore it to shreds, Butler, despite protests and threats, hanged him in front of the building. Mumford became a Confederate martyr, as did Mrs. Philip Phillips, who laughed and jeered at a funeral procession for a Yankee lieutenant—and was thrown into military prison on Ship Island.

As military governor Butler showed a racial attitude more liberal than one might have expected of a Hunker Democrat. He abolished segregated streetcars, put white workers next to black and established a "Native Guard" regiment of blacks as well as two regiments of loyal poor whites. The only segregation he recognized was between Unionists and Secessionists.

In all, Butler did a creditable job of running New Orleans. Yet always, as in Massachusetts, the scent of corruption followed him; there was a sense of chicanery, of underhanded transactions. He maintained that contraband trading with the enemy was necessary in order to obtain supplies; still, the profits in such trade for those around him were enormous. But that Butler himself stole, or made money on official transactions, is not credible. His mills in Massachusetts were bringing in huge profits; his law firm was prospering through his subordinates. He was too well off to have to speculate or peculate. Yet those around him did, and he knew it. Southern heirlooms picked up by Yankee officers for pittances at auctions went north by the carload. Butler's brother Andrew drove a sharp trade in cattle, sugar, cotton and other Confederate commodities; he was said to have made between $500,000 and $2,000,000 in such enterprises.

European nations objected violently to Butler's cavalier treatment of their New Orleans consulates, and complained to Secretary of State William H. Seward. Finally, in December 1862, Lincoln removed the controversial general for reasons that were obvious to many, although they were never really spelled out. In his farewell address to the citizens of New Orleans, Butler struck a familiar pose: "I saw that this Rebellion was a war of aristocrats against the middling man, of the rich against the poor; a war of the land-owner against the laborer; the few against the many; and I found no conclusion to it, save in the subjugation of the few and the disenthrallment of the many. I therefore felt no hesitation in taking the substance of the wealthy, who had caused the war, to free the innocent poor, who had suffered by the war."

Butler, the unemployed general, returned North as the hero of the Radicals—indeed, he had moved the full arc from Hunker Democrat to abolitionist Republican. Radicals like Benjamin Wade and Thaddeus Stevens began to see him as a Presidential possibility.

It took almost a year for Lincoln to decide what to do with his obstreperous general. Butler was now doubly important politically, both as an old Democrat and as a new Radical. It was necessary, Lincoln saw, to give him some position, if only to keep him out of politics. Late in 1863 Butler was given command of the Department of Virgina and North Carolina.

The following April, the army's newly appointed general-in-chief,

U.S. Grant, conferred with Butler on Grant's proposed spring offensive against Richmond. Grant was dubious about Butler's military ability and bolstered him with Major Generals Quincy A. Gillmore and William F. "Baldy" Smith. Lincoln was considering burying Butler in the obscurity of the Vice Presidency, but when Simon Cameron relayed the offer of second spot on the Republican ticket for 1864, Butler turned it down: "Tell him. . . I would not quit the field to be Vice President, even with himself as President, unless he will give me bond with sureties, in the full sum of his four years' salary, that he will die or resign within three months after his inauguration." Events were to give the statement a macabre tone: Mr. Lincoln was dead within a few weeks of his inauguration.

In Grant's battle plan Butler's forces were to form the fourth prong of an attack on Richmond, thrusting from Fortress Monroe up the James River to attack from the rear. Butler's troops occupied Bermuda Hundred, only twelve miles from Richmond, without opposition. Caught off guard, the Confederates had left their capital defended by only a skeleton force. Had he been a daring commander, Butler might have committed his forces at once and taken the city there and then. But, bluffed as to the strength of the defenses, wary before the unknown and with a civilian's fear of casualties in a bloody frontal attack, he hesitated. And Smith and Gillmore proceeded with a nonprofessional caution that made failure certain. A makeshift Confederate force drove Butler back to the Bermuda Hundred neck. Butler later blamed his subordinates, and even had Gillmore arrested for "military incapacity." To Smith's plea that the amateur general be got rid of, Grant replied sadly that he could not. Butler was still too strong politically.

Butler had one more chance for military triumph. Wilmington, North Carolina, the last port of entry for supplies to the South, lay within his department. If he could seize Fort Fisher, on the promontory that was the key to Wilmington, the city would fall and the Confederacy would face starvation. Butler concocted a scheme for putting the fort out of action by exploding a ship full of gunpowder directly in front of it.

Grant took a dim view of the idea, but he allowed Butler to go ahead and try it. Butler insisted on leading the military-naval expedition himself. When it came, the explosion was so ineffective that the Fort Fisher garrison thought a blockade runner had burst a boiler. Of the 6,500 troops Butler took to capture the fort, only one third landed on shore. Even so, these were enough to have taken the fort—had not Butler again lost his nerve. Alarmed at news that the fort was receiving reinforcements, he ordered a precipitate retreat. Seven hundred of his men were stranded, and had to be rescued by a disgusted Admiral David Porter, who had directed the naval part of the operation. The crew of Porter's flagship manufactured a leather medal for Butler: on one side was a pair of running legs and the stars of a major general; on the other, the legend "In commemoration of his heroic conduct before Fort Fisher, Dec. 1864." On January 9, 1865, Lincoln ordered Butler to "repair to Lowell, Mass."

Hours after Lincoln's assassination Butler joined in caucus with Radical Republican leaders determined to get rid of "Lincoln influences." Elected to Congress in 1866, Butler became head of the Committee on Reconstruction, and one of the South's most unforgiving opponents. In the coming years his best efforts were directed at impeaching Andrew Johnson, whose conciliatory attitude he regarded as treasonable. The President's removal of Secretary of War Edwin M. Stanton, contrary to the Radical-sponsored Tenure of Office Act that required senatorial consent for such actions, gave Butler and his colleagues the pretext they had been waiting for. Johnson, for his defiance of the Radicals, should be impeached—and Ben Butler would spearhead the proceedings.

All Butler's legal adroitness went into the trial. His grating voice opened the proceedings in a savage four-hour speech to the Senate, sitting as the court of judgment. A *Harper's Weekly* reporter observed him as:

> a man whose large pudgy body seemed literally bursting out of his extraordinary swallow tail coat, exposing a broad expanse of not too immaculate linen, and whose massive bald head with its little fringe of oily curls was probably familiar to every occupant of the galleries, for Benjamin F. Butler had not hidden his light under a bushel. There was power in the man's coarse, big-featured face, force and aggressiveness in every line, but his curiously ill-mated eyes with their half-closed lids, his hard mouth and small, drooping moustache, all combined to create an uncomfortable impression of cunning and insincerity, and his whole personality was unattractive.

When the Senate failed by one vote to give the necessary two-thirds majority for conviction, a Washington newspaper put out an extra edition headlined SUICIDE OF BEN BUTLER.

But suicide, physical or political, was far from Butler's mind. The postwar era gave him a renewed sense of life. His voice became one of the most feared—and applauded—in the capital. He now made Negro rights and fiat money the cornerstones of his philosophy, whether out of conviction or expediency no one knew. He maneuvered one of the first civil-rights bills through Congress, and fought for the suppression of the Ku Klux Klan. After an Ohio-born carpetbagger had been horsewhipped by night riders in Mississippi, Butler brandished the victim's bloodstained shirt in the House; the phrase "waving the bloody shirt" came to mean appealing to Civil War sentiments for political reasons.

Butler went out of his way to be friendly to the new black congressmen and to blacks generally—so much so that he was hailed at a black banquet in New Orleans as a general with a "white face, but a black heart."

Butler and Grant reached something of a détente after Grant reached the White House. The President favorably reappraised Butler's war record, and Butler became one of the administration's chief spokesmen. Yet privately, Butler considered Grant an ignoramus.

Butler took a noisy and active part in setting up carpetbag governments in the South and in supporting them with Northern bayonets. but for all his publicly vengeful attitude toward the South, he could be privately and quietly kind. When the destitute widow of Mumford, the man he had hanged in New Orleans, appealed to him, Butler found her a job.

Conservative Republicans of Massachusetts, their Whig instincts still intact, continued to have little use for Butler. And when he embraced the ultimate State Street heresy of greenback currency, of paying off war debts in depreciated paper, Boston Brahmins persuaded one of their own—Richard Henry Dana, author of *Two Years Before the Mast*—to run as a hard-money Democrat against him in the next congressional election. Butler, sniping away at the "Codfish aristocracy," beat Dana six to one.

Forcing his Klu Klux Klan bill through Congress in 1872 was one of Butler's great victories, one that brought him to the height of his national political power. On that crest he attempted to win the nomination for governor, but his entrenched enemies in Massachusetts were able to thwart his ambitions in the Republican conventions of 1872 and 1873. In 1874 they even succeeded in preventing his renomination for Congress, though by waving the bloody shirt he got himself re-elected two years later.

Somehow Butler still found time for his private concerns; he was a much-sought lawyer with a flourishing practice. In a suit over prize money for Confederate ships seized during the war, he won an award of $1,500,000 for Admiral Farragut and his crews—the highest damages sustained up to that time by the Supreme Court. Yet for all his legal eminence, Ben Butler remained the impudent young man who had once tweaked the reporter's nose. When a judge asked him testily if he was trying to show contempt for the court, he replied that he was trying to conceal it.

With law and politics came business ventures. In addition to his mills he now owned a granite quarry and the United States Cartridge Company. He speculated in land, in mines, in a barge company. Conflict of interest never troubled him. If he could use his influence to further his enterprises, so much the better. To ''Butlerize'' was a word coined by his enemies meaning to make off with everything in sight. Butler's activities—and his toadlike bald head and bloated face— became the delight of cartoonist Thomas Nast.

True to his New England heritage, Butler loved the sea. He built a summer home near Gloucester, overlooking Ipswich Bay. He relaxed by sailing his yacht *America*, the famous cup-winner and Confederate blockade-runner. He dressed his crew in snappy uniforms and often participated in the races off Newport, Rhode Island. A spanking nor'wester was an exhilaration: alerted by the Coast Survey when a storm was brewing, he would don his oilskins and put to sea.

In 1878 Butler announced that he was through with both major parties and allowed himself to be nominated by the Greenbackers for the governorship of Massachusetts. But at the same time he was moving back toward the Democratic party of his youth (he even came out for pensions for Confederate veterans); his real goal was to become the Democratic gubernatorial candidate. He arranged for his supporters to pack the convention hall, and he was in fact nominated—to the disgust of the conservative Democrats, who walked out to nominate their own man. The split insured a Republican victory. Conservative Republicans were delighted at Butler's defeat. Mild-mannered President Hayes wrote that it was one of the best events since the war; he considered Butler ''unscrupulous, able, rich, untiring, the most dangerous and wicked demagogue we ever had.'' Butler was an unsuccessful gubernatorial candidate again in 1879, and the following year he refused to run for any office.

Ben's wife, Sarah, had died of cancer in 1876; in 1881 his son Ben-Israel succumbed to Bright's disease. Butler was again nominated for governor by the Democrats and Greenbackers, but in that sad year the candidate's sharp tongue and rasping voice were muted. He scarcely campaigned at all and seemed indifferent to his inevitable defeat.

But by 1882 his spirits were largely recovered, and this time the perennial Democratic gubernatorial nominee had the backing of the likes of Wendell Phillips, Susan B. Anthony and prison reformer Burnham Wardwell. And, at last, Butler was successful.

In spite of the fair promise of his inaugural address—he said he would reform the criminal code and the state penal institutions, abolish the poll tax, give women the vote and lower the hours of labor while increasing wages—the new governor was able to do little in the face of a Republican legislature and governor's council. Harvard again became his whipping boy following his "exposure" of the previous administration's selling of paupers' bodies from the Tewksbury almshouse to the Harvard Medical School. "The selling and tanning of human skins," he declared, "was an established industry in Massachusetts!" Breaking a 250-year tradition, Harvard refused that year to give the governor an honorary doctor's degree. Butler attended the commencement anyhow; so indignant was the president of the alumni association that he resigned in order to avoid receiving him.

In the election of 1883 Butler charged that the Republicans were importing "repeaters" from outside the state to defeat him, and he ordered his 9th Massachusetts Regiment (mostly Irishmen) to guard the polls. He prepared a magnificent display of fireworks on Belvidere's grounds to celebrate his re-election. There was no celebration. Massachusetts voters had tired of his bombast, and Butler was through in state politics.

As he resumed his legal practice, nebulous thoughts of the White House occurred to him; in 1884 he accepted the Presidential nomination of the Greenback and Anti-Monopoly parties, hoping that this splinter movement would enhance his chances at the Democratic national convention, to which he was a delegate-at-large. But the resurgent white South would have nothing to do with Spoons Butler. He could not even find a spokesman to place his name in nomination. After the Democrats nominated Grover Cleveland as their hard-money candidate, Butler toured the country in a gaily painted private railroad car, telling workers that if Cleveland were elected they would starve. When he spoke in Detroit, hecklers tossed tin spoons on the stage, and elsewhere he was jeered as the "Benedict Arnold of American politics." He received a mere 175,000 votes out of ten million, which ended his political career with a humiliating anticlimax.

Butler devoted his remaining years to law, which he said was like chess; and when money and popularity no longer mattered, the game itself was still intriguing. He took many unpopular cases—he defended Chicago's Haymarket Square anarchists, for example—that paid him little or nothing. He grew rheumatic, hard of hearing and flabby (his daughter Blanche put him on a diet and reduced his weight to 220 pounds).

His enemies and the anti-Butler legends endured, and their target began to grow solicitous of his reputation. In 1892 his thousand-page autobiography was published. *Butler's Book* was an enormous undertaking for an old man, yet the Butler swagger, shrewdness and military partisanship are stamped in its pages like a watermark. The book interestingly described his relations with Lincoln and Grant, and vindictively carried on his feud with the West Point generals whom he accused of sabotaging his military career. The postwar years he crowded into a single chapter.

Ben Butler died in 1893 while in Washington preparing a case for the Supreme Court. Eight veterans (two of them blacks, on one of whom Butler had pinned the Congressional Medal of Honor) accompanied his body back to Lowell. He lay in his coffin in the drawing room at Belvidere, a rose in his buttonhole, and, thanks to the undertakers, a smile on his face. He was buried on a bitter-cold January day; a service was held at St. Anne's Episcopal Church, to which be belonged but in whose creed—as he had admitted to Sarah—he had ceased to believe.

The funeral cortege, led by a hearse with six black-plumed horses, extended a mile and a half. All the bells of Lowell tolled as the coffin was drawn across the Merrimack bridge to the cemetery, and the crowds were so great that half a dozen onlookers were injured in the crush. In attendance were state politicians and men of prominence from the governor on down, even the codfish aristocracy—who kept their fingers crossed against the appearance of any future Ben Butler.

Time has shown Ben Butler to be one of the most arresting political figures that Massachusetts has ever produced; certainly the most caricatured and most vilified; possibly the most astute. "God made me only one way," he once said. "I must always be with the under-dog in the fight. I can't help it; I can't change it, and upon the whole I don't want to." Butler may have Butlerized, but he also helped the immigrant workers when Know-Nothingism ran high in his state. Whatever his subsequent war record, he rallied the Breckinridge Democrats to the Union at a critical moment. He spoke out for civil rights far in advance of his day. Even his Greenback heresy of man-aged paper money would become orthodox reality after World War II. Those who thought themselves the better people, both in the North and in the South, despised and distrusted him, and he capitalized on their hate. The workers and the shanty Irish and the blacks loved him, and not without reason.

Though Belvidere still perches serenely on its hill above the Mer-rimack, Lowell's textile mills have been gone since the Depression; the gray industrial city has forgotten Butler. Two miles across the river there is a cemetery within a cemetery, a plot surrounded by a locked fence, the grave of an ex-governor and ex-general. There is a headstone of polished granite, but there is no flag to go with it.

Charles Ponzi in a dapper pose just before his financial bubble burst.

CHARLES PONZI AND THE
BOSTON BUBBLE

SEEN FROM THE HIGH OVAL WINDOWS OF BOSTON'S CITY HALL ON THAT sultry June morning in 1920, the line of stiff-brimmed straw hats bobbing along School Street resembled a roiled, wheat-colored stream. Among the straws were dark blotches of cloth caps, women's brighter hats and even the official visors of the police. On the honky-tonk outskirts of Scollay Square the stream grew denser and contracted into the cleft of Pi Alley. Then it flooded left down City Hall Avenue past the blank, rusticated side of City Hall and left again beyond the pigeon-spattered statue of Mayor Josiah Quincy. The stream dissolved into a jabber of individuals who stormed up the dark stairway of Twenty-seven School Street, just below City Hall, to wedge themselves, seething and shoving, along the corridor and into the office of the Securities and Exchange Company.

For all its imposing name the Securities and Exchange Company consisted of one man, the dapper, dynamic five-foot three-inch Italian immigrant and financial wizard known as Charles Ponzi, who, it seemed in that Boston summer, had conjured up the secret of perpetual money. He had started the Securities and Exchange Company with a few hundred dollars borrowed from two discreetly silent partners, Louis Casullo and John Dondero. Lend me your cash, he promised in the prospectuses he mailed out, and in forty-five days you will get it back with 50 percent interest; in ninety days you will get it back doubled. And since December, when fifteen investors lent him $870 and the following month happily drew out $1,218, he had been keeping his promise. In December Ponzi had paid only 40 percent interest. By February he had raised the rate to 50 percent for forty-five days, 100 percent for ninety. The good news spread, and in March, 110 Bostonians left $28,724 at the unpretentious office on School Street. April brought 471 hopefuls with $141,671. Four times that number paid almost a half million dollars in May, and during June 7,824 persons trudged up the stairs to the Securities and Exchange Company to pay in $2.5 million in cash and receive forty-five or ninety-day notes in return. In the latter part of the month Ponzi claimed to be receiving $500,000 and paying out $200,000 a day, and traffic in School Street had come to a standstill.

It was a very simple, the money wizard explained, merely a matter of knowing how to take advantage of the various and varying exchange rates in different parts of the world. He had conceived his scheme, so he said, when he received a business letter from Spain enclosing a reply coupon—issued as a convenience by international postal agreement— which was exchangeable at any United States post offices for a six-cent stamp. Ponzi was struck by the fact that the coupon in Spain had cost the buyer only the equivalent of one cent. As he told a Boston *Post* reporter interviewing him in his lush Lexington mansion at the height of his dollar-checkered career, "I looked the coupon over. I thought about its value on this side of the Atlantic and its value on the other side. I said to myself: 'If I can buy these stamps in Spain for one cent and cash it for six cents in the United States just because the rate of money exchange is higher here, why can't I buy hundreds, thousands, millions of these coupons? I'll make five cents on every one—of this particular kind—so why not?' Then...I investigated the rate of exchange in many of the other foreign countries. My original theory, 'why can't I make money this way?' grew more real. Then it became a fact.'"

Ponzi explained to the reporter that his operations were being conducted in nine unspecified foreign countries. His agents were bundling international reply coupons in massive quantities back and forth among these countries, although he had now stopped redeeming foreign coupons in the United States. The scheme might not, he admitted, be considered ethical, but it was positively legal. And the idea was foolproof. He said he had just set up thirty branch offices throughout New England and was preparing to open an office in New York.

Each morning at eight o'clock his Japanese chauffeur brought him from Lexington in a cream-colored Locomobile limousine to his School Street office. Each morning an ever-larger crowd was waiting for the cocky little man with the bouncing step and elegant manner. Police cleared the way for his car. Men cheered him, and office girls blew him kisses. He smiled and bowed, tipped his hat and sometimes on getting out of his car made a little speech. He exuded jauntiness, from his pointed shoes to his wide, pointed lapels, from the razor-sharp crease of his trousers and his sleeves to the pearl stickpin in his striped moiré tie. Nonchalantly he swung a gold-headed Malacca cane and smoked a Turkish cigarette in an ivory and gold holder. His manner and his manners never failed. "A born aristocrat," his young wife said of him. For his thirty-eight years and certainly for the hard rows he had already hoed, he looked amazingly fresh. There was no sign of a wrinkle on his high forehead. He had a wide mouth above a jaw of almost Mussolini set. His eyes were genial and sympathetic. His voice was soft and convincing, with just the trace of an Italian accent. Face and voice inspired trust and among some a permanent devotion.

Ponzi was born in Parma in 1882. His family was upper-class and his father a general in the Italian army (or so he said). As a boy he attended a boarding school founded by Napoleon's ex-empress, Marie Louise. When he was eighteen he became a student at the University of Rome, but spent more time in cafés and at theaters and fashionable parties than in libraries and at lectures. In November 1903, after three years of this gay nocturnal existence, his Roman uncle sent him to America with a one-way ticket and a thousand lire (then worth about two hundred dollars).

Having lost all but two and a half dollars to a cardsharp on the voyage over, Ponzi wandered from Boston to Pittsburgh, New York, Providence, Montreal and various points in the South, passing fourteen years in such employments (when he was working at all) as dishwasher, waiter, clothes-presser, shop clerk and Italian interpreter. His English had become almost glib by the time he turned up in Massachusetts again in 1917.

In Boston he took a job typing and answering foreign mail for the J. R. Poole Company, merchant brokers, at sixteen dollars a week. On February 4, 1918, he married Rose Gnecco of Somerville, a second-generation Italian-American half his age, the daughter of one of the Gnecco brothers, fruit dealers in Boston's Italian North End. He quit his job with Poole in September to go to work for his father-in-law. But in January 1919 the fruit firm went bankrupt, with liabilities of eleven thousand dollars and assets half that. Ponzi tried to convince the Gneccos that if he could have the use of the assets, with his knowledge of importing and exporting he could double the money and more than pay off their debts in a year. The dubious Gneccos refused. Ponzi at that time had a little upstairs back room in the School Street building of the Tremont Trust Company, where he liked to tuck himself away and scheme his schemes. There it was, in August 1919, that he received his letter from Spain and evolved his Great Idea.

As the summer of 1920 wore on, the lines to School Street lengthened. The persistent and impatient crowd that blocked off School Street traffic all day long was made up of people from the city fringes— the Italian North End, the South End lodging-houses and the small suburbs. Periodically Ponzi distributed free coffee and doughnuts to them. Whenever he saw a pregnant or elderly woman in the hot sun, he would take her inside ahead of the others through a side door. Tucked visibly behind the twin-pointed handkerchief in his coat pocket he carried a certified check for a million dollars. With that sum, he told people, he could live in all the comfort he wanted for the rest of his life. Anything he got above that million he intended to use to "do good in the world." The money now came into his office so fast that it filled all the desk drawers and spilled over into a dozen wastebaskets. Sixteen clerks, hired to do nothing but sort out the cash, tallied it and stacked it in closets until it reached the ceiling. When Police Commissioner Edward Curtis sent three inspectors down to Twenty-seven School Street to investigate, Ponzi talked two of them into buying his notes. Others were investigating, too: the chief post-office inspector; state and federal attorneys; and the later-disbarred Suffolk County district attorney, Coakley's associate Joseph Pelletier. Ponzi welcomed them all, and none could see anything illegal in the Security and Exchange Company.

Ponzi now brought his mother, Imelda, over from Italy and provided her with a French maid. As his finances expanded he bought into the Hanover Trust Company, where he had first deposited his money, and became a director. As an ironic reminder of his clerical days he took over the J. R. Poole Company. He invited a group of New York financiers to the Copley Plaza Hotel at his expense and conferred with them about his newest plan to organize a $200-million corporation with a chain of "profit-sharing banks" in which depositors would share with stockholders in the net profits. His earnestness was convincing, contagious. A highly respected judge, Frank Leveroni of the Boston juvenile court, became his lawyer. With what would seem redundancy he hired a long-time Boston advertising man, William McMasters, as publicity agent.

The bubble expanded, glittering, iridescent, irresistible now even to the covetous from State Street and Beacon Hill. Some plungers put down as much as $25,000, though most people bought only a few hundred dollars' worth of Ponzi notes in return for handfuls of small bills. By the last week in July Ponzi was taking in several hundred thousand dollars a day. His name was in headlines all over the country; he became something of a national hero. Newsreel cameramen flocked to his Lexington home and recorded him strolling across the lawn with his wife and his mother. There were armed guards at the mansion entrances and rumors of millions locked away in vaults in the cellar.

Although city, state and federal officials in their overlapping investigations had turned up nothing against Ponzi, a less official but much more efficient investigation was being carried on in the editorial office of the Boston *Post*. Young Richard Grozier, the assistant editor and publisher, was convinced that Ponzi has never bought so much as a dime's worth of international reply coupons and that he was merely taking in money at one wicket to pay out at the next. If nobody else was able to show Ponzi up, Grozier determined the *Post* would.

On Sunday, July 25, Grozier discussed Ponzi and his scheme with Clarence Barron, the Boston financier and publisher of the financial daily *The Boston News Bureau* (later *Barron's Weekly*). Barron admitted that it was theoretically possible to make money by manipulating international reply coupons but said he was sure it would be impossible to turn over more than a few thousand dollars that way. To talk of running them up to Ponzi's ten million dollars was, Barron said, ridiculous. He added that it was odd for Ponzi to put his own funds into banks paying only around 5 percent when he was offering 50 percent to other people. Not even if Rockefeller made an offer like Ponzi's would anyone with any financial sense put his money into it. The Wizard of School Street was, in Barron's opinion, just another goldbrick salesman.

Monday morning the *Post* headlined Barron's views on the front page. The result was a run on the Securities and Exchange Company. A line of a different temper and intent soon choked School Street, but Ponzi, jaunty and self-assured as ever, saw to it that everyone in the line who wanted his notes cashed got his money back. By afternoon he had turned the run into a stampede of new investors. Meanwhile, he calmly admitted that his story of the coupons was just a blind. Its purpose, he said, was to keep Wall Street speculators from catching on to his moneymaking methods, which were his secret. He told Grozier that no investigation could hurt him, that he had money enough to pay off his investors in full any time. In spite of Grozier's warning columns in the *Post*, Ponzi continued to prosper. Crowds welcomed him as he walked down Washington Street along Newspaper Row past the *Post* building. When someone shouted "Three cheers for Ponzi!" they were given with a roar, and as they died down he shouted back, to their laughter, "Three groans for the *Post*!" "Who's the greatest Italian that ever lived?" someone else called out to him. "Columbus," Ponzi called back, "because he discovered America." "But you discovered money!" came the reply, with many cheers. McMasters told reporters that Ponzi was planning to give the city an Italian hospital and had already pledged $100,000 for an Italian orphanage. Ponzi himself said he was considering running for mayor or governor, not stressing the fact that he was still an alien.

Late Monday afternoon, July 26, 1920, District Attorney Pelletier announced that Ponzi had agreed to suspend accepting any more investment money until his books could be audited. The district attorney did not hint at any fraud and was careful to say that there was no charge against Ponzi; it was just that his operations had become so vast that an audit was in the public interest. Meanwhile Ponzi, unperturbed, continued to pay any notes that fell due and to redeem later notes at face value.

By the time the deposits closed on Monday at Twenty-seven School Street, 30,195 persons had paid in $9,582,591 since December 1919 with a promised return of $14,374,818. The average investor had put down $300. Some from the little streets, however, had turned in their life savings. The confidence record seems to have gone to a woman from Quincy who sold all her real estate and invested $33,000. Richard Engstrom, who had sold Ponzi his Lexington house, turned in $20,000. Judge Leveroni proved his faith, if not his judgement, by investing $5,400.

Even after the deposit wickets of the Securities and Exchange Company had been battened down, Ponzi was still a hero to the man in the street, the more so now because he seemed to have the bankers and the big people arrayed against him. He still continued to pay off any notes due, still drove into Boston daily in his Locomobile, as fresh and confident as ever. One day, to relax, he went for a plane ride at the Lynnway Airport. It cost him thirty dollars for thirty minutes, and he gave the pilot a ten-dollar tip and said he planned to buy a plane of his own. However, he had by this time become something less than a hero to his publicity agent. A disillusioned McMasters went round the corner to Grozier to tell him that Ponzi was "as crooked as a winding staircase" and agreed to write the whole story for the *Post.* It appeared under McMasters's name in a special edition on August 2. Ponzi was, according to McMasters, "hopelessly insolvent"; his debts were now between $2 million and $4.5 million.

McMasters's article started another and more persistent run on the Securities and Exchange Company offices. Again School Street was a bobbing mass of straw hats. Yet even now the little investor kept his faith in Ponzi, the man of the people, the one man who dared to stand up to the big bankers and show he could beat them at their own game. Ponzi protested that if only the authorities would let him alone, he would pay 100 percent interest in ninety days on all the money he had accepted. His supporters passed out handbills up and down School Street, defending their man and denouncing the "unscrupulous bankers" who were attacking him. Speculators edged up and down the lines of those waiting to get their money, offering to buy the notes on the spot at a discount. Ponzi followed, radiating reassurance, warning the impatient that anyone selling his notes then was giving up his certain profits. An employee of a Boston brokerage house declared that his firm had asked an Italian bank if Ponzi had credit, and the reply had come: "To any amount." That story spread and grew.

By passing out hundreds of thousands of dollars without a tremor, Ponzi kept the crowd with him. He paid with checks on the Hanover Trust Company, to which he was now indebeted for a quarter of a million. About the same time he acquired a personal poet laureate, one James Francis Morelli, a sometime vaudeville hoofer with a knack for making rhymes. Morelli had a desk at the Securities and Exchange Company and a salary of three hundred dollars a week. One of his efforts advised:

If they should ask you to sell
your notes,
Step forward and exclaim:
"No indeed, I'm sorry, lad,
'Cause my notes bear Ponzi's name."
Just step in line, and wait
with ease,
And avoid all kinds of commotion
For Ponzi has as many dollars as
There are ripples in the ocean.

Ponzi thumbed his nose at Grozier's office as he walked by on his way to the courthouse to bring a five-million-dollar libel suit against the *Post*. But the clouds were gathering. Early in August Massachusetts Bank Commissioner Joseph Allen closed down the Hanover Street Trust Company over the protest of the bank's officers. Ponzi supporters, undaunted, reviled the commissioner. In spite of the *Post* and McMasters and the commissioner, Ponzi was still the poor man's Midas who could trounce the bankers at their own game.

Abruptly, predictably and astonishingly—like John Law's Mississippi Scheme and the South Sea Bubble before it—the Ponzi bubble burst. Grozier, after receiving an anonymous tip that Ponzi had once been jailed in Quebec, sent a reporter, Herbert Baldwin, to Montreal. After two days of poking about in the Italian district and then checking his information at police headquarters, Baldwin discovered that the Boston financier was none other than an ex-convict, Charles Bianchi, alias Ponsi, who in 1908 had been sentenced to twenty months in the St. Vincent de Paul Prison for forgery.

On August 11 the *Post* broke the story in banner headlines. In 1908 Charles Ponsi had arrived in Montreal to organize a financial operation much like his later Boston scheme. With Joseph Zarrossi, the owner of a small cigar factory in a settlement of Italian immigrants, he had set up the banking office of Zarrossi & Company. Ponsi, as manager, announced that the company would pay depositors the highest rate of interest in the city. Immigrants flocked to the new bank with their savings. Ponsi paid the interest with the capital of the newest depositors. Zarrossi & Company also accepted remittances to be forwarded to Italy—money that somehow never arrived. When the police and the bank examiners finally closed in, Zarrossi decamped to Mexico. But Ponsi was so successful in placing the blame on his absent partner that he might have gone free if he had not lightheartedly borrowed a blank check from the Canadian Warehousing Company, traced the manager's signature on it and filled it out to the plausible figure of $423.68. It was this minor feat of penmanship that sent him to St. Vincent de Paul.

The *Post*'s account of Charles Ponsi's Canadian career was flanked by a Montreal rogues'-gallery photograph of a mustached Ponsi and a photograph of Boston's Ponzi with a mustache painted on. The two looked almost identical. Before running the article Grozier sent two reporters to Lexington to show it to Ponzi, who laughed and said it was all false. The Montreal convict was somebody else, he assured the reporters. He himself had never been to Montreal, had never been arrested and would bankrupt the *Post* with libel suits if any such story ever came out. Nevertheless Grozier, after a telephone talk with his reporter, who was still in Montreal, decided to go ahead and print.

Laggard city, state and federal officials now began to bestir themselves. Everyone, it seemed, wanted custody of Ponzi at once. He was arrested by a United States marshal on August 13 at his Lexington home. The house itself was impounded and searched in vain for hidden vaults and the bookcase shelves that, according to common talk, were stacked with Liberty Bonds. Before the examination of Ponzi's company books was finished, the School Street office had been shut down, but the auditor estimated that there were liabilities of over seven million dollars and assets of less than four million. His estimate was optimistic. Few of the investors in the Securities and Exchange Company ever saw more than a fraction of their money again.

Ponzi's fall brought about one of the most tangled legal situations Massachusetts had ever known: criminal trial and civil trials; bankruptcy hearings; hearings before the bank examiners; suits by Ponzi and suits against Ponzi. The Hanover Trust Company never again opened its doors; its president, Henry Chmielinski, a leader of Boston's Polish community and founder of the Polish *Daily Courier,* was ruined. Another bank that had lent Ponzi money, the Tremont Trust, collapsed later, as four other banks eventually did. More of Ponzi's past began to leak out. After he had served his time in Montreal he had gone to Georgia. It seemed that there, in 1910, he had been sentenced to two years in the federal penitentiary for smuggling alien Italians into the country.

Now, on November 30, 1920, Ponzi was indicted in Boston's federal court for using the mails to defraud. Massachusetts wanted to try him for larceny. At a retaining fee of $100,000 he engaged the deftly unscrupulous Daniel Coakley as his defense counsel. In spite of the fee and in spite of a reputation for slipping his clients out of apparently impossible situations, Coakley advised this client to try to avoid further state prosecution by pleading guilty to the federal charge. Ponzi's face was livid and his voice high-pitched as he stood up in court to admit his guilt. Rose, among the spectators, fainted twice. Her husband was sentenced to five years in the Plymouth County Jail, used by the federal government because it had no jail of its own in Massachusetts. Ponzi became the most famous prisoner the old brick county jail had ever held. At times he seemed more a commuter than an inmate, traveling back and forth to Boston with the sheriff to attend innumerable bankruptcy proceedings, hearings of receivers and various civil suits brought against him. For some months he was in the Massachusetts General Hospital, recuperating from a stomach operation. In the jail he was a model prisoner, spending his spare time studying law. For all Coakley's scheming, Ponzi while still at Plymouth was indicted by the Commonwealth of Massachusetts on twenty-two counts of conspiracy and larceny. During his long state trial he defended himself with considerable ability, maintaining that often persons who had the means took a chance because they heard of large profits. "But," he told the jury, "the promise of a profit is not larceny; it is merely a promise, and a promise may or may not be kept according to the circumstances." Acquitting him on four counts, the jury disagreed on the rest, making another trial necessary.

Of the fifteen million dollars that Ponzi had taken in, eight, at least, were never accounted for. When his assets were finally distributed, his noteholders received twelve cents on the dollar. Yet even while he was in jail, many of those he had bilked remained loyal to him, still believing that if the authorities and politicians had let him alone, he would have paid all the money he had promised.

Apparently Ponzi himself did not regard his Securities and Exchange Company wholly as a swindle. Carried away by euphoria as the wave of green bills surged over the counters, he had come to think that once he had accumulated sufficient capital to buy his way into the international financial world, he could make enough to pay off his investors. One of the silent partners, Louis Casullo, had taken a prudent trip to Italy with over a million dollars, and the other, John Dondero, had disappeared with a trunkful of money. But Ponzi had stayed on to the end, confident that he could overcome any crisis, hypnotized by his own wizardry. Just before the debacle he was negotiating for a merger—or so he thought—with the Bank of America in California.

After three and a half years at Plymouth Ponzi was released on parole and at once rearrested by the Massachusetts authorities. He was tried again in February 1925, convicted as a "common and notorious thief" (in the quaint phraseology of the Massachusetts statutes) and sentenced to seven to nine years in a state prison. Pending his appeal he was released on $14,000 bail. A month later he disappeared.

He turned up in Florida in the middle of the land bubble. Using the name Charpon—a partial anagram of his name—he organized the Charpon Land Syndicate and was soon selling underwater lots at ten dollars an acre, sight unseen, to buyers who in that hectic mid-twenties summer of pyramiding trades needed no more assurance than a blueprint. After this swamp went down the drain, Ponzi was indicted for fraud. The court in Jacksonville, Florida, found him guilty and sentenced him to a year. On June 3, 1926, he again jumped his bail.

The trail led to Texas. Five days after he left Florida, he dodged the waiting authorities at Houston and shipped as a common seaman aboard an Italian freighter bound for Genoa. On June 28, when the freighter touched at New Orleans, a Houston deputy sheriff was waiting for him. Florida and Massachusetts both wanted him, but the Texas governor sent him back to Boston.

In February 1927 he began his term for larceny at the Charlestown State Prison, across the river from Beacon Hill, where his compatriot, Bartolomeo Vanzetti, was undergoing the final year of his imprisonment. While at Charlestown Ponzi continued to study law. He spent much of his time writing vain appeals to the governor for commutation of sentence in order to escape deportation. In 1934 his seven years' minimum was up, and as his behavior had been excellent, he was freed. Florida had forgotten about him.

Ponzi was now fifty-two years old. Prison had aged him. What was left of his hair was turning white. His face had sagged, and his dapper figure had grown pudgy, though he still carried himself on the grand manner. Rose was still waiting for him. Through all the years, even the Florida interlude, she had stood by him. Together they went to see the new governor, Joseph Ely, to plead against the deportation threat that was now beginning to loom large over Ponzi's head. While his wife worked as secretary for the owner of the Cocoanut Grove nightclub, he spent his days in the law library of the Federal Building, trying to discover some legalism that would let him stay in the country. Meanwhile he paid a visit to the city room of the *Post*. There he shook hands with the city editor, talked of old times with some nostalgia but no resentment and then left. On the way out he walked past the Pulitzer Prize plaque the Post had won for exposing him.

There were no conjuring paragraphs to be found in the law library, and Governor Ely was as adamant as his predecessor had been. On October 7, 1934, the U.S. Immigration Service put Ponzi aboard the *Vulcania* in Boston Harbor for a single passage to Italy. He still had enough friends to give him a rousing send-off from the dock. As he went up the gangplank, he raised his arm in the Fascist salute.

Back in Italy he became an English translator for a small export house in Rome. He revisited the cafés of his student days; his photograph, showing him at ease over an apéritif, appeared in the American press. In his spare time he began writing his autobiography and apologia. Rose had expected that after he found work in Rome he would send for her, but he never did. After two years of waiting she lost patience and divorced him. She never remarried.

Shortly after Ponzi's divorce Mussolini offered him a job in Brazil with Italy's new airline. From 1939 to 1942 he served as branch manager in Rio de Janeiro. In 1942 he lost his job because, he claimed, of his protests against "wide departures from the organization's original, strictly honest commercial operations." A group of airline officials had, in fact, been smuggling currency. They had not included him in their group, and when he found out what they were doing, he tipped off the Brazilian government with the expectation of getting 25 percent of the fines. Then as an afterthought he offered to come to America to tell the government what he knew about the operation.

The United States government did not want him. As the tide of war turned against Italy the airline closed down. No money came to Ponzi from any fines. For a while he unsuccessfully tried to run a lodging house in Rio de Janeiro. Through the war years he made a meager living giving English lessons while he drew a pittance from the Brazilian unemployment fund.

The year 1949 found him, semiparalyzed and partly blind, in the charity ward of a Rio hospital. Flanked by an old man with a hacking cough and a quiet, senile black man who spent his days staring at the ceiling, he still tried to work on his autobiography. Somehow he had saved up seventy-five dollars, enough to keep his body from the potter's field. He died in January 1949, leaving behind his unfinished manuscript, "The Fall of Mister Ponzi."

Group photograph of the Martha Baker School's second grade in 1917. The author is second from left in the top row. Ben Tilly in his Dutch clip is in the front row (see arrow).

THE END OF MATTAPAN MACKY

W E STARTED OUT TOGETHER IN THE MATTAPAN SECTION OF DOR-
chester, in the now boarded-up Martha Baker School. His
name was really Tilly, but I always think of him by his
nickname, Macky, though he never attained the insouciant bravado
of Gay's Captain Macheath. I doubt if the Anglo-Norman label under
which I first knew him in kindergarten had been in his family long.
By itself the name was as old as American history. A signer of the
Mayflower Compact was a Tilly, as was a captain tortured and murdered
by the Pequots in King Philip's War. Consonant with its Norman roots,
it is borne by one of the recurring characters in the *Comédie Humaine.*

Macky had a swarthy complexion and off-blond hair, a contrast one
sometimes finds in gypsies. I suspect his ancestors were Sicilians,
although I never thought about his origins when I knew him. In his
adult years all his associates were Italians, extending to the local heads
of what would later be known as Cosa Nostra. In 1975 he was killed
in a car crash near the Morton Street railroad bridge in Mattapan at
two in the morning, ironically enough almost in front of the police
station where he had first been arrested as a juvenile and only a few
hundred yards from the three-decker where he had lived as a boy. "It
was a straight accident," the police captain told me when I talked with
him. "Nothing like you're thinking. No gang stuff. That's just a bad
corner by the bridge. He was going seventy, swung over to the left and
another car clipped him. You see the notice in the *Globe?*" The captain shifted his cigar and the whites of his eyes popped. " 'Tilly was

engaged for several years in the contracting business in Brighton.' He sure was!''

I dropped in on Macky's wake at the Danny O'Connell Funeral Home. Until quite recently Danny (the Liberator) considered tuxedos *de rigueur* for translating his clients. But in these less formal times I found Macky laid out in a white suit, striped shirt and purple flowered tie, as if he were ready to take the next plan for Miami. Three feet above his nose a rhinestone-studded cross sparkled in the beams of a concealed ceiling light, and his hands clutched a jet-and-silver rosary. A crash at seventy miles an hour must have given Danny a lot of reconstruction work. But he was up to it, even to the obligatory smile, though I could find no trace of my old schoolmate in those patched, waxy features. For a Cosa Nostra finger-man the floral decorations were muted, although the ailing chief, Raymond Patriarca, had sent a six-foot set piece of white and yellow roses wired to resemble the open pages of a book and inscribed with red carnations: THE BIBLE. I paid my anonymous respects to Macky's wife, either his fourth or his fifth.

Thinking of Macky primped in his satin-lined coffin, my mind goes back over the years to Miss Lowe's kindergarten class. For some reason I go to the dressing room, Miss Lowe is already there. She is gentle; the only teacher I ever liked at the Baker school. Only this morning she is not gentle. She is holding Macky and shaking him, and he is howling. As she shakes, crayons, blocks, a ringtoss, pencils, three lead soldiers and other kindergarten objects fall in driblets from his rompers. I am only four, but I know Macky has been stealing. I am too appalled to speak. For the first time I have seen a thief.

At that time we were living on the top of Dorchester Hill in Mattapan. Macky and his brother Joe lived below the far side of the Hill on the second floor of a Morton Street three-decker. Even in kindergarten there was a quality about him that made me afraid, something that went beyond the physical fear that I and the other Hill children felt for the Mulvey Street Gang in the Hollow by the cemetery. His husky child's voice already had overtones of menace, as if he were practicing ''Stand and Deliver.'' I have a group photograph of our Martha Baker first grade. Macky sits in the front row in the spring sunshine, slightly scowling but impassive, as if he had already learned to give away nothing of himself. His hair is cut with bangs across his forehead in a kind of bob that covers his ears, a style then known as a Dutch clip. Lower-class boys then, often to the age of six or seven, had Dutch clips, although the style was on its way out. Of our twenty-two boys, only five still wore their hair that way. Macky is wearing a kind of romper suit instead of the knickerbockers that most of the other boys are wearing. I think the sinister effect derives from his eyes, feline and singularly sallow against the swarthiness of his complexion.

Macky's mother never came to school. That was not unusual. Hill mothers sometimes did. Morton and Mulvey Street mothers did not. But there was something strange about Macky's father. He was never seen coming home from work like other fathers. In fact most of the time he was never seen at all. Then when after a long interval he did appear, his hair was always close-cropped. A "prison clip" someone more knowing than myself whispered. Macky and his brother Joe continued to steal all through the Martha Baker's three grades. And on their way home over the Hill they would snatch up whatever they came across: tricycles, express wagons, even dolls. Afterward they would deny so glibly and tearfully that they had taken anything, that grown-ups believed them—or at least felt uncertain.

I remember a day in the third grade just as we were leaving at noon when Miss Sykes caught Macky rifling her purse, which she kept in her desk drawer. Miss Sykes, the stern headmistress, was not at all hesitant about laying hands on a wayward child—as was common enough for a teacher at that time. Macky squealed like a rabbit as she came up behind him and grabbed him. He struggled and bit her hand. She took him by the scruff of the neck and hoicked him out the front door. "Don't come back without your mother," she told him. He stood on the brick walk, defiant, his pallid eyes flashing. Suddenly he began to shout at her, a flood of Anglo-Saxon monosyllables that I had absorbed at a distance from the Mulvey Gang, that I understood vaguely and that I also knew must never be used in the presence of a grown-up. Yet here was Macky shouting all of them at Miss Sykes. Having always thought of her authority as absolute, I expected her to strike him down. To my astonishment she did nothing at all, merely stood in the doorway and repeated very quietly: "Don't come back without your mother." Then, noticing me, she said almost gently: "You go home, Francis." As I walked up the concrete footway to the Hill I could still hear Macky shouting the unmentionable words.

The memory is like a few feet of old film run through a projector. What happened after that, whether Macky's mother came to the school, whether Macky even had a mother, how he was punished, I do not know. I have another segment of mental film from that same year: Macky scuttling down the street chased by the fat man in the white apron who ran the corner Greek store that sold college ices and banana splits and Paige & Shaw chocolates. My last school memory of Macky runs several years later when I was in the third or fourth grade. I had made myself a kite shaped like a five-pointed star from a diagram I had found in *The Boy Mechanics Handbook* and had taken it one spring afternoon to try it out for the first time from the top of the Hill near the old white oak. There wasn't enough wind that afternoon for me to get my kite off the ground. As I struggled with it, Macky and Joe came along, watched me for a moment, and then with disarming friendliness offered to help, ''I'll hold your kite here,'' Macky told me, ''and you run with the string.'' I was always rather guileless, even with boys like Macky. He held the kite above his head, and I turned and ran. I had the merest glimpse of its star shape as it began to climb into the April sky. What I did not notice was that Joe had taken out a jackknife and cut the string. I ran for about thirty feet without ever feeling the kite pull. Then as I turned I saw Macky and Joe trotting over the crest of the hill, my star kite bobbing along behind them on the end of its abbreviated string.

Since that spring afternoon I never saw Macky again until the spring of 1971. After the three grades of the Martha Baker School he moved on to the Roger Wolcott School across from the Morton Street bridge while I was shifted to the Edmund Tileston School near Mattapan Square. School-leaving age was then only twelve, and I think Macky left on his twelfth birthday or sooner. According to a recent Massachusetts commissioner of correction there are no criminals, merely victims of a hostile environment. One should then, I suppose, be sorry for Macky, should grant that anyone brought up from kindergarten on as a sneak-thief was bound to be a criminal, should be angry rather against Miss Lowe and Miss Sykes for not having managed to shape him differently. Yet, even as I looked down on what was left of him in his coffin, I could not feel pity. Something of my child's fear of that small figure in the Dutch clip with the pallid hazel eyes still lingered. Perhaps it was this old fear, this child's uneasiness, that induced me to follow his career over the years, at least as it appeared in the papers. It was spectacular enough—robberies, holdups, an armored car hijacked with a machine gun, a Macheath-like trail of females. Yet, since he never had a legal occupation and since the papers record only his failures and missteps, most of his history is like the submerged nine-tenths of an iceberg.

His juvenile record is not available, but I know he was caught several times breaking and entering, shoplifting and purse-snatching, that he worked for a while as a delivery boy for a bootlegger, and that after stealing a car in Roxbury he ended up in the Lyman School, a reform school for boys near Framingham. His adult record begins at almost the earliest possible date, three weeks after his seventeenth birthday, with *Ind Exp 1/10 Pr*—"Indecent Exposure-Probation." Obviously the police had long had their eye on him, for his record continues month after month with petty to trivial offenses, mostly motor vehicle violations: not slowing down at an intersection, speeding, operating to endanger the lives of the public, and so on. When he was eighteen he was convicted of stealing a car and was given a suspended sentence. That same year he also received suspended sentences for assault and battery and for drunkenness.

In 1930, for the first time since his Lyman School days, he ended up behind bars, sentenced to a year in the house of correction for robbing a store. However, after an appeal the case was placed on file and Macky released. He must have been then about twenty. Beyond minor violations, all placed on file, I do not know what he did for the next three years. He now lived in Roxbury, was married, but never seemed to appear twice in public with the same woman. In 1933 he made the headlines for the first time when he and Joe and two others with Italian names were indicted for the machine-gun holdup of a mail truck in the North Station in which about $100,000 had been stolen. A jury in Suffolk County, where juries have a long reputation for broad-mindedness, found him not guilty. That same year he was charged with snatching a bag containing $50,000 worth of diamonds from an out-of-town jewelry salesman in the Back Bay Station, but again a jury failed to convict him. Later in the year the police of Portland, Maine, caught him robbing a jewelry store on Congress Street. Since there is nothing about this in his record, I presume it never got to court. The next year he and Joe were in court charged with holding up the Glenwood Coal Company in Charlestown, but Macky managed to "prove" that he had been in New Hampshire on that day. In 1935 he was caught breaking into a bank in suburban Melrose and this time was given two years in the house of correction, some months of which he actually served before being parolled. Once outside he joined Patriarca, then in his

Cosa Nostra salad days. Together they held up the Robin Hood Shirt Company in New Bedford. But this time something went wrong. They were both arrested, convicted and sentenced to three to five years in state prison. After eighty-four days Patriarca was released, chiefly on the grounds that he had been good to his aged mother. After loud protest by the Bar Association, Governor "Chowderhead" Hurley excused himself by saying he had signed the pardon inadvertently. Coakley had put it on his desk. But the protest was hard on Macky. He had to sit in state prison for almost two years—his longest stretch—until he was parolled. But before his trial, while he was still out on bail, he was identified as one of two men who robbed a jewelry store in Newton, forcing the proprietor at pistolpoint to open his safe, and then after cutting the telephone wires making off with $20,000 in goods and the proprietor's car. For some reason the case was placed on file.

A few months after his second parole he was picked up with burglar tools and a revolver, and though the case was filed, he was returned to state prison for violation of parole. I happened to know the commissioner of correction who personally drove him back. "Quite agreeable," the commissioner told me. "Not the type one imagines—though professional criminals often are not." A year later Macky was let out on a good conduct release. During that time his third—or possibly his fourth—wife divorced him in the grounds of his being a habitual criminal.

It was after Macky's second release from state prison that the good years began for him. Whatever he was doing, his invisible means of support came from outside Massachusetts. Within the state he conducted himself circumspectly. True, at the beginning he did have a little further difficulty about burglar's tools found in his car, but the judge was again understanding and placed the case on file. Macky even managed for once to go legitimate, getting a liquor license for a store in Brighton. He drove a white Cadillac convertible and acquired a new ultrablonde wife who looked like a model. Up until then he had always lived on obscure semislum streets in Roxbury and Dorchester. But now, as if for his blonde's sake, he bought the Concannon house at the top of Mount Vernon Street in suburban West Roxbury.

Before World War I Mike Concannon, a Protestant Irishman, had set up a tool shop in the back of his house in Roslindale where he manufactured artificial arms and legs. The casualties of the war had enlarged his shop to a factory and made him a prosthetics expert as well as a rich man. After the war he had gone to England on his arms-and-legs business and with his wife had visited the Cotswolds, becoming possessed by the stone houses of Broadway and Chipping Camden and Stow-on-the-Wold. When he got back to Roslindale he determiend to build a Cotswold house in neighboring and wealthier West Roxbury. He enlisted a competent traditional architect and spared no expense. Unlike the so-called English-style houses of brick with fake half-timbering, round towers and gumwood interiors, his house was authentic. From its rough-cut stone exterior to its walnut-panelled living room-library it followed the Cotswold design, not only in proportion but—as imitations rarely do—in atmosphere. It was a beautiful house. Of course it looked absurd on woodenly suburban Mount Vernon Street, even on a double lot. Mike Concannon died a month after moving in, and his widow left for St. Petersburg. My Aunt Dorothy, who lived three streets away, gave me the neighborhood gossip after the house was sold. "Someone named Tilly has bought that Concannon house," she told me. "I don't know what he does, but they seem like nice quiet people. They've built a swimming pool and they have cookouts for all the neighbors. The wife is quite striking looking, very blonde; I think she's younger than he is."

"Do they call him Macky?" I asked her.

"As a matter of fact they do. Why?"

"Oh, nothing," I said, thinking that they could find out for themselves.

They found out several months later when four masked men, using tear gas, held up the Harvard Cooperative Society in Harvard Square. Just as they were bolting for the door with their loot, one of them lost his mask. The face underneath was Macky's. This time the case against him seemed clear-cut. Nevertheless a jury failed to agree, and he was again turned loose. Not long afterward he was arrested in Boston for having stolen some $160,000 worth of jewelry from a Denver, Colorado, art gallery. He had flown back the day of the theft and tried to establish an alibi by talking publicly to police and various bartenders that evening. But the police found some of the jewelry in his bedroom, and the next day his lawyer turned over the rest without comment. The lawyer was a former Massachusetts legislator known at the State House as "the Skull," a bald, cavernous man with a skin of yellowed parchment stretched tightly over a face that, but for its appraising eyes, looked like a death's head. The Skull flew to Denver with the extradited

Macky and managed to get him acquitted there on the grounds that the grand jury indicting him had been illegally empanelled. Macky arrived back in Boston "with a big grin on his face" according to the *Record-American*. Acquittal it might be, but it finished him in West Roxbury. No one on Mount Vernon Street would sit beside his swimming pool or go to his cookouts. Finally the blonde disappeared. A few weeks later there was a FOR SALE sign on the front grass. That same year Macky paid a seventy-five-dollar fine for registering bets. A year later he was arrested in Brookline for "open and gross lewdness" on the complaint of two eighteen-year-old girls who said he had pulled up beside them in his car, exposed himself and then attempted to molest them. For this he received two months in the house of correction. He did not appeal. "There's something fishy here," a Boston criminal lawyer told me when I mentioned my old schoolmate's latest caper. "Macky's not the type to go picking up high school girls in the park that way. He's got all the stuff he needs down in the North End. Either he was framed or else—and this is what I think—he wants to be locked up for a couple of months for his own safety." Whatever the reason, Macky left the house of correction after serving his time and, for all I know, disappeared for the next five years.

Then in August 1970 three men with machine guns held up the driver of a truck about to deliver a $68,000 payroll to the Chelsea Naval Hospital just north of Boston. A month before, Macky had been arrested for "breaking and entering with intent to commit larceny." What he intended and where I do not know, having only the hieroglypic of his record: *B&E Dt w/iCom Larc 82*. It was while he was out on bail that the Naval Hospital delivery holdup occurred. For the breaking and entering he was given two years. After he had begun his term at the Norfolk State Prison Colony, an old-time convict named "Buzz" Daly—rumored to have been connected earlier with the Brinks robbery—confessed that he and Macky and one of the Angiulo brothers had held up the Naval Hospital truck. Then, prudently, he asked to be placed in protective custody. Macky was taken from Norfolk to stand trial with Angiulo, a local lieutenant of Patriarca's.

On an impulse I spent an afternoon at Macky's trial, held in the federal courtroom on the fifteenth floor of Boston's Post Office Building. The legal cliché that a man is innocent until proven guilty scarcely applied to Macky. For him the reverse would have been more nearly true. The ratio of what he had done to what he had been caught

doing was probably about ten to one. It would be most unlikely that
he would ever appear in court charged with what he had not done.

The trial was not one to arouse much public interest. Indeed after
the first day it was not even reported in the Boston papers. When I
arrived the courtroom was only about a third full, the usual collection
of hangers-on: the idle, the dubious, the involved. Looking around
the room I thought of Dickens characters that often seem such an ex-
aggeration of life. Perhaps they weren't after all. For even if a Zola
had written of those I saw in the courtroom, from the judge to the
deputy sheriffs to the spectators, describing them with cold naturalism,
they would have seemed as wildly exaggerated as anything in *Pickwick
Papers*. The judge himself, peering over his half-spectacles, grinning
a detached monkeyish grin, was perplexingly familiar. I had seen him
before. But where? Then I remembered. I had seen that face many
times during the war in the *London Daily Express*'s Giles cartoons.
At my right the defense lawyer, the Skull, shuffled through his papers
while chewing gum with spasmodic clicks, his skin like yellowed par-
chment, gorilla eyes sunk in a wrinkled head. To the left I noticed
an intent brass-bed blonde with bouffant hair, wondered if she could
be one of Macky's doxies. But Macky and Angiulo I could not spot
at all. With Patriarca presently in prison, the Angiulos were said to
be running Cosa Nostra in New England. If it was so, I wondered why
this Angiulo would be directly involved in a holdup instead of leaving it to underlings. Still, Patriarca and Macky had been hunting
partners.

When I reached the courtroom, the state's key witness, Buzz Daly,
was already on the stand testifying that he had received the holdup
money from Macky and had handed it over to Angiulo. The Skull,
looking more than ever like death warmed up, cross-examined him,
tracing back Daly's long record of assault and battery, holdups,
muggings, brawls, robberies. Daly, a heavy, broken-nosed man in his
sixties, could have been a punch-drunk ex-prizefighter. That face was
not one I should have cared to meet coming down a dark empty street.
Yet he stuck to his story, while the Skull clicked his dentures and sparred
with him. At first I could not locate Macky. Defendants are harder
to spot in court than in the unenlightened days when they sat in the
dock. Such an enclosure has come to be considered prejudicial to the
defendants, demeaning them in the eyes of the jury. Now they sit in
ordinary chairs and it is difficult to tell them from lawyers, at least

it was for me where I was sitting. I asked a sheriff's deputy, a bleary-eyed man with crude, fat features, which one was Macky. "Dunno, dunno!" he said in obvious irritation at my question. Later I would see him leading Macky from the courtroom down the corridor, pals together.

At a short recess I managed to find out that the defendants were sitting in three leather chairs in front of the brass railing. I did not know the name of the third defendant, but he looked a cruder variety of Naples pimp, a man in his thirties with yellow, apelike teeth, wavy hair, long nose, padded shoulders and fists that seemed designed for knuckle-dusters. Angiulo, second in line behind his dark glasses, had the withdrawn Mafia air. Then, after over half a century, I saw Macky again. In his rogues'-gallery mug shots, taken in his thirties and forties, the Martha Baker Macky, his pallid cat's eyes glittering beneath the Dutch-clip bangs, was still recognizable. But with another twenty years added on, I should not have known him. For one thing he was short, a full head shorter than I, though in our schooldays he had been taller. At sixty he looked a plump sixty-five. His receding hair was greased and brushed back, and he had grown wispy sideburns. Nor did his complexion seem as swarthy as I remembered. His eyes, masked by heavy tortoise-shell bifocals, were no longer to be defined; his oval head ended in a singularly long jaw. He was nattily dressed, though in the style of several years back—narrow lapels, narrow tie, pointed shoes. An initialed handkerchief peeped from his breast pocket. One would not have said that he was Italian, or that he was not Italian, but unlike Daly he looked mild. I could imagine him kiting checks or stealing credit cards, but hardly slugging a jewelry salesman in an alley or holding a submachine gun barrel against a payroll guard or tossing a smoke bomb into the Harvard Coop. Age too—at sixty—was taking its toll, apparent in the slackness of his torso, the hunch of his shoulders. Another decade would see him an old man. He glanced at me once or twice through his bifocals with unseeing eyes, and I wondered if he could still remember running over the hill with his brother, trailing my star kite behind him. Unlikely. Probably he had even forgotten my name.

To me Daly was convincing. Apparently he failed to convince the jury, for two days later I read that Macky had been found not guilty and that before the jury went out the judge had freed Angiulo for lack of evidence. That afternoon was the last time I ever saw Macky alive. How much he served of his remaining Norfolk sentence is not on record, though to judge by his earlier history no great part of it. I have his record only through 1968. His last six years are to me a blank. But that incomplete record is spectacular enough in all the intricacy of its legal code numbers: *Occupation; salesman, chauffeur. Aliases; 9. Wives; 4. Court entries from January 1927 to September 1968; 56. Time served; a handful of months.*

I think of Macky in his coffin under the rhinestone crucifix. Perhaps he was a victim of his early environment, shaped by family and circumstance to be a criminal. Perhaps it was in his genes. I do not know. I merely see a star kite with an awkwardly knotted tail mounting up into a cloudless April sky over the crest of Dorchester Hill, then dropping down, disappearing from sight forever.

These psychic photographs were taken in December 1923. The above picture shows the purported materialization of Margery's father. In the second picture Margery is obscured by a psychic haze out of which a face, identified as her husband's grandmother, emerges. Margery's husband, Dr. Crandon, is shown at the right.

THE WITCH OF BEACON HILL

NEVER IN THE AMBIGUOUS HISTORY OF SPIRITUALISM IN THE UNITED STATES has there been a medium who achieved such a reputation for psychic phenomena and caused such extended controversy as the woman known as Margery, who suddenly manifested her abilities in Boston in the spring of 1923. Margery, it was claimed, performed under the spirit-control of her dead brother Walter. His voice first spoke through her, though later independently of her vocal cords. During a series of Margery's séances extraordinary occurrences took place. Flowers and other objects materialized from nowhere. Ghostly bugle calls sounded. At times ectoplasmic rods sprouted from the medium's body that were capable of touching persons in the dark, moving objects, producing lights and making wax impressions of themselves. J. Malcolm Bird, associate editor of *Scientific American,* who later wrote a book on Margery, became her partisan as did Hereward Carrington, Sir Arthur Conan Doyle and others. Houdini the magician, after attending five of the séances, denounced her almost hysterically. In the next few years hundreds of newspaper and magazine articles appeared about her. A committee from *Scientific American* and one from Harvard investigated her. Their findings were varied. Concerning Margery herself there has never been a final conclusion.

What made Margery's case unique beyond spiritualist phenomena was the quality of the people involved. Doctors, professional men and members of the Harvard faculty were among the regular sitters at her séances. No financial consideration ever entered into the mediumship;

in fact the expenses of many of the investigators were paid by Margery's husband.

Margery was the Canadian-born wife of Le Roi Goddard Crandon, a well-known Boston doctor and surgeon-in-chief of a local hospital. Dr. Crandon, a Harvard graduate of the Class of 1894, had been for some years a lecturer in surgery at the Harvard Medical School. The Crandons lived in a four-story Federalist town house at 10 Lime Street, just at the foot of Beacon Hill. It is a small street of dissimilar houses harmonized by the passage of time, and its antique intimacy makes it seem rather fitting for psychic adventures.

The name Margery was a pseudonym invented for Mrs. Crandon at the outset of her mediumship to protect her from publicity. In her ordinary daily life she was matter-of-fact about her psychic powers and would sometimes jokingly refer to herself—a personable woman in her thirties—as a witch, adding that if she had lived 250 years earlier she would probably have been hanged.

Margery the medium had her origins in Dr. Crandon's library. Early in 1923, more or less by chance, he happened to occupy himself with books on spiritualism, at first in a desultory way and later with more concentrated interest. Although his wife did not take spiritualism seriously, they talked about it together, and one day as a joke she went with a friend to a Boston clairvoyant. She did not identify herself, and she was astonished when the medium, in a trance, told her that a spirit by the name of Walter was present. The messages that he then transmitted from Walter consisted of small personal incidents from her girlhood.

A short time after this the Crandons, with four of their friends, made a private attempt at spirit communication, gathering around a table in the Lime Street living room under a red light. Before long the table began to rotate and then tilt. One by one the sitters were sent from the room. Only in Mrs. Crandon's absence did the table remain dead. A code of responses was soon established by which the table-tipping intelligence, who maintained he was Walter, could reply to questions. Subsequently Walter began to communicate by a series of raps, and then after some time his voice asserted itself through Margery. About this time Dr. Crandon constructed a cabinet for his wife, and her séances were conducted with the sitters joining hands in a circle.

Walter's presence was usually announced by a sharp whistle. His voice now became a standard feature of all Margery's séances, and the table-tipping and the raps were discarded. Over the months her mediumship seemed to follow its own curious progression. At one point all the clocks in the house were stopped at a time predetermined by Walter. At another séance Walter announced he would play taps, and shortly afterward the notes were faintly heard in the lower part of the house. Sometimes the furniture in the living room would move. Once, after he called attention to the possibility, a live pigeon was found in the next room.

Finally Dr. Crandon claimed that he had observed "faint aurora-like emanations" projecting from the region of Margery's fingers. This was the beginning of the ectoplasmic materializations that were to produce organs and hands of various kinds. A wax cast was made of one of these hands. Others were photographed. Walter registered his thumbprint in wax. The ectoplasmic limbs rang bells. Accompanying these materializations were psychic lights that floated about the room glowing and fading.

In 1922 *Scientific American* offered to pay $2,500 for any objective demonstrations of psychic phenomena and appointed an investigating committee of five prominent persons interested in this subject. The members were Dr. Daniel Comstock, formerly professor of physics at the Massachusetts Institute of Technology; Dr. William McDougall, professor of psychology at Harvard and president of the American Society for Psychical Research; Dr. Walter Franklin Prince, former clergyman and research officer of the society; Dr. Hereward Carrington, the author and psychic experimenter who had tested the European medium Palladino; and Harry Houdini, the magician and escape artist. J. Malcolm Bird, who had first brought Margery into contact with the committee, served as its secretary. During 1924, in the course of the committee's investigations, three articles, essentially favorable to Margery, appeared in *Scientific American*. These spread interest in her mediumship quickly and widely.

The report of the committee a few months later was, however, unfavorable. Mr. Bird accepted the Lime Street séance phenomena as genuine, as did Dr. Carrington. Houdini, with a showman's eye for publicity, published a lurid pamphlet denouncing Margery. Dr. Prince was not convinced. Yet it must be said that his and Houdini's attendance at the séances was scanty. Dr. Comstock was present more often than any of the others. He found difficulty in making up his mind, and concluded merely that "rigid proof has not yet been furnished." Dr.

McDougall also seemed hesitant during the séances, but in his report he wrote: "As long ago as November...I was inclined to observe all the phenomena I had observed as produced by normal means...Since that date...the inclination has grown steadily stronger in the main, in spite of some minor fluctuations, and has now become well-nigh irresistible." The report and the committee were sharply attacked by the growing number of Margery's defenders.

In the summer of 1925 another briefer investigation was conducted by a group of younger members of the Harvard faculty, this time in a room of Emerson Hall in the Harvard Yard. Walter made the transition from Lime Street easily, but the principal Emerson phenomenon was Margery's trance production of an ectoplasmic hand. For these séances she wore luminous bands on her legs as controls, but during one sitting it was discovered that she had slipped a foot out of the band and was free to manipulate it. Afterward a committee member, by a similar free use of his foot, managed to duplicate all the phenomena except the production of ectoplasm. The ectoplasmic hand impressed itself on a lump of plasticine, which on later examination showed skin markings and lint microscopically identical with that in the medium's slipper. At another Emerson séance two observers noted that the medium had worked both hands free, and one of them detected her conveying objects from her lap and afterward returning them.

At a subsequent series of séances with an English representative of the Society for Psychical Research, Margery produced varieties of ectoplasm including a much more embryonic hand than the earlier one, spongy and feeling like blancmange. This hand was photographed under red light. When these photographs were examined by Dr. W. B. Cannon, professor of physiology, and Dr. H. W. Rand, professor of zoology, both at Harvard, they reported that the so-called ectoplasm was composed of the lung tissue of some animal.

There were rumors that the Harvard group had disagreed about Margery. To correct this the members issued a statement that they were "in absolute agreement; that the only conclusion possible is that trickery accounted for all the phenomena; and that the only possible difference of opinion is to what extent the trickery is unconscious."

Perhaps the most directly damaging evidence against Margery was the discovery in 1932 that the wax impressions shown for six years as Walter's psychic thumbprints were really those of a Boston dentist. The dentist, still alive and practicing, admitted that he had once made several such impressions in dental wax at Mrs. Crandon's request. To this charge the Crandons never replied.

My later friend, the poet Robert Hillyer, who was at that time an English instructor at Harvard, became a regular attendant at the Lime Street sittings along with another young Harvard writer, S. Foster Damon. With Damon, Margery developed an almost maternal relationship, and he came to her for advice on all his personal problems. Subsequently he wrote a glowing book about her. Robert had just published his fourth book of verse, *The Hills Give Promise.* What he experienced in the séance room at first convinced him, and he gave Margery a copy of his new book in which he had written: "I have seen, and I have believed." In the course of further sittings, however, he came to change his opinion and in the end very much regretted that he had given Margery the inscribed book.

"At one séance," he told me, "Margery produced an ectoplasmic hand and we were asked to feel it. As soon as I touched it I knew it was the hand of a dead person. It was small, either a child's or a woman's, but dead. I understood then. Dr. Crandon was a surgeon, and he could sneak such things out of the hospital."

"But," I asked him, "if it was a fraud, why did they do it?"

"It was a weird business," he said. "Crandon was much older than his wife, and he was an educated man of some standing. She had neither education nor background. There may have been some sort of psychological conflict in that, each trying to prove something to the other. Of course he faked, but perhaps he felt that in spite of the trickery there was something real behind it all. He may have believed in Walter. I don't know. After that night I never went near Lime Street again."

It was in the second autumn of the war, in 1940, just before I left Boston to join the Canadian Army, that I happened to be asked to 10 Lime Street. I was surprised to learn that Margery still lived there. In the ominous quiet of an America preparing its first peacetime draft, the controversy she had caused a decade and a half earlier seemed remote and irrelevant. Yet though the fashions of publicity had passed her by, Margery still continued her sittings with her followers. Dr. Crandon had died the winter before.

A Dr. Richardson introduced me. He had been a friend of the Crandons from the beginning of Margery's mediumship. Just after World War I he had lost his two sons in a polio epidemic and this had turned him toward spiritualism. To his satisfaction, at least, he had found his boys again in all the brightness of their youth at Margery's séances. On our way to Lime Street he showed me a spirit photograph of Margery in a trance with a cloud like a double exposure above her head on which were the blurred outlines of two faces. These faces, he told me, were his sons beyond doubt.

We arrived at eight o'clock of a rainy, line-storm evening. Margery herself opened the street-level door for us, shook hands and led the way to an upstairs drawing room. She was an overdressed, dumpy little woman, amiable, yet with a faint, elusive coarseness about her that one sensed as soon as she spoke. Dr. Richardson said that in recent séances they had been trying to reach Dr. Crandon, and that tonight they hoped to get a wax imprint of his fingers. The room was a homely one with chintz curtains, leather and fabric armchairs, imitation upright Chippendales, a tapestry brick fireplace with a sofa in front of it at one end and lengths of bookcases at the other. On a side shelf was a silver-framed autographed photograph of A. Conan Doyle, and another of Sir Oliver Lodge. Near the window stood an old-fahioned Victrola. There were eight or ten people standing about.

"Everybody ready?" Margery asked us. We arranged our chairs in a circle. Margery sat in the center in a straight-backed chair. "Let's have a little music," she said as we settled down.

Someone turned on the Victrola. She squatted there with her eyes half-closed, and there was no sound but the rasp of the needle and then the notes of "Ah, Sweet Mystery of Life" scratched out of the wax grooves.

The song ended, and as the mechanism shut itself off Dr. Richardson turned out the lights. For several minutes there was no sound at all. The tension hung suspended, like that empty moment before the bull comes into the arena. Then I noticed Margery's breathing. At first it sounded no more than a repeated sigh, but with each breath she took it deepened until it became a stertorous moan. Only once before had I heard such sounds—when I passed a hospital room where a man was dying.

Then, breaking in suddenly over this animal noise that stopped abruptly, came a rush of air and an ear-cracking whistle, and after this a man's voice talking very fast. The sound seemed to come from a spot several feet above Margery's head.

"Almost thought I couldn't make it," said the voice nasally. "Lots of interrupters, lots of trouble, plenty of them."

Dr. Richardson spoke back. "Walter," he said, "we have a new sitter with us I'd like you to meet. This is Mr. Russell."

"How do you do," I said awkwardly, in what I thought was his general direction, realizing as I said it that my voice sounded strained and artificial.

"How do *you* do," said Walter mimicking me. "I don't think you do very well. Is that a Harvard accent you have?"

"You mustn't mind Walter," said Dr. Richardson. "He's often rude, but he doesn't really mean a thing by it."

"That's what the Doc thinks," said Walter.

A woman in the darkness opposite asked if Dr. Crandon could give them any message.

"Roi's busy," Walter answered her. "He said to say he was OK, but he's still tied up. He can't come through yet."

"When do you think he can?" Mrs. Richardson asked.

"Not for a while yet, not for a while yet. Keep your shirt on." Walter's voice was edged. "Leave him alone. Give him time. He's got his troubles, too."

There was more talk and then Dr. Richardson asked Walter about the fingerprints.

"Not tonight, Doc," said Walter. "Next time, maybe."

Then there was silence, as if a radio station had gone off the air, and a few seconds later Margery's voice broke in casually. "Will you turn on the lights?" Although pitched in another key, the tone bore a certain resemblance to Walter's.

The lights went on and we stood up blinking, while Margery smiled at us in an indolent, good-natured way, stretching her plump arms and yawning. As we left she shook hands with each of us at the top of the landing. "You must all come to tea next Sunday," she said. "I have a feeling it's going to be important. All of you, next Sunday—but not before five o'clock. I have to see about Roi's grave earlier." She giggled. "The landscape gardeners have made an awful mess of it, planted hydrangeas. Roi hates hydrangeas. Now don't forget—next Sunday at five."

It was the only time I ever saw Margery. At that séance there had been no wandering lights of ghostly music, no bells ringing, no psychic touch I could feel, no ectoplasm or even fingerprints. In a committee sense there had not been enough phenomena for anyone to pass judgement, yet Walter's voice was real, and he was the core of the matter, the leading spirit—if one could excuse the play on words. Those earlier productions of ectoplasm had been a contrivance, part of the paraphernalia that Dr. Crandon had assembled. A less gullible medical man than Dr. Richardson was afterward to describe the psychic rods sprouting from Margery's body as some sort of animal intestines stuffed with cotton. The lights and the bells and the rest Houdini could have managed as well.

That left Walter, a spirit with a taste for Victor Herbert, brash and crude of speech, a kind of poolroom johnny from the other world. As an audible actuality he was capable of three interpretations. Either he was a disembodied entity that had once been Margery's brother; or he was a subconscious element of Margery developed in a trance; or he was merely Margery's normal self playacting.

If one were to believe the first interpretation, as did Dr. Richardson, that glimpsed other world must be a shabby, static place. For Walter, since parting from his body, showed no development in mind or personality or tastes.

In regard to the latter two interpretations, the first seems more likely. For Margery to contrive such a conscious Walter-fiction during hundreds of sittings over a period of years would be too demanding a feat. Walter was a complete individual. He never hesitated, never lacked for words, never stepped out of character. Rather than to assume that Margery was merely a clever actress, it seems a more likely assumption that her trances at least were genuine and that Walter was a second personality developed in them.

Several years after that Lime Street séance, while I was in an infantry reinforcement unit in England, I happened to pick up a pink paperback copy of *Whitaker's Almanack* in the mess anteroom. While I waited for dinner, I thumbed through it—the events of the year before, tides, eclipses, weights and measures and finally a list of noted people who had died during the year. There, under November's obituaries, I suddenly noticed: "Mrs. L. R. G. Crandon, the medium Margery, at Boston, Massachusetts, U.S.A.

It was not quite, however, my last contact with Margery. One heat-struck August afternoon just after the war, I happened to be walking along Cornhill behind Boston's City Hall. As a relief to that empty, sun-bleached street I stopped under the shadow of the awning in front of Colesworthy's secondhand bookstore. On the sidewalk was the usual tray of twenty-five-cent books. Glancing over them I saw one with a faded brown cover that looked familiar, though I could scarcely decipher the lettering of the title, *The Hills Give Promise*. I picked it up and opened it. There on the flyleaf, just as I had somehow expected, was Robert's neat, almost prim inscription: ''I have seen, and I have believed.''

John Boyle O'Reilly's earnest and sensitive face is somewhat obscured by the walrus moustache of the period.

A FORGOTTEN POET:
JOHN BOYLE O'REILLY

D URING THE LATTER PART OF THE NINETEENTH CENTURY JOHN BOYLE
O'Reilly was perhaps the most celebrated Irish exile of all those
who settled in America. As a poet, novelist, editor, wit and
defender of his countrymen, he did much to mitigate the antagonisms
between Puritan and Catholic America that had been so intensified
by the Irish migrations of the Famine years. He was a man gifted with
a singularly winning personality who, arriving penniless in America
as an escaped convict, soon made a national literary reputation for
himself. The established New England circle of Longfellow, Lowell,
Whittier and Holmes regarded him highly. His quick success together
with his natural optimism blinded him to some extent to the deeper
racial and economic conflicts underlying the new republic. Men of a
sadder vision like O'Donovan Rossa saw things more clearly. But
whatever O'Reilly's insufficiencies he became in his lifetime one of
the most respected of Irish-Americans and one of the better-known
poets of New England and of the United Staes.

He still exists as a name, but he is no longer read. His two novels,
his little volume on *Athletics and Manly Sport* and his four books of
verse are forgotten. Sometimes an ageing Boston politician will quote
a few swinging lines from *The Exile of the Gael* on St. Patrick's Day,
and on the anniversary of O'Reilly's birth the Charitable Irish Society
of Boston still places a wreath on his statue in the Fenway. To the present generation, however, he has become a figure on a monument. Most

of the older anthologies include the eight lines of *A White Rose,* the little mannered lyric which has alone survived from his four volumes. It is in the *Oxford Book of English Verse,* but the more recent *Oxford Book of American Verse* excludes it, as does Louis Untermeyer in his various collections. Such versifying, so far removed from the idiom of our own time, no longer arouses emotional response. O'Reilly's roses seem made of wax:

> The red rose whispers of passion,
>   And the white rose breathes of love;
> Oh, the red rose is a falcon,
>   And the white rose is a dove.
>
> But I send you a cream-white rosebud
>   With a flush on its petal tips;
> For the love that is purest and sweetest
>   Has a kiss of desire on the lips.

As a poet he is bounded by his era, the era of Mrs. Hemans and Jean Ingelow, both of whom he resembles on a somewhat lower level. As a man and a leader, however, and in particular as an example of the phenomenon of the Celt in America, he deserves to be remembered. If his talents had only equalled his character he would have been a great poet.

O'Reilly was born at Dowth Castle near Drogheda in 1844, close to the Boyne and four miles west of Tara. The castle then housed the Netterville Institution and contained a national school of which his father was headmaster. At the age of eleven O'Reilly left school and became a printer's devil for the *Drogheda Argus,* where he worked the conventionally long hours of the early Victorian period—from six to nine in the morning, from ten to two and from three to seven or eight in the evening. However, the work was not hard, and the boy had none of the young Dickens's sense of grievance at his early employment.

Four years later, at the death of the Argus proprietor, O'Reilly crossed over to England to live with his relatives at Preston. There he found a job in the office of the *Guardian* where he stayed on until he eventually became a reporter. The three and a half years he spent at Preston were among the happiest of his life. They are reflected in the serene description of an English small town with which his first novel, *Moondyne,* opens, reflected too in the fact that despite the imprisonments

and hardships he later endured at the hands of the English government he bore no enmity to England or its people. All the characters
of *Moondyne*, including its autobiographical hero, are English rather
than Irish.

A year after his arrival in Preston, O'Reilly joined the 11th Lancashire
Rifle Volunteers. This brief taste of spare-time military life pleased him,
and by the time he was seventeen he had become a noncommissioned
officer. Yet at the same time, influenced by the numerous emigrant
Irish from the neighborhood of Liverpool, he was becoming interested
in Fenianism.

When he reached the age of nineteen he made his choice. He left
Preston to return to Ireland as a trooper in the Tenth Hussars. At that
time a third of the ranks of the British Army was Irish. According to
O'Reilly's biographer, James Jeffrey Roche, he entered the British
military service with the object of overthrowing the monarchy. This led
the historian, William Lecky, after the book appeared, to accuse O'Reilly
of violating his soldier's oath and betraying his trust.

Neither version fits the facts. O'Reilly was still an unformed young
man when he joined the army. His state of mind was not that of a
conspirator, but ambivalent. On the one hand he liked the life of a
trooper. He was proud of his dark blue hussar's uniform with its plumed
busby. A smart and able soldier, he enjoyed the martial aspects of life
in the Prince of Wales' Own. On the other hand, in his barrack existence, he drew closer to the dissident nationalism that now expressed
itself through the Fenian movement among the rank and file of the
British army.

O'Reilly's was the case of a man with divided loyalties, loyalties that
were incompatible and yet—such is the illogicality of the human
mind—managed to exist side by side. Although he was proudly conscious of his Irish nationality, he had nevertheless lived happily in
England. He loved Ireland and he loved the life of a hussar. There was
probably no ulterior thought in his mind when he enlisted. While a
hussar he did take the Fenian oath with a number of his barrackmates.
But when the group of which he was a member was betrayed by an
informer, and he himself was arrested at the Island Bridge barracks
in February 1866, the charges against him were not of conspiring but
of "having come to the knowledge of an intended mutiny in Her Ma-
jesty's Forces in Ireland and not giving information of said intended
mutiny to his commanding officer." This mutiny was mostly harebrained

talk. The real case against O'Reilly was that, having knowledge of it, he would not betray his comrades. His Fenianism was a feeling of emotional solidarity with his fellow countrymen, not a manifesto. Years later he was to write: "I never realized the Fenian movement until I found myself in prison for it."

A formal sentence of death was passed on him which was commuted the same day to life imprisonment and later to twenty years. While waiting shipment to England he was placed in Mountjoy Prison. Some time before this he had begun to versify, and he now composed two poems, "The Irish Flag" and "The Irish Soldiers," which he scratched on the wall of his cell, adding the defiant note "written on the wall of my cell with a nail, July 17, 1866. Once an English soldier; now an Irish felon; and proud of the exchange." In spite of the defiance the verses were feeble.

After a few weeks he and his companions were marched through the streets of Dublin in chains and shipped to England. First he was sent to Millbank where Mitchell and Davitt were imprisoned and which he describes at some length in *Moondyne*. Then later he was moved to Chatham where after an attempted escape he was put into one of the gangs wheeling bricks at Portsmouth. Dartmoor, the man-killer of its day, was his last English prison, from where he again tried to escape. Four months later the order came for his transportation to Australia. He was then sent by way of Portland to the convict ship *Hougoumont* with a number of other Irish political prisoners. In *Moondyne* O'Reilly describes the *Hougoumont* in the rhetoric of the period: "Only those who have stood within the bars, and heard the din of devils and the appalling sounds of despair, blended in a diapason that made every hatch-mouth a vent of hell, can imagine the horrors of the hold of a convict ship." During the long voyage the prisoners, with the aid of the prison chaplain, were able to publish a weekly paper, *The Wild Goose,* which O'Reilly helped edit.

The voyage ended in the Roadstead of Freemantle, the little Australian town enmeshed in surrounding woodlands with the great stone prison high above it. From Freemantle O'Reilly was sent thirty miles along the coast to the convict settlement of Bunbury where he was assigned to a road party of common criminals. Australia seemed a strange and semitropical land, and even in his captivity he marveled at it, at the great stretching landscape, and the flowers and brightly colored birds under the enormous southern skies. The convicts were not bound. On all sides of them the bush extended endless miles, a barrier more formidable than chains. Even if a man could escape the camp and the native trackers, he could not live. Yet before O'Reilly had been there many weeks he began to plot another escape. He was determined somehow to make his way through the wild bush country to the sea. "It is an excellent way to commit suicide," the missionary priest, Father McCabe, told him when he learned of his plans. There must have been unusual qualities of O'Reilly that made the bush priest single him out from the mass of criminals. "Don't think of it again," he told the young man. "Let me think out a plan for you."

O'Reilly's subsequent flight from Australia was one of the great escapes of the nineteenth century, an amazing adventure even to those who have become accustomed to the intricate dangers of later escapes. Father McCabe's plan was for O'Reilly to be smuggled from the convict camp and across the bush to the seacoast where he could be secreted aboard an American whaler scheduled to touch at Bunbury for water. When the time came and an intermediary brought the priest's alert, O'Reilly broke away from camp to a bush rendezvous. He was then taken on horseback by stages to a remote beach on the west coast. From the beach he was to have been rowed out to the whaler as it passed on its return. The first attempt failed. Although the whaler was sighted they did not succeed in reaching it with their skiff. The following day O'Reilly rowed out alone, still unsuccessfully searching, but after much hardship he was forced back to the beach where he endured several days of thirst and privation. Then for some weeks he was secreted in the remote home of a friendly settler until another American boat should arrive. Finally Father McCabe managed to make arrangements with the captain of the bark *Gazelle* from New Bedford. This time the attempt succeeded and O'Reilly in his small boat reached the *Gazelle* just out of sight of land.

It was almost impossible to escape from Australia in those days, and O'Reilly's flight gave him a prominence he had never had before. Two months later the *Gazelle* put into the harbor of Roderique, a small British island in the Indian Ocean. There the forewarned governor appeared with a police guard to demand the surrender of the felon O'Reilly. The *Gazelle*'s officers maintained that he had committed suicide—and although the governor was not really taken in by this implausibility, he had the humanity to accept it. O'Reilly then adopted the name and papers of a seaman who had deserted. When they reached the

Cape of Good Hope he was transferred to another American bark, the *Sapphire* of Boston. As a Mr. Soule he arrived safely at Liverpool where he stepped on English soil again only long enough to secure passage to America. Unhindered and unsuspected he took his place on the regular passenger list outward bound for Philadelphia. The second day out, in clearing weather, they sailed close enough to shore so that O'Reilly could see the familiar outline of the Irish coast. It was the last glimpse he was ever to have of Ireland. Years after he wrote of this moment: "Home, friends, all that I loved in the world were there, almost beside me—there 'under the sun' and I, for loving them, a hunted outlawed fugitive, an escaped convict, was sailing away from all I treasured—perhaps, forever."

On his arrival in Philadelphia O'Reilly was met at the boat by a Fenian delegate who asked for Boyle O'Reilly the poet, and was surprised and at first somewhat dubious at the unpoetical appearance of the young man facing him. O'Reilly did not stay long in Philadelphia but soon moved on to Boston, where he was to live out the rest of his life. He was received into that city by Dr. Robert Dwyer Joyce, whose long-forgotten *Deirdre* and *Ballads of Irish Chivalry* were then considered signs of a Celtic rebirth in the United States. Joyce, together with Patrick Collins, later mayor of Boston, took the young man in charge and found him a job as reporter and general writer with the Boston *Pilot*. The *Pilot*, a weekly newspaper, was the most influential Irish-Catholic journal in the United States, the spokesman for the waves of immigrants who had been pouring into the country since the Famine years.

In no great time O'Reilly became the *Pilot*'s editor and one of its owners, a position he held until his death. His last dozen years in America were serene and successful. He married, and his home life was happy. His reputation became for a time international. In 1882 he was chosen to read his poem "America" at the reunion of the Army of the Potomac with General Grant presiding. Grant later asserted that it was the grandest poem he had ever heard—which may well have been true. Dr. Joyce claimed that O'Reilly's fame was co-extensive with the English language. "Few men have felt so powerfully the divinus afflatus of Poesy," Cardinal Gibbons wrote of him. "The bitterest prejudices of race and creed seem to have been utterly conquered by the masterful goodness of his heart and the winning sweetness of his tongue."

O'Reilly was the first Irishman of the mass immigration period to bridge the gap between the immigrants and the Yankee descendants of the Puritans. The young man's magnetic quality that had so impressed Father McCabe in Australia attracted all the elements of the Boston community to him. At the centenaries of O'Connell and of Emmet he was the commemorative speaker. He delivered the principal American address on Moore's birthday. When Parnell visited New York in 1880 it was O'Reilly who formally welcomed him, as later he was to welcome Justin McCarthy and other Nationalist members of the English parliament. During O'Reilly's editorship the *Pilot* published poems by Yeats and Hyde, still young and unknown, as well as pieces by the emergent Oscar Wilde. Wilde wrote to O'Reilly: "I esteem it a great honor that the first American paper I appeared in should be your admirable *Pilot*."

In his later American years O'Reilly was accurately described as "a quiet unobtrusive gentleman of conservative vein and a devoted Christian." Although during this time he helped organize the expedition of the whaler *Catalpa*, which rescued six other prisoners from Australia, it was the last echo of his Fenian past. Fenianism, which ended tragically in Ireland, ended farcically in the United States with the comic opera invasion of Canada by the American Fenian Army in 1870. O'Reilly, who had gone along with this overgeneraled expedition as a reporter, wrote a lengthy and critical account of the whole absurd, mismanaged affair. He himself became a gradualist and a leading American supporter of Home Rule. He was not a physical force man. His nature was much more that of a reconciler than a revolutionary. Each St. Patrick's Day he had the *Pilot* building twined with strands of green and orange. In the New York disorders that accompanied the annual Orangemen's parade he condemned both sides.

O'Reilly was the most prominent of a group of poets of Irish birth and American adoption who saw themselves as the inheritors and bearers of the Celtic tradition, who felt themselves each one as did the young Yeats,

> True brother of a company
> That sang to sweeten Ireland's wrong,
> Ballad and story, rann and song...

Even the names of the others are forgotten, those "recent Celtic minstrels of his greater Ireland"—Miles O'Reilly, Maurice Egan "the

sweet true poet," Father Ryan, John Augustus Shea, Patrick Sarsfield
Cassidy and the rest. Their Irish patriotism was sincere if derivative,
but when it was applied to verse it found expression in bombast and
a series of rhymed clichés such as filled the pages of O'Reilly's *Irish
Anthology*:

> . . . Till the castle be wrecked and the last red coat of its
>   myrmidon hordes be gone,
> The Irish race, through time and space, shall
>   ever go marching on.

Almost any page will furnish similar examples. O'Reilly himself could
write in "The Exile of the Gael":

> No treason we bring from Erin—nor bring we
>   shame nor guilt!
> The sword we hold may be broken, but we have not
>   dropped the hilt!
> The wreath we bear to Columbia is twisted
>   of thorns, not bays;
> And the songs we sing are saddened by thoughts of
>   desolate days.
> But the hearts we bring for Freedom are washed
>   in the surge of tears;
> And we claim our right by a People's fight
>   outliving a thousand years!

His American set pieces have a similar tone-deafness. Much of the
bulk of his verse is made up of long and improbable narrative poems,
most of them with an Irish background, but some dealing with America
and Australia. All his books are interspersed with weak little lyrics.
O'Reilly wrote easily, naively, and to the readers of his time effective-
ly. The fault was in his stars, not in himself, that he was not a poet.
    O'Reilly's two novels were incidental accomplishments. The first,
Moondyne, A Story of Convict Life in Australia, appeared serially in
the *Pilot.* It is in a sense a dream autobiography, interspersed with
many of O'Reilly's actual experiences. The plot is a conventional Victorian one with any manner of coincidences, apostrophes to female
virtue, bold heroes, dark villains and so on. Yet, after one accepts the
tradition, the story moves on and holds one's interest. There are authentic glimpses of Western Australia as it was when it was a penal colony,

living descriptions of the bush landscape and of the four-month voyage in the convict ship. The story concerns an escaped convict, Moondyne Joe, who bears O'Reilly's old number, 406. This convict managed to make his way into the mountains of the Vasse where he was given the name Moondyne by the natives "which had some meaning more than either manhood or kingship." After a lengthy period during which he discovers gold in the Vasse, Moondyne Joe reappears as the wealthy and mysterious Mr. Wyville, a kind of Australian Count of Monte Cristo whose holdings—the deeds of which have been received through the Colonial Office—are so vast that they include a rectangle with the northern and southern limits the 33d and 34th parallels of latitude and the eastern and western boundaries the 115th and 116th longtitude. The setting of *Moondyne* alternates between London and Australia. Indirectly it reflects the political atmosphere of the days of the elder Chamberlain. All the London characters of the novel, although highly connected, are republicans. Lord Somers the Colonial Secretary deplores the monarchy as does his friend Mr. Hamerton who has renounced his hereditary title. No Irish characters appear in *Moondyne*'s pages. The secondary hero, Will Sheridan, who becomes a company agent in Australia and who is another facet of O'Reilly, is a Catholic, but this is treated as quite an incidental matter. What is most surprising about the book is the complete absence of bitterness on the part of the author towards England and the English.

The King's Men, written by O'Reilly with the collaboration of several others, is a novel projected into the future, a genre made familiar by Bellamy and continued to our own day by George Orwell. The action of *The King's Men* opens in the year 1940. At this point in the history of the British Isles, Home Rule has been operating for some time in reverse, for the Republic of Great Britain and Ireland is now in its seventeenth year under the presidency of O'Donovan Rourke. The deposed George V is now in exile in Boston, Massachusetts, holding an emigré court in a shabby hotel in the South End where he is attended by the Dukes of Norfolk and Wellington, Lord Gladstone Churchill and the Archbishop of Canterbury. Although the novel has the involved Victorian love plot, it has in addition a secondary plot concerned with a Royalist attempt to restore the lost monarchy. A small and ineffectual group of aristocratic reactionaries takes the desperate step of raising the royal standard at Aldershot, hoping to rally the army to them. Their gesture fails miserably. When the news of their action reaches

London the outraged citizens blow up the Albert Memorial in their indignation. George V fails ignominiously to back his supporters, and without even the satisfaction of his loyalty they are seized and sent to Dartmoor.

The King's Men is chiefly a vehicle for O'Reilly's republican sentiments. It has no real literary value, although there are amusing touches such as the exiled George V having difficulties with his hotel bill, the appearance of Lord Gladstone Churchill and the Albert Memorial going up in smoke. The account of prison life in Dartmoor is realistic enough, drawn as it was from O'Reilly's own experience. Why he should have needed collaborators in this book is difficult to see. Whatever their contribution, however, the general pattern of the writing and the imprint of thought were his. It was his last attempt at fiction.

O'Reilly as a man represented the best of Ireland in America. That is his lasting significance. He and others like Patrick Collins, Dr. Joyce and Hugh O'Brien, the first Irish mayor of Boston, were men of culture and integrity who, like the Germans of 1848, had come to the United States as political exiles. With their abilities and their firmness of character they assumed the leadership of their fellow countrymen. Those semiliterate masses who had swarmed across the ocean were, however, driven by economic necessity and not by political idealism. They had been forced to leave a broken land to become the lowest level of the new-world proletariat. The Irish immigrants in the eastern seaboard cities lived and died like animals. Their somber fate played itself out obscurely, below the levels of literary understanding.

Against the fact of mass migration such high-minded men as O'Reilly were powerless. Individualistic by outlook, they could not grasp the sociological and economic significance of this mass phenomenon. They themselves were incorruptible. But they failed to comprehend that the wretched immigrants in their slums would not be bound by the restrictions of English common law as applied by the entrenched descendants of the Puritans.

Idealists like O'Reilly expected the newcomers to accept the ethic of the community to which they had come, even though it excluded them from every level but the lowest. They did not see that the only way up for the immigrants lay in the rejection of this ethic and an assertion of political power. The Irish urban masses wanted jobs and some kind of protection against the dark days for which the laissez-faire attitude of the community offered no assistance. Those needs the rising political bosses supplied through a deft manipulation of the Irish vote.

So it was that the men of the great Irish tradition, men like O'Brien and Collins and of whom O'Reilly was the honored leader, were followed by the little venal men, the Honey Fitzes, the Coakleys and their blackmailing rings, the "Bath-house John" McCoys, the Dowds and the O'Dwyers. Curley, who liked to quote O'Reilly, admitted disarmingly in his approved biography that there wasn't a Boston City Hall contract that didn't have something in it for him during his four terms as mayor. The tradition of Emmet ended in the tradition of Tammany Hall. For men of the integrity of O'Reilly and Collins this was the ultimate disillusionment. In his later years Collins turned to drink. O'Reilly, out of some inner despair, killed himself at the age of forty-five.

O'Reilly is buried in Holyrood Cemetery in Brookline, six miles from Boston. A seventy-ton mass of conglomerate, the local Roxbury pudding-stone, marks his grave at the cemetery's highest point, overlooking Chestnut Hill. Near him is his friend Patrick Collins and just below his friend and biographer, the poet James Jeffrey Roche.

Down the hillside the graves of the more prosperous Irish of the last fifty years line the winding paths, their relative financial status indicated by the number of cubic feet of polished granite placed over them. Beyond the paths is a wall and beyond that the humming traffic of the Worcester Turnpike.

John Boyle O'Reilly lies on this eminence facing a twentieth-century America unaware of him. His vision was not a sustaining one. The pattern of the Celt in the new world took other shapes. High above the turnpike the great mass of conglomerate appears lonely and remote, and few passers-by know what it commemorates, the failure of a noble spirit who lies there in a foreign land.

The alleyway where Evelyn Wagler was set on fire.

DEATH IN DORCHESTER

AT HALF PAST NINE OF AN EARLY SEPTEMBER EVENING IN 1973 THE YOUNG woman in the flowered dress walks along Blue Hill Avenue down the slope from Franklin Park. Behind her the trees in the park, though somewhat bedraggled, still hold their summer greenery. Most of the small stores she passes on the Avenue are empty, boarded up since the riots of six years ago, their fronts pasted over with now tattered and faded Black Power posters and smeared with crude slogans. Only the liquor stores, those hardiest of weeds, have managed to survive here, their windows bricked down to slits and protected by layers of steel mesh.

The young woman is pretty in a casual way. Her errand is obvious. She is carrying a red two-gallon can of gasoline from a Grove Hall filling station to a car stranded somewhere in the no man's land of streets between Dorchester and Roxbury. There are few if any pedestrians in sight. People no longer walk along Blue Hill Avenue, particularly in the evening. As she nears a dilapidated corner house beyond a line of boarded-up or shuttered stores, six young blacks step out of the darkness into the blue-white range of the arc lamps. Shouting obscenities they encircle her, shove her from one to the other like a rag doll, force her down the narrow alley between the corner house and a decayed apartment block. There in the litter of a vacant rear lot they order her to pour gasoline on herself. She refuses. They beat and kick her until she finally gives in. When she has drenched herself to their satisfaction, one of the gang flicks a lighted match at her. She takes fire like a torch, and they run off laughing and jeering.

After vainly rolling on the ground to put out the flames, she staggers down the alley, her clothes and hair ablaze, and screams her way past half a dozen closed shops to the open liquor store. Customers and clerks pull off her burning clothing. A police car that happens to be cruising by takes her to City Hospital. She has second and third degree burns over all her body. Four hours later she is dead.

She was Evelyn Wagler, a twenty-six-year-old German-born Swiss, married but separated from her husband, the mother of a six-year-old boy. A drifter, she had lived in communes, with Woman's Liberation friends, on Chicago's tough South Side, worked as a carpenter, a waitress, a truckdriver. Five days earlier she had arrived in Boston after hitchhiking from Chicago and taking odd jobs along the way. She moved in with four women she had known previously—three black and one white— who lived in the upper floor of a three-decker on the edge of Dorchester. She was looking for a job when her borrowed car ran out of gas. Before she died she managed to tell the police that she had been confronted on the avenue the day before by three of the same gang. They had warned her: "Whitey, get out of this part of town!" It was just more of the same sort of street jive, she told her roommates, she used to hear in Chicago. Neither she nor they felt particularly alarmed. After her death her estranged husband explained to reporters that she had been killed "by the system, a system that creates ghettos and racial hatred." Her body remained in the morgue unclaimed.

Boston's Mayor Kevin White, after asserting that there was nothing inherently racial in this torch murder, offered a $5,000 reward for information leading to the arrest and conviction of the murderers. A week later no one had been arrested, and Evelyn Wagler's name had disappeared from the newspapers.

The tale would have been one to which I should have reacted in transitory horror and then inevitably have pushed aside as new tales intervened. But Dorchester, where Evelyn Wagler died, happens to be the section of Boston where I grew up, the place of my first memories, the only part of the earth that has come to seem instinctively home to me. So I felt her death as something personal, as if we were somehow related. Blue Hill Avenue was for me *the* Avenue before I knew there were other avenues, a Via Appia running die-straight from the Blue Hills to Boston on the horizon that to my child's eye was London and Paris and Rome and all the world's fabled and fabulous cities.

We lived a mile or so the other side of Franklin Park on Dorchester

Hill, bordering on Blue Hill Avenue, a segment of Dorchester that still kept the Indian name of Mattapan, Place-of-the-Ford. That hill of my childhood is an obscure drumlin, one of the several hundred left by the glacier in the Boston area. But for me it was the hub of the universe. From the row of pignut trees on the Hill's crest one could look north to the hazy tentacular city four and a half miles away and sometimes on bright afternoons catch the glitter of the gilt State House dome. On gray days the sky itself seemed held up by the granite obelisk of the Custom House tower. East lay the harbor islands, beyond the yellow bulk of the Dorchester High School. From my bedroom window I looked west beyond New Calvary Cemetery in the hollow to the vague ridge of the Canterbury Hills with their promise of continental distances beyond, enhanced by the red sun-ball as it sank each evening below the Bellevue water tower.

Until the Boston Elevated Street Railway Company extended its line from Grove Hall to Mattapan in 1908, Dorchester Hill was a supernumerary bit of property owned by Wellington Holbrook, a feckless *Mayflower* descendant who lived on the bits and pieces of his diminished inheritance. Thanks to the Boston El, Mattapan became a streetcar suburb and Holbrook was able to develop his empty drumlin into a settlement of one- and two-family houses, run up as cheaply as possible on postage-stamp-sized lots. With passing vanity he changed the Hill's old name to Wellington Hill. It became a bourgeois community of those who considered themselves simply Americans but who would later be labeled WASPs—clerks, salesmen, petty officials, minor professional men and the occasional teacher.

Ironically enough, the year of the Mattapan carline extension was the year of the great Chelsea fire that destroyed most of that sordid industrial adjunct of Boston, obliterating the slum streets along the Mystic River inhabited by Jewish refugees from Polish Russia. Before 1880 there were fewer than five hundred Russian Jews in Massachusetts out of a foreign-born population of 350,000. Between 1900 and 1914 they formed the largest racial block coming into the state. After the Kishinev pogroms of 1903 and the 1905 massacres, this migration became a stampede. Of 100,000 new immigrants coming to Massachusetts in 1913, 21,000 were Jews from the Polish Pale. They took to peddling and junk dealing, a haggling existence to which they were adapted by their harsh and limited life in the Pale. To Boston's small group of wealthy, long-established German Jews they seemed as remote as lunar visitors. Following the destruction of the Chelsea ghetto, its inhabitants migrated across the Mystic River ten miles south to the sections of Dorchester already solidly built up with wooden three-deckers. Speculative builders ran up more three-deckers to meet the demand.

With the advent of World War I, shops with kosher signs began to spread down Blue Hill Avenue, each year creeping closer to the Hill. District after Dorchester district became solidly Jewish. As soon as a few Jews bought into a street, the other families would become restive, FOR SALE signs would appear in their windows, and in a few seasons they would have moved away. Dorchester was becoming, not a ghetto, but a *kahal*, an expanding Jewish community, soon to be the most densely populated area of greater Boston.

For some time Dorchester Hill remained a nativist island surrounded by an alien sea. The outcome was only a matter of time. Finally in 1920 the Robinsons on the Hill quietly sold their house to a Jewish family. Prices of houses, like all prices, had soared just after the war, and the Robinsons could not resist doubling their money. I remember the sense of indignation, the neighborhood talk of banding together to buy the house back. Of course nothing came of it. The neighborhood "changed." More Jewish families moved in. No others would now buy on the Hill. But the change was a gradual process, lasting over a decade, and some of the more rooted and stubborn Hill natives stayed on until they died. Between the old and the new there was little social mingling, although the children soon played together. There was dislike, even latent hostility, but no conflict. The newcomers were extremely law-abiding, even litigious.

Most of the Jews who moved to the Hill were foreign-born, and in the rush before the more restrictive immigration laws they were willing to spend their last dollar to bring in their assorted relatives. We stayed on for six years after the first invasion, and I became used to the sight of full-bearded old men—like the Rabbi Sheshevsky who bought a two-family house not far from us—in long black coats and wide black hats. On summer evenings they sat on their front porches with *yarmulkes* on their heads, and the old women wore wigs that sometimes peeped askew from beneath their shawls. Shops along Blue Hill Avenue proliferated—meat markets, delicatessens, fish markets, hardware and dry goods stores, shoes, tailoring. There were too many, and some of them failed. The arson rate was high. Near Franklin Park there was the Hebrew School Haschachar, and whenever I walked by on a spring afternoon I could hear the murmur of the scholars' voices like the hum of bees. Only on Friday evenings was the Avenue quiet, empty. The rest of the time it gyrated with an ever-shifting crowd. In front of the shops were pushcarts with flaring kerosene lights, and always on summer evenings the throngs of talking, laughing, gesticulating foreigners, their language as thick as the delicatessen smells. So it all seemed to me; the Avenue a fascination. As I walked back to the Hill on a winter afternoon from skating on Franklin Field, I felt an abounding sense of life pulsing along those crowded sidewalks, a contagious vitality in those rudely pushing shoppers.

The Dorchester *kahal* became the center of Boston Jewry. In those years before the New Deal, the Jews voted Republican in opposition to the Irish Democrats. By the late thirties the more prosperous Jews were leaving Mattapan and Dorchester. The children and grandchildren of Chelsea peddlers and ragmen, of Blue Hill Avenue tailors and fishmongers and delicatessen proprietors, had through their relentless pursuit of education become lawyers, doctors, professors, financiers, members of all the professions. From the three-deckers and two-family houses of Dorchester they had moved to spacious single homes in Brookline and Newton. There were Jewish sections of those towns, but the *kahal* itself had vanished.

After World War II Dorchester and the Hill remained undividedly Jewish, but the population was thinning. Those who stayed behind were those who had not made it, the has-beens, the failures, the elderly. Dorchester remained a slightly obnoxious memory. The proud marble bulk of Temple Mishkan Tefila loomed up across from Franklin Park an empty shell, its name and substance having been translated to Newton Center.

Sometimes on a summer evening in the early fifties when I happened to be driving in to Boston from Wellesley, I would park my car near the Martha Baker School, where I had attended the first five grades, then like a revenant walk up the Wellington Footway to the Hill and along the streets with the uneasy familiarity of a dream, past the houses I once knew, the gabled house where I once lived. The Hill's crest line of pignut trees had been replaced by the brick solidity of the Solomon Lewenberg Junior High School. Who he was I had no idea, but then I had never known who Martha Baker was. But I did know that the Lewenberg School had the highest scholastic standing of any junior high school in the city. On such a lingering summer evening the Hill people sat on their porches, in their minute yards, even on their front steps, calling back and forth in a lighthearted neighborliness that I, the revenant, found myself wishing I might share, that someone might nod to me as I passed.

In those years when I took the Blue Hill Avenue streetcar daily and transferred at Egleston Square to the El on my way to the old Roxbury Latin School near Dudley Street, the black area of Boston was a static one, extending from the Dover Street to the Northampton Street El stations and stopping there. The "colored" district, everyone called it then, and it stayed within those limits for a generation. That colored world seemed stranger to me than Blue Hill Avenue and more remote. Not for decades should I ever know anyone with a skin darker than my own.

After World War II the Northampton Street barriers gave way. Then, as in so many cities and for much of the same complex of reasons— welfare and otherwise—Boston's black population suddenly expanded, bursting its static boundaries, flowing to Dudley Street and then across Roxbury to Dorchester. A number of old Yankee families had persisted in the large and solid Victorian mansions of the Roxbury Highlands, and the Jewish invasion had flowed round rather than through them. The black tide of the fifties and sixties drove out the Yankee lingerers when they were faced with what they had never encountered with the Jews—violence.

On casual trips to Boston in the sixties I would sometimes drive up Blue Hill Avenue to watch the progress of the black tide. It was easy to spot. For some reason lower class Jewish families never had window curtains but merely shades or Venetian blinds. Where on lower Blue Hill Avenue the windows in the drab brick apartment buildings had been neat though bare, they suddenly became smeared, the blinds twisted askew, the shades torn and stained. Blacks had arrived. One could trace the tide by the condition of the windows. It seemed to move at about half a mile a year. By the time it had covered the down slope from Franklin Park to Franklin Field, though there was still a mile to go, I knew the Hill was about to "change" again.

In the Roxbury-Dorchester riots that followed Martin Luther King's murder, most of the shop windows along Blue Hill Avenue were smashed as far as Franklin Field and even beyond. The boarded-up fronts remained. A few proprietors did reopen because their little shops were all they had. But their customers dwindled away and they found themselves threatened and challenged by young blacks, robbed in their shops, mugged on the street. These tough teen-age gangs soon made the Avenue a street of peril. No longer did flaring lights welcome the customers into the shop interiors. Old men still huddled in the G & G Delicatessen, drinking tea out of glasses and reading Yiddish papers, but each time I dropped in there were fewer of them. The Jewish wave that I had seen crest and break so long ago had receded, leaving only a few pebbles behind. Now the second wave was cresting, always thrusting—more by the accident of geography than anything else—against the retreating Jewish remnant. According to the census, Dorchester Hill had 1,204 residents in 1960, of whom ten were black. Ten years later the Hill had become half black. That year, while there was still time, I decided to call at my old house and ask how they felt about their incoming neighbors.

It was a strange feeling to walk up the steps to the long porch. Not for forty-three years had I been in that small gabled house. In 1926 I had walked down those very steps, happy to be quitting what I considered a socially inferior neighborhood, not realizing until years later how much of myself I was leaving behind. As I rang the bell I could see my reflection in the square of plate glass set in the oak front door, even the small hole in the left-hand corner that I had made with a BB-gun.

I was too late. A young woman with a café-au-lait complexion opened the door. Awkwardly I explained that I used to live there as a boy. She was very gracious, showed me into the living room furnished in what can best be called Sears-Roebuck Mediterranean—massive carved chests with huge knobs, similarly carved chairs, and a television-stereo to match. Where our bookcase had been was an artificial fireplace with an electric heater behind which a red bulb flickered. A Naugahyde sofa filled the space once taken up by our Hallet & Davis upright piano. The young woman told me she was a nurse. Her husband worked for Boston Edison. They had come from Roxbury because they needed more space for their child, room for a garden. "We wanted to move into an integrated neighborhood," she said, "but since we moved in a year ago the others have been moving away, a regular stampede. The man next door is white. I asked him if he was going to stay and he said he didn't know. I know though!" I told her about the early days of the Hill, of Holbrook and of the coming of the Jews. Then she asked me if I would care to see the rest of the house. We went through, room by room. I was haunted by memories—the kitchen's phantom Glenwood coal range with its iron scrollwork and nickel trim where I used to toast my feet while memorizing French irregular verbs before leaving for school. Finally we stood in my small room. Her little son, now taking a nap there, with the friendliness of happy children stretched out his arms to me. By the window that overlooked the Canterbury Hills had been my desk where I sat night after night construing my twenty lines of Vergil, stumbling through *L'Avare* or puzzling over the problems set in Hawkes, Libby & Touton's *Revised Algebra*. Perhaps, I thought, this small boy perched on the edge of his bed would one day be studying his lessons at the same window with less distaste (I hoped) than I had had for academic learning.

As I drove down the Hill I was aware of a very bustle of remodeling and repairing going on; reshingling, reroofing, painting, modernizing. Plumbing of 1908, old bathtubs, sinks and stoves, were stacked in the yards waiting to be carted off. Even if the Hill was about to turn all black, it was not going to go the way of the apartments on the Avenue. These were people who cared. Three years later I saw another scene. The Hill had indeed turned completely black, but the refurbished houses were falling apart—gaps in the shingles, peeling paint, clogged and rusted gutters, cracks in the foundations, unkempt hedges and overgrown yards, litter, rubbish. Some houses were still neat and cared for. Yet the general tone was one of slovenly deterioration. Our house was among the dreariest, the garage doors torn off, cellar windows gaping, shades ripped down altogether, the porch sagging. A FOR SALE sign announced that it had been taken over by the Federal Housing Administration and gave Blue Hill Avenue "realtor" George Sampson as the agent.

Curious about my old house, I went to Sampson's office. He turned out to be a friendly, soft-spoken man, light brown in color with rosy cheeks that gave his complexion a slightly orange tint. When I told him I merely wanted to inquire about the Hill and my old house, he couldn't have been more helpful. As he explained it to me, after the 1968 riots two dozen banks banded together in the Boston Banks Urban Renewal Group—BBURG—and agreed to put up $20 million to help low-income families buy their own homes through federally insured mortgages. The bankers established an arbitrary district in Dorchester, the BBURG line, within which they would write mortgages and outside which they would not. Dorchester Hill was almost within the dead center of that line.

The practical result of BBURG for the Hill and surrounding Dorchester was instant blackness. Blacks could get mortgages only within that area. No one else would think of buying there. For the blockbusting real-estate operators and speculators, BBURG's announcement was a treasure trove. They panicked the remaining Jews into selling their houses at any price, repaired the bought-up buildings hastily and cheaply, and sold them at inflated prices to the incoming blacks from the Roxbury slums, who could take them or nothing. "Many of our people never owned houses before," Sampson told me. "They really didn't know what it meant. They weren't used to budgeting, making regular monthly payments. Most of them weren't handymen and didn't understand much about maintenance, and they paid too much and signed up for what they couldn't afford."

"Have there been many foreclosures?" I asked him.

"Quite a few. And when anyone's about to have his home foreclosed, he isn't too fussy about keeping it up."

I did not come back to Blue Hill Avenue until the week after Evelyn Wagler's death. Nor did I linger on Dorchester Hill, for the Lewenberg School was letting out shortly and that was dangerous ground then. The school was all black now, tumultuous, its proud standards obliterated. Now, when school let out, the remaining shops on the Avenue closed for an hour. I was not going to risk having my car rocked over with myself in it, as had almost happened to me one earlier afternoon. Yet in my brief Hill transit what had struck me was the aura of fear. Many of the better-kept houses now had protective grillwork on the windows and doors. Others were surrounded by chain-link fences. No longer was it Jewish fear of blacks, but blacks fearing blacks, men fearing other men.

Later I found the same permeance of fear along the Avenue, almost deserted in the twilight. A few shops huddled behind gratings or even behind the steel shutters that I had seen before only in Europe. Only the Brown Jug still kept its doors open at the corner of Morton Street. The stark yellow-brick Morton Street synagogue and school had been abandoned. The Morton Theater had become a club of sorts, the Liberty Theater a warehouse, the Franklin Park Theater at the Avenue's summit the New Fellowship Baptist Church.

Day after day for five years I had taken the Blue Hill Avenue streetcar

on my way to Roxbury Latin. From afar I used to look at the elms that
overarched the Avenue near the Franklin Park Theater's spire. Always
they reminded me of the small framed picture of elm-arched Clovelly
that my mother kept in the upper hall. So familiar was Clovelly-
Dorchester, four decades removed in time. The present was inexorable.
At Franklin Field I noticed that the Talbot Tailors and Cleansers had
a sign in the iron-latticed window: BEWARE OF ATTACK DOG. Almost
across the street was the Dunkin' Donuts where a man had been stabbed
to death a few weeks earlier.

Beyond the park I stopped for a moment opposite the spot where
Evelyn Wagler had been cattle-prodded down the alley to her death.
The alley was only a few feet wide, fenced in but with a gap large
enough to squeeze through. The back area was open to a side street
that ran off the Avenue beside the dilapidated green corner house.
Someone in that house or the apartment next to it must have heard
her screams, must have looked out a window, must have seen. But
no one ever came forward to say so. I drove round the block in the
now semidarkness. There was the same conjunction I found on the
Hill and all over Dorchester: ramshackle houses, empty houses, derelict
houses, the yards overgrown with pig and ragweed and ankle-deep in
debris; and, in between, houses as well-groomed, with yards as green
and tidy, as the most proper "executive" suburb. Except for a few
children skipping rope, the only figures I saw were those of young black
males anywhere from sixteen to thirty, standing or leaning against
doorways or store fronts, eyeing the world, and me in particular, with
challenging, hostile glances. I drove round the block twice, and the
second time these young men in their slouch hats watched me more
narrowly, stabbed out their cigarettes with contempt as I passed, and
I could sense their latent threat like a declaration of war. Unemployed,
unemployable, they were as scornful of liberal panaceas as they were
of me. These, or such as these, could have set Evelyn Wagler afire.
What did they want from life? Unformed, consumed by an anger as
vicious as it was undefined, I don't suppose they knew themselves.
Their satisfaction was that they brought fear with them.

For the last time I drove back along the Avenue, down the long
slope from Franklin Park. Great Blue Hill lay directly ahead on the
horizon, the nipple of the weather observatory on its summit outlined
against the gray sky. Just as I used to notice from the streetcar in my
schooldays, Blue Hill seemed to recede into a kind of infinity as one

moved downhill toward it. Blue Hill Avenue itself was empty, a scarecrow boulevard, like an artery drained of blood. I could see a planet over the dark hulk of the Lewenberg School, Venus or Jupiter I wasn't sure which. I knew then that, when everyone else had forgotten her, I should not forget Evelyn Wagler. I knew that I should not come that way again.

Author's Postscript

More than anyone else the late Frank Maloney, curator of documents and relentless collector of manuscripts and memoirs at the Boston Public Library, is responsible for this book. For years he kept urging me to gather my assorted Boston articles under one cover. These dozen pieces I wrote over two decades, the last piece as late as 1987. Some of the earlier ones I would add to briefly here. I do not want to leave unrecorded Curley's hundredth anniversary, observed in the somewhat bleak aula of Boston's new Gropius-designed City Hall, a structure that to my mind resembles a cubistic version of East Prussia's Tannenberg War Memorial. For Curley's birthday there was a massive cake shaped like a cartwheel and trimmed with green frosting and shamrocks. Pieces were given to all-comers, including myself. Like most commercial wedding cakes it had much sweetness but no taste. Still, it was a pleasantly nostalgic gesture by the present mayor. Nor would I neglect the life-size replica of Curley—in the modern vogue for informal statuary—sitting in bronze insouciance on a bench in City Hall Plaza.

Like the Kennedys, Curley had nine children, and when he eclipsed Fitzgerald as mayor it seemed as if he might be founding a dynasty. None of his children, however, had their father's freebooter *élan*, and only two survived him. George Curley, who outlived his father by only a few years, became a nocturnal wanderer in the half-world of Boston Common. Francis X., the Jesuit and sole living Curley, later left the order. When I last heard about him he was on welfare, living somewhere in Boston's South End where his father had originated.

Joseph Kennedy is buried not far from John Boyle O'Reilly, his dynasty secure. Today the Kennedy Museum and Library on Columbia Point, white and gleaming and surrounded on three sides by the sea, with a glass shell like a crystal cathedral soaring eight stories above the atrium, has become a pilgrimage point for tourists. In time one might almost expect miraculous cures to take place there.

Margery, the Lime Street medium, died in 1941 at the age of fifty-six. In her last years she had become an alcoholic and, in fact, drank herself to death. During those months before she died Nandor Fodor, an unorthodox Hungarian psychiatrist with an interest in psychic phenomena, spent much time with her. As she neared the end he asked her if, for the sake of truth, she would tell him what had been genuine in her séances and what methods she had used to effect the rest.

"Why don't you guess?" she told him. "You'll all be guessing for the rest of your lives." A doctor who subsequently bought the Lime Street House told me he had discovered various concealed wires in the moldings as well as acid stains on the floors.

In the years that have elapsed since Evelyn Wagler's murder not so much as a suspect has ever been turned up. Yet undoubtedly there are those in the black community who know. I remember her because I must.

I regret I could not have included here my Harvard classmate and dearly missed friend Bill Harrison, who lived and died in the South End and who for a number of years edited Boston's black weekly, *The Chronicle*. Once put up by the Communists as candidate for attorney general of Massachusetts, he was shunted aside by them in his last lingering illness. I helped arrange his funeral. I saw no comrades there.

Several of these chapters have appeared earlier in somewhat altered form in my book, *The Great Interlude*. The others came out variously in *American Heritage, Antioch Review, Boston Magazine, Country Journal, Horizon, Irish Writing, Metro-Boston, National Review* and *New England Galaxy*. Boston, the city above all American cities that is a state of mind, is the cement that holds them together.